MW01268375

1	2	3	12	13	14
4	5	6	15	16	17
7	8		18	19	20
9	10	11	21	22	23

SAUGATUCK
AREA
SOLDIERS
IDENTIFIED
from the
preceding
FRONT *pages*

(see also BACK
pages 200-201)

1 Levi Loomis

2 James G. Butler

3 Elisha Mix

4 Nelson Wade

5 F. B. Wallin

6 Francis B. Stockbridge

7 George W. Bailey
3rd Michigan Infantry

8 Scott W. & Jonathan P. Eddy
44th Indiana Infantry

9 Charles C. Billings
3rd Michigan Cavalry

10 Frederick H. May, just after
the Civil War

11 Dr. John P. Parrish,
6th Michigan Infantry
Although he held the rank of
private, Parrish worked in the
hospital, as wardmaster, cook
and, later, pharmacist and
seldom wore a military uniform.

12 Henry Blakeslee
19th Michigan Infantry

13 George N. Dutcher
5th Michigan Cavalry

14 *An unidentified soldier with*
the battlefield guidon of the 5th
Michigan Cavalry which was
retired after it was mistaken for
a Confederate flag and caused
men of the 5th to fire at their own
scouting party.

15 Tim Daggett
19th Michigan Infantry
in 1909 after he was no longer
as "rough" and "wicked" as
described by a former comrade

16 John Nies
2nd Michigan Cavalry

17 Brigadier General Elisha Mix
In his G. A. R. uniform, ca.
1890

18 Dr. W. T. Hoy
3rd Michigan Cavalry

19 William H. Dunn
10th Michigan Cavalry

20 William White
5th Michigan Cavalry

21 James W. Billings
U. S. Signal Corps

22 Edward Penfold
13th Michigan Infantry

23 Dr. E. B. Wright

LINCOLN'S "READY-MADE" SOLDIERS
Saugatuck Area Men in the Civil War

Kit Lane

SAUGATUCK-DOUGLAS HISTORICAL SOCIETY

2005

This book is the seventh in a series of publications funded by the Saugatuck-Douglas Historical Society Publication Fund, which was established in 1996 through the generous donations by members to document the history of the Saugatuck-Douglas area. Other titles include:

Painting the Town: A Century of Art in the Saugatuck Area, 1997

Heroes, Rogues, and Just Plain Folks, 1998

Raising the Roof: The History of Architecture and Buildings of the Saugatuck-Douglas Area, 1999

Lost & Found: Ghost Towns of the Saugatuck Area, 2000

Storm, Fire, & Ice: Shipwrecks of the Saugatuck Area, 2001

Off the Record: The Photographs of Bill Simmons, 2002

Snapshots: A Saugatuck Album, 2003

BOOK DESIGN: Ken Carls

THE AMERICAN CIVIL WAR WAS A HORRIBLE, BLOODY TIME. It was the hardest kind of war. Not only was the enemy close enough to see and hear at the height of battle, he looked much like you, spoke the same language and, indeed, his life was probably similar to yours. Unlike the aerial bombing and guided missile attacks of the 20th and 21st Centuries, the Civil War was a personal kind of war. ¶ According to the imperfect statistics of the time 373,458 men died in battle in the Civil War and nearly twice that number from disease. For four long years the two sides killed each other, not so much over a piece of ground, as a determination to maintain and expand an ideology or a way of life. The South fought for the rights of the states to prevail over the power of the central government and to perpetuate slavery which had become an important part of Southern economic policy. The North fought to maintain the Union, to keep as a unified whole the country our forefathers had put together, and, in the end, to banish the constitutional framework that allowed one human being to own another. ¶ No area of the country was more zealous for the Northern cause than Michigan. It was a young state, celebrating its 24th year in the Union. Allegan County was only slightly older having entertained its first settlers in 1830, seven years before statehood. Union soldiers from Saugatuck and the western side of the county included the offspring of the area's earliest residents. Major James G. Butler was the son of William G. Butler, the first settler in the county and the founder of Saugatuck. Captain George N. Dutcher was the oldest son of William F. Dutcher, the founder of Douglas. There were also Private Albert H. Fenn, the son of Elam A. Fenn, the founder of Fennville; Private William McCormick, the son of the first settler in Manlius Township and Private Edwin R. Crawford, the first white child born in Glenn. Also included in Civil War rosters were Peter H. Billings,

John Darius Billings and Robert McLaughlin all young survivors of an 1841 shipwreck on the Kalamazoo River in which their mothers and four of their siblings perished. By a curious collection of circumstances Andrew Plummer, the first white child born in Saugatuck Township to live to maturity, saw service with the Confederate infantry. ¶ Abraham Lincoln once remarked that in Michigan soldiers seemed to be born "ready made." Smart-looking regiments arrived in Washington from the state on a regular basis and they didn't seem to require as much training as similar recruits from other areas. There was some truth to this. The rigors of the Michigan frontier were excellent training for the trenches. Well over half of the recruits in Allegan County were farm boys who had been riding horses all of their lives; it is no wonder that more than 40 percent of men serving from the area entered cavalry regiments. Most of these recruits had grown up in the forests and fields hunting deer, rabbits and other small animals – superb training for the infantry. A few were even accepted into the exalted sharpshooters regiment. These farm boys were hankering for adventure, for some action that did not involve plowing or harvesting. Most had never been outside of their own state. ¶ Economically the war meant little to Michigan. Few people from the state were involved in the slavery and rum trade that made money for the ship owners and merchants of the East. The cotton industry of the South had little impact on the Michigan businessman aside from an occasional length of calico to clothe a wife or daughter. Western Michigan was known as a northern Bible belt, the home of many fervent adherents to fundamental Christianity. They were concerned with slavery as a moral issue, although they expressed some reservations about the possibility that freed slaves might actually move north and live among them. Many favored the idea of freeing the slaves and returning them to Africa. ¶ Despite the blood and horrors of the reality, there is a romantic aura hovering around the Civil War that began as soon as the boys started wandering home after the conflict. There were numerous efforts to recapture the spirit and some of the experiences that were part of the wartime life, including veterans' encampments and regimental reunions. Sometimes old veterans from both sides of the conflict met on the old battlefields and took their old positions. Only this time there was no killing, and all joined in a post "battle" chicken dinner. ¶ The Civil War is still being re-enacted. Modern-day men, in the costumes of that era, meet again to hold mock battles. Their wives and sweethearts dress in hoop skirts to soothe the brows of the "wounded." Regiments journey to these wartime dramas from throughout the United States. There are even American Civil War re-enactors in Europe, all attempting to recreate the romance of the times, without the bloodshed. ¶ Michigan historian Bruce Catton, after three decades of studying the war and writing about it, concluded that this romance is an important part of the real Civil War, the division that brought unity to a large, but eventually vigorous country. He wrote that Lee rode right into legend when he left Appomattox Court House in April of 1865. Catton explained that the essence of the legend that Lee and the Confederacy left behind, was "that they suffered mightily in a great but lost cause." ¶ The "lost cause" created a channel through which pent-up emotions could be discharged. Because the cause, however noble and honorable, was considered lost there was no need to continue the fight or seek revenge somewhere down the road. The issue was over, it had been decided. The lost cause was something to be cherished, to be revered, to be the outlet for emotions, but not to be the center of a new outbreak of fighting. ¶ Union General Ulysses S. Grant won the military war, but it was Confederate General Robert E. Lee who, by his decision to surrender in the most gentlemanly and honorable way, paved the way for the peace. The world is full of civil wars that have left such bitter feelings that they surfaced decades, and even centuries, later in renewed hostilities and bloodshed – Northern Ireland, the Middle East, and Yu-

JAMES W. BILLINGS

goslavia are three clear examples. In America, especially after the bungled reality of reconstruction, there was bitterness in the South, but no attempts to renew the struggle. The question of secession and slavery had both been settled, and the nation moved on. ¶ Both sides, the winning and the losing, honor those who served. There are monuments North and South and they are very similar. In some cases the manufacturers of statues that grace the top of Civil War monuments used the same mold for the Confederate soldier as they did for the Union man. Only the designations on the hat differed. Also the descriptions below the figure. Popular phrases on monuments in the North were "Defenders of Our Union" as the Ganges monument states, or "Defenders of Our Nation," the words on the Allegan statue. ¶ In the town square in Centreville, Alabama, the monument erected to the Bibb County soldiers speaks of the lost cause, and gives even the people from Michigan who read it some feeling about how the country, after the terrible fighting and bloodshed, was eventually able to move on:

TO OUR CONFEDERATE HEROES

These are the men who, by the simple
manhood of their lives
by their strict adherence to principles
of right by their sublime courage
and unspeakable sacrifice even to the
heroism of death have preserved for
us through the gloom of defeat
a priceless heritage
of honor

In this retelling of the events and the stories of the American Civil War, it is the aim of the Saugatuck-Douglas Historical Society to concentrate not so much on the war as a whole, but on the action as experienced by the men of the local area, mostly those from Saugatuck and Ganges Townships. ¶ The committee would like to thank libraries in Michigan, Indiana, Ohio and Illinois, as well as many local citizens and descendants of Civil War veterans who searched their trunks and attics and discovered letters, articles and artifacts, some that they did not even know they owned. More than 60 never-before-published letters were discovered in this effort, many of them rich with the emotion and detail that make the war come alive for the 21st Century reader. In addition, area soldiers served as wartime correspondents to the *Allegan Journal* a weekly newspaper published in the Allegan County seat, and others later penned autobiographies which included an account of their wartime service. Another source of first-hand accounts was the military and pension records of the individual soldiers in the National Archives. These records also contain muster rolls, correspondence and copies of orders that give a fairly detailed account of a man's service. ¶ More than 450 enlistees were discovered by name including a number of men who served in regiments from other states and moved to the Saugatuck area after the war, many as a direct result of wartime acquaintances from southwestern Michigan. About half of these enlistees were actually living in the Saugatuck-Ganges area when they went off to battle, and they are our primary focus. ¶ The effort in this narrative is to let the men themselves tell their story, with only enough framework added to make the text a coherent whole and flesh out the lives of the men doing the writing and the fighting. Sources are described at the end of the text. Handwritten letters, especially those written behind earthen breastworks under fire, are often bereft of meaningful punctuation and the spelling is erratic. Enough of this has been left to give the reader the flavor of the writing, but some commas, capital letters and paragraphing have been added to make the old letters easier to read and understand.   ❖ KL

1861

THE IDEA OF SECESSION from the United States of America was not new. New York State several times threatened to secede. South Carolina was on the brink during the tariff crisis of 1832. Oregon and California kept making noises in that direction. Texas had actually existed as a sovereign state for nearly a decade before admission to the Union in 1845 and many Texans wanted to return to that status. But when the legislature of South Carolina voted to secede from the Union on December 20, 1860, it was the first state to actually carry through on the threat and insist on an answer to the question, whether withdrawal would be permitted by the remaining states.

"LIBERTY AND UNION, NOW AND FOREVER"

Michigan began the year 1861 with the inauguration of a new governor, Austin Blair, an attorney from Jackson. In his inaugural address on January 2, he declared: "Michigan is loyal to the Union, the Constitution and the Laws and will defend them to the uttermost." He offered "to the President of the United States, the whole military power of the State for that purpose . . . . Let us abide in the faith of our fathers — 'Liberty and Union, one and inseparable, now and forever.'" Blair also recommended that the budget for the State militia, $3,000, "be materially increased." ¶ On March 4, 1861, Abraham Lincoln was sworn in as president and noted in his inaugural speech:

> I have no purpose, directly or indirectly, to interfere with the institution of slavery where it exists . . . . No State upon its own mere motion can lawfully get out of the Union. I shall take care, as the Constitution itself expressly enjoins upon me, that the laws of the Union be faithfully executed in all of the States . . . . In your hands, my dissatisifed fellow country men, and not in mine, is the momentous issue of civil war. The government will not assail you. You can have no conflict without being yourselves the aggressors.

With the possibility of military action pending, an act was approved by Governor Blair on March 16, 1861, which authorized him "to accept and muster into the military service of the State" two regiments to place Michigan in a State of readiness to answer the expected call from the federal government for aid – but the act included no funds.

BOOM TIME IN SAUGATUCK

Economically, Saugatuck was booming for the first time in its short history. The settlement was only 31 years old, and had grown only slowly. William G. Butler, his wife and two children had arrived in 1830 and lived in the area alone until 1834 when others began trickling in. By the 1850 federal census the population had risen to 235 in the entire township. ¶ The area was still very much dependent on lumbering and other wood-related industries including tanning of leather and shipbuilding. Earlier efforts at making the timbers of its virgin forest pay had been hampered

MOORE'S MILL
PL. I

16

1861
1862
1863
1864
1865
AFTER THE WAR

by the high shipping costs to reach the consumers in Detroit, Buffalo and other major centers of population in the
East. As Chicago and Milwaukee and other communities
on the western Great Lakes developed, the Saugatuck area
had more convenient customers for its output of leather and
lumber products. Thus, for the first time in its history industry was turning a healthy profit and the population was
growing. ¶ The 1860 census, taken as the country was on
the verge of war, showed 816 residents in Saugatuck Township (then known as Newark Township) which included, in
addition to the settlement on The Flats that would later be
Saugatuck, Dudleyville and Douglas on the south bank of
the Kalamazoo River, and Singapore, a sawmill community near the mouth of the river. ¶ A brand new lighthouse
had been constructed near the mouth of the Kalamazoo
River in 1859, with a fifth order Fresnel lens. This wooden
structure was 150 feet northeast of an older, partially stone,
structure that had been built in 1839. The old lighthouse
had been undermined by river and wave action and toppled
in 1858. The building constructed in 1859, later used as a
summer cottage, stood until it was destroyed in a tornado
April 3, 1956. ¶ Residents hoped that the new lighthouse
was an indication that the federal government would fund
some kind of harbor improvements in the near future. The
natural channel of the Kalamazoo River was tortuous and
shallow. Because the river entered Lake Michigan flowing
against the prevailing winds with no protection, the mouth
was wide and tended to shoal in a storm. In 1859 Francis
Browne Stockbridge, who would later be a U. S. senator,
and lumberman Otis R. Johnson formed O. R. Johnson
& Co. which owned both a lumbermill in the settlement
of Saugatuck and one, later two, in Singapore as well as a
store downtown. They added their voices to those already
clamoring for harbor improvements. ¶ In Ganges Township, south of Saugatuck, there were 759 residents in 1860,
most engaged in farming although there was an operating
tannery at Plummerville and some small sawmills which
manufactured lumber for domestic use. Also by 1860, the
cultivation of fruits for the market was just beginning. The

SAUGATUCK
CA. 1864
PL. 2

LIGHTHOUSE
PL. 3

SAUGATUCK
AND
GANGES
TOWNSHIP
MAPS
PLS. 4 & 5

1861
1862
1863
1864
1865
AFTER THE WAR

17

1861

1862

1863

1864

1865

AFTER THE WAR

new orchards were mainly peach trees, but included apple and cherry trees with some grape vines and small fruit. Onions were also an area specialty. ¶ Manpower was much in demand. If the family didn't need him at home, a young man could make good wages "working out" on neighboring farms. Mill hands and other village workers were even more reluctant than farm boys to give up a steady job for the life of a soldier, but all were paying close attention to the newspapers and telegraph wires. ¶ In the December 10, 1860 issue of the *Allegan Journal*, while South Carolina was still examining its options, the editor noted:

> The South Carolina "secession" movement does not appear to very greatly derange our business affairs here in Allegan. Farmers are actively engaged in bringing in all kinds of farm produce. Our streets are literally crammed with sleighs, loaded down with wheat, corn, oats, shingles, wood and everything usually produced on the farm. The last was an abundant harvest, and our farmers are now reaping the rewards of their honest industry.

FORT SUMTER LOST, BOYS START DRILLING

In the first military action, April 12, 1861, Confederate shore batteries fired on Fort Sumter, in the harbor at Charleston, South Carolina. News of Fort Sumter reached Detroit about the time of its surrender the following day. Three days after Fort Sumter fell, Lincoln put out a call for 75,000 men for three months feeling that the rebellion would be wrapped up by that time. At his home in Jackson, Governor Austin Blair was advised by telegram from the War Department that Michigan's quota was one infantry regiment. Communities vied for the privilege of participating in that first regiment. George W. Bailey, one of the early enlistees, later wrote:

> On the fair grounds at Allegan during the latter part of April and for part of May, a squad of Allegan county volunteers were quartered and when that nucleus increased it took a military form. Officers were elected to lead or direct future movements. And who of that band was more worthy to lead as captain than our young, patriotic Christian comrade, Chauncey J. Bassett, supported by first Lieutenant Henry Stark of Otsego, a veteran 'who had smelled powder' a few years previous in Mexico and Alfred

Wallin of Saugatuck, second lieutenant. After these came the required number of non-commissioned warrant officers and then we were on 'a war footing.' Lacking in three things only of bringing the rebellion to a speedy and permanent close – first, muster into U. S. military service; second, arms and ammunition; third, brought face to face with the rebellious horde who scoffed at our patriotism and insulted our dignity by calling us 'Northern mudsills' and 'Lincoln hirelings' all of which caused our loyal blood to boil.[1]

The Allegan County men, drilling under the direction of Daniel A. Marbelle who had been in the band in the regular Army, were informed early in May that the quota for companies called for three months was full. Judge William B. Williams went to Detroit to intercede for the company, but was unable to sway the governor although he did report that the elected officers could go to Dearborn and drill, expecting that if the war did not come to a swift conclusion there would be another enlistment call in August or September. ¶ The 1st Michigan Infantry was made up of small detachments of "home guard" which had some previous experience with guns and marching. Ten companies were mustered: two from Detroit and one each from Jackson, Coldwater, Manchester, Ann Arbor, Burr Oak, Ypsilanti, Marshall and Adrian. Shortly after its organization it was obvious that the war would not be over in three months. The reorganization of the 1st Michigan Infantry with enlistments, this time for three years, began June 28, 1861, before the return of the original regiment. Several Allegan County men later served in the 1st Michigan Infantry.

"WE PLEDGE OUR LIVES, OUR FORTUNES
AND OUR SACRED HONOR"

On April 29, 1861, a meeting was held in Saugatuck at Morrison's Hall. The details were reported in the *Allegan Journal* under the headline:

UNION MEETING AT NEWARK

A National mass meeting of the citizens of Saugatuck and vicinity was held at Morrison's Hall on Monday evening April 29. ¶ Levi Loomis of Ganges, was called to the chair and J. G. Butler elected Secretary. Messrs Geo. Harris, F. B. Wallin, E. Mix, and Nel-

1861
1862
1863
1864
1865
AFTER THE WAR

19

NEWSPAPER
NOTICE
PL. 6

son Wade were chosen a Committee on Resolutions who reported the following which were unanimously adopted. ¶ Whereas, A portion of our country is in open rebellion against the Government, and with arms are opposing the constituted authorities and bidding defiance to the Laws; therefore ¶ Resolved, That we cannot admit the right of Secession, for it involves our own destruction, or in other words, secession is rebellion, and as such should be put down by all the powers of the Federal Government. ¶ Resolved, That like our forefathers, we pledge our lives, our fortunes, and our sacred honor to sustain inviolate the Union and Constitution, purchased by their blood, ¶ Patriotic speeches were made by F. B. Wallin and F. B. Stockbridge of Saugatuck. Hon G. Meyers of Allegan, followed by the presentation of an Enrollment list and the names of twenty of the audience were immediately subscribed. After a few national songs from the glee Club, the meeting adjourned, giving 3 cheers for the volunteers, 3 for Gen. Scott, and 3 for the Union.

Levi Loomis, pres't
James G. Butler, sec'y

The men who were prominent in the meeting are a cross section of western Allegan County's most influential citizens. Chairman Levi Loomis was a Ganges farmer and former mill operator who had come to Allegan County in 1835 settling first at Swan Creek. He was married in 1837 and moved with his wife to Singapore, a sawmill settlement near the mouth of the Kalamazoo River. They purchased farmland in Ganges Township in 1839 and were among the first fruit growers in the county. At 51, Loomis was too old for active service, but two of his sons enlisted in the Union army. One would not return. ¶ James G. Butler was the son of William G. Butler who had founded the settlement at Saugatuck in 1830. His father had died in 1857. James had attended high school in the East and was a 21-year-old student at the University of Michigan when the war began. The 1860 census identifies him as a surveyor. He would enlist in the Union cavalry in September of 1861 and rise to the rank of major. ¶ Elisha Mix, a member of the committee of resolutions, had moved from New York City to Allegan County in 1853 with Elam A. Fenn, who would eventually found Fennville. Al-

LOOMIS
BUTLER
MIX
WADE
WALLIN
&
STOCKBRIDGE
FRONT I - 6

though he was 44 years old he enlisted in the cavalry and left the service at the end of the war a brigadier general, the county's highest ranking officer. ¶ Others on the committee included: George H. Harris, whose family owned a drug store in Saugatuck, he would enlist in the 6th Michigan Infantry in August 1861, as a corporal, but finish the war as a white officer with the 96th U. S. Colored Infantry in Louisiana; Nelson Wade, the brother of Jonathan Wade, one of the first settlers in what was then known as Dudleyville; and Franklin B. Wallin, one of the sons of C. C. Wallin & Sons, a firm with tanneries at Dingleville (now mostly Clearbrook Golf Course) which later bought the Gerber tannery in Douglas. Although Wallin was 29, a prime candidate for military service, he had broken his shoulder at the tannery and could not enlist until it healed. He never served, but he was a gifted orator and much in demand at patriotic occasions. ¶ Francis Browne Stockbridge also spoke at the meeting. He was a partner in the firm O. R. Johnson and Co. which owned sawmills at Saugatuck and Singapore. He served in the Michigan Legislature 1869 to 1872 and was elected to the U. S. Senate, a position he held until his death in 1894. According to a county biographical volume, during the Civil War "although not in active service, he was on the staff of Gov. Blair, and gained the rank of Colonel."[2] ¶ They gathered at Morrison's Hall, a meeting place on the second floor of S. A. Morrison's general store, located near the intersection of Butler and Culver Streets. The store was later operated in partnership with his son-in-law, John Francis, until it burned in 1879.

REFUGEES FROM MISSOURI

The war in Missouri was particularly nasty and uncivilized. In May of 1861 Brigadier General Nathaniel Lyon had captured an entire camp of Confederates and marched them through the streets of St. Louis to prison. When a crowd on the streets attempted to interfere he shot nearly two dozen civilians before being allowed to proceed unhindered. This may have been the incident that prompted the action described below. ¶ According to Saugatuck historian May Francis Heath, "Just as the Civil War broke out, two young girls came to Saugatuck to get away from the city of St. Louis until the war cloud blew over. They were Margaret and Mary Whalen. Mary became the bride of Wiliam Coulson, a millwright of Douglas, and Margaret became Mrs. James Naughtin and these villages were their homes for the rest of their lives." The Naughtin family cleared land and set an orchard. near Wallinville. James Naughtin died in 1887 and his widow married Henry Holt, a veteran of the 13th Michigan Infantry.

MORRISON'S HALL PL. 7

SLAVERY, THE "HUMILIATING ELEMENT," DROPS THE MASK

On May 3, 1861, Lincoln put out a call for additional troops, a total of 500,000 men for three years. Michigan's quota was about 20,000. Although many States would declare then, and later, that the war was strictly about States' rights and the preservation of the Union, Governor Blair made it clear in a May 7, 1861 speech that, to himself and much of Michigan, slavery was an important issue from the beginning. He told the Michigan Legislature:

> African slavery, the great and only disturbing element in our institutions, after having ruled the country for sixty years and during that time driven the free States from one humiliating concession to another . . . has dropped the mask and taken up arms . . . . It cannot be that this wicked rebellion will succeed. Utterly without cause . . . it can have neither the sympathies of mankind nor the favor of God.

He closed with a plea for funds noting that "considerable expenses have already been incurred and paid from the voluntary loan of citizens to the State." ¶ Even though the average Michigan man knew little about slavery and slaves, they understood the patriotic call to "Preserve the Union" and eligible men flocked to enlist, concerned that the war would be over before they got there. On May 13, 1861, there was a rally at Grand Rapids for the 3rd Michigan Infantry. New enlistees from the Saugatuck area were Alfred M. Gardner, 22, a farm laborer; Ed Goble, who enlisted at Saugatuck, a Corporal, but was a resident of Van Buren County; Perry Goshorn, 27, a farmer near the shore of the lake that bears his name; Jerome Kibbe, 28, a Saugatuck Township farmer; Joseph Shuler, 25; and John Simkins, 23. Recruits from Ganges were David Davis, 22; Nelson T. Davis, 24; Albert Hamlin, 22; and Joseph L. Payne, 22. And from nearby in Allegan county, Sylvester Gay, 32; Calvin Hall, 37; James Reeve, 25, a sawyer at the Fennville mill and James Rhodes, 21, a laborer on his family's farm in Manlius Township, answered the call.

"THANK GOD FOR MICHIGAN!"

On May 16, 1861, the 1st Michigan Infantry arrived in Washington D.C. by rail, and was reported to have been "the first Western regiment at the Capitol." When he was told of the regiment's arrival, President Lincoln, who was concerned for the defense of Washington, was said to have remarked, "Thank God for Michigan!" ¶ Company I of the 3rd Michigan Infantry was recruited from the lakeshore townships of Allegan County. Just before the regiment was ready to be accepted it was decided that the number in each company would be increased from 83 to 101. The details of a May 31 meeting held to recruit additional men were reported June 10, 1861 by the Saugatuck correspondent for the *Allegan Journal* under the headline:

OFF FOR THE WAR

Hon. John Haire, member of the Legislature from Ottawa County, arrived at our town last Wednesday evening. He came in the vocation of recruiting officer in search of soldiers to go into immediate service. He had no difficulty in obtaining the quota of men assigned to him by Captain George Wetherwax, the gentleman in command of Company I. This Company belonging to the Third Regiment, was accepted some time ago and will be mustered into the United States service at Grand Rapids next week . . . . As soon as it was known that the mission of Mr Haire to our town was to get men to fight and not play soldier, the boys did not hesitate, but came up to the scratch eager to sign the muster roll and be marching. Through the kindness of Messrs. F. B. Wallin and John H. Billings, the boys were carried gratis to their place of destination – Grand Rapids , the rendezvous of the Third Regiment, where they will be mustered into service, armed and equipped, and go into encampment either at Grand Rapids or Fort Wayne immediately. The boys carry with them the best wishes of all, and their friends and relations would unite in prayer – God bless our brave young volunteers.

Because the railroad had not yet been built to Allegan, county enlistees usually had to march to Kalamazoo or Grand Rapids, where they either went into temporary training camps or boarded the train for Detroit. For the 3rd Michigan Infantry unit, Franklin B. Wallin, who ran a tannery near Saugatuck, and John H. Billings, who operated the stage between Allegan and the lakeshore (and whose son, Charles, was among the enlistees), provided transportation for the new men to join the regiment encamped

1861

1862

1863

1864

1865

AFTER THE WAR

24

in Grand Rapids. ¶ On June 4, 1861, as final preparations were being made to muster the 3rd Michigan Infantry into federal service, George W. Bailey and two Allegan friends walked through the night from Allegan to Grand Rapids to enlist. Bailey had been a member of the first company that had collected on the Allegan Fairgrounds hoping to become part of the three months' regiment. He was the son of Leonard Bailey who, with his brother Jacob, had come to Clyde Township from New York to build a sawmill on section 10. The mill operated from 1838 to 1840 when the brothers left for other businesses. Leonard married and moved to Allegan where his oldest son, George, was born in 1841. ¶ There was tremendous community pride in the men being sent to battle. The Sunday before the official mustering in of the 3rd Michigan Infantry new Private George W. Bailey wrote later,

G. BAILEY
FRONT 7

> I was agreeably surprised by a visit from father and mother, who drove over from Allegan, and who brought with them pies, cakes, baked chicken and other food enough to feed the half of my company, which was distributed among my old friends in Company I from the lakeshore.

The next day an Allegan businessman visited them bringing two more recruits. The regiment left Grand Rapids June 13, 1861 for Washington commanded by Colonel Daniel McConnell of Grand Rapids. They went by train to Detroit and boarded a steamer to Cleveland, Ohio, where another train carried them through "Secesh" country to Washington D. C.

NAVAL MANEUVERS OFF SOUTH CAROLINA

Many Great Lakes sailors, and those who would eventually sail on Lake Michigan, were part of the U. S. Navy which soon after the action at Fort Sumter set up a blockade along the Atlantic coast to limit traffic in and out of Southern ports. Patrick Devine, who would later be based in Saugatuck, was coxswain aboard the U. S. Navy steamer Union on June 18, 1861 when the vessel captured the sailing ship Amelia which was attempting to run the blockade. According to the captain's report:

On the morning of the 18th of June, being off the harbor of Charleston, a sail was discovered in the offing to windward about 12 miles, standing in shore, and apparently under easy sail. I was directed to go in pursuit. Chase was immediately given and as we approached she changed her course, and stood from us; but seeing that we were gaining upon her, and while in the act of firing a gun, she tacked and stood for us. Upon coming up, she proved to be the ship Amelia from Liverpool, belonging and bound to Charleston with an assorted contraband cargo. I took possession and convoyed her to the anchorage . . . . She came very near getting in and would have done so if the pilots of Charleston had kept a bright lookout. The captain of the Amelia says there are several American vessels bound to Charleston under English colors, so I beg of you to lose no time in sending us down a steamer or two.[4]

The Amelia was the Union's third prize since June 1 and she would add one more before being seriously damaged in a collision with the Spanish vessel Ne Plus Ultra on July 2. Devine had arrived in America from Belfast, Ireland, in 1860 and served on saltwater ships and in the shipyards of Philadelphia before the war. He enlisted in the Navy in April of 1861 and continued in service until the winter of 1862 when, as he later wrote, he "went on shore, got on a spree and was left behind." Later that year he re-enlisted in the Navy using the alias "John Manning" and served on the revenue cutter Forward until the end of the war. Devine moved to Saugatuck and was an active crewman on the Great Lakes for the Brittain boats and others.

THE FIGHTING BEGINS

The first area soldiers saw action on July 18, 1861, when the 2nd and 3rd Michigan Infantry participated in a reconnaissance action at Blackburn's Ford, Virginia, and encountered a force of Confederate soldiers firing from a wooded area. The first Michigan man wounded in the war was Private Mathias Wollenweber of Wayne County, near Detroit. ¶ The first major battle of the war occurred at Bull Run, a small river southwest of Washington, near Manassas Junction where two armies of green, untrained recruits met on July 21, 1861. The North "won" the morning skirmish, but lost ground in the afternoon, ending in a rush back to the

1861
1862
1863
1864
1865
AFTER THE WAR
25

north bank of Bull Run. The retreat was further hampered by the carriages of citizens who had ridden out from town to watch the battle. The 1st Michigan Infantry fought with the Third Division, Second Brigade and did well by green recruit standards. The 2nd, 3rd and 4th Michigan Infantry regiments were in the field but not actively engaged. According to official records, they "had the honor of covering the retreat." Senator Zechariah Chandler of Michigan was a spectator and gave President Lincoln an eyewitness account.

ORGANIZING THE 6TH MICHIGAN INFANTRY

On June 19, 1861 Alfred C. Wallin of Saugatuck, who had been elected lieutenant by the first company of men which had drilled at the Allegan Fairgrounds in April, enlisted in Co. G, 6th Michigan Infantry at its organization and was mustered as second lieutenant. Company G was dubbed the "Littlejohn Light Guard" named in honor of Judge Flavius J. Littlejohn of Allegan. In addition to Wallin, Chauncey J. Bassett of Allegan and Henry Stark of Otsego, who had also been elected officers of the first group which had drilled at the Allegan fairgrounds, went as captain and first lieutenant. Wallin's family ran tanneries on Moore's Creek on what would later be Clearbrook Golf Course near Saugatuck and had an interest in the tannery at Douglas. Alfred, the third Wallin brother, was only occasionally active in the business. He had been attending law school when the war broke out. ¶ The officers of the 6th Michigan Infantry spread out into the countryside to find men to fill its ranks. At a rally at Ganges on August 5 and 6 at least 10 township men enlisted in Co. G including John B. Bartell, Frederich Dailey, George W. Dailey, Enoch Davis, John J. Maine, George H. Newcombe, Charles E. Plummer, John Rollins, Enoch Simpson, Osborn Swaney, Theodore Weed and Frank Whipple. George Newcombe was discharged on writ of habeas corpus on August 29, nine days after his enlistment. This may have been because his parents caught him falsifying his age. All of the others were farm laborers in the Ganges area, most from family farms. William Henry Parrish, of Pine Plains (later Valley) Township, enlisted August 5 at Allegan. ¶ Enlistment for the 6th Michigan Infantry continued in Saugatuck from August 9 to 19. The drive netted Corporal George H. Harris of Saugatuck, who had been part of the first war meeting; Levi Higby and Robert Payne of Ganges, and Frank Seymour, 26, a Clyde township farmer, who traveled to Allegan to enlist on August 16. On August 19, apparently having missed the enrollment at Ganges, Benjamin Fry, a Ganges township farmer, went to Allegan to enlist as corporal in Co. G. One

PROFILE OF A SOLDIER

Who were these volunteers, ready to risk life limb, and, in many cases, the fortunes of their families, for the abstract cause of "union" or "freedom?" ¶ The two main communities under study here, Saugatuck and Ganges Townships, each furnished roughly the same total number of men. About 110 in Ganges and 111 in Saugatuck have been confirmed by using the Michigan rosters and other sources. An additional 48 men with lakeshore ties were included as area soldiers for the purposes of this study, most from Manlius and Casco Townships, but a few also from Laketown, Fillmore and Clyde. ¶ The populations of Saugatuck and Ganges Townships were not very different in number. The 1860 federal census shows Saugatuck Township at 816 people and Ganges Township at 759. In percentage of total population, 13 percent in Saugatuck and 14 percent in Ganges enlisted, or were drafted, as soldiers. In both cases, this does not count the 18 individuals identified as serving in the Civil War-era U. S. Navy. ¶ In both townships, about two-thirds of those enlistees for whom we can identify marital status were unmarried. The Ganges soldier is slightly more likely to be a bachelor (69 percent in Ganges to 67 percent in Saugatuck). Married soldiers in both townships nearly always also left behind at least one child. The only exceptions were a handful of soldiers who married quickly before they left for the training camps like Charles

C. Billings of the 3rd Michigan Cavalry who married September 5, 1861 and enlisted September 6. And Captain Isaac Wilson, also of the 3rd Michigan Cavalry, who married while he was home on furlough in 1864. ¶ Along with the higher percentage of unmarried enlistees, Ganges had more very young men. Thirty-one (or 28 percent) of the soldiers from Ganges were under 20 years of age. Most of these were young men still living and working on the family farm, often the younger or youngest of the male siblings. Only 22, or 20 percent of the Saugatuck men were in the same age bracket. ¶ Other age groups: 20-29 years, Saugatuck, 51 percent; Ganges, 46 percent; 30-39 years, Saugatuck, 21 percent; Ganges 19 percent; and 40 and over, Saugatuck, 9 percent (including a 55 year old), Ganges, 2 percent. ¶ In Ganges Township, a whopping 82 percent of those who enlisted were engaged in farming (18 owned their own small farms, 40 were farm laborers). Other occupations recorded in Ganges were five day laborers (mill or dock workers), one teacher, two clergymen, three carpenters and two millers. ¶ In Saugatuck Township, only 35 percent were engaged in farming. There were 13 day laborers, eight who were described as "works in sawmill," two carpenters, two students, four blacksmiths, two engineers, three lumbermen and one each: fisherman, painter, clerk, brewer, teamster, saloon keeper, raftsman, bricklayer, jobber, photographer, pharmacist and printer.

of the last enlistees was John P. Parrish, the 44-year-old father of Private William Henry Parrish of Co. G. Although the 1850 census describes John as a physician, he enlisted as a wagoner. ¶ On August 20, 1861, the 6th Michigan Infantry was mustered-in at Kalamazoo. Recently arrived recruits included William J. Bailey of Ganges and John B. Smith who enlisted at Saugatuck that day. There were two companies from Niles and one each from St. Joseph, Schoolcraft, Dowagiac, Marshall, Saline, Allegan, Charlotte and Albion. The regiment numbered 944 officers and men, commanded by Colonel Frederick W. Curtenius of Kalamazoo. They boarded the trains and headed east on August 30.

A "WATERY" GOOD-BYE IN INDIANA

S. & J. EDDY
FRONT 8

Scott Wilmoth Eddy, who would later move to Ganges, enlisted in the 44th Indiana Infantry at Warsaw, Indiana. He had wanted to go during the first call in April, but his father would not give his permission, so Scott had to wait until he turned 18 on June 14. The company left on August 20 for the training camp at Fort Wayne. Eddy wrote later:

> Then came the leave taking. The people got us a fine dinner at the hotel. Everybody was there to see us off. Now it was some sight to see fathers and mothers and sweethearts and friends bidding their boys goodbye. Not sure they would ever see them again. It was a watery time. I think there were about 80. I said I wasn't going to shed tears. I was going home and met Fanny Eddy, a little girl then. She kissed me and said, goodbye, and burst out crying. I couldn't hold out; and the tears come now; and I haven't thought of it in years
> . . . . So many young boys. I had never been out of the country. did not know one card from another. The train came. It was made up of flat cars. We had to go on it and we got dusty and black.[5]

Three Eddy brothers, Scott, William and Jonathan, fought in and would survive the war.

RECRUITING HORSEMEN AND FOOT SOLDIERS

From August 28 to September 21, 1861, West Michigan enlistment opened for the 2nd Michigan Cavalry. Volunteers included James Hutchinson, later a Saugatuck engineer; Uri M. Nichols, a Ganges Township farmer; Oscar D. Robinson, a Saugatuck riverboat captain; John Nies

1861
1862
1863
1864
1865
AFTER THE WAR
28

of Fillmore Township, later a Saugatuck hardware store owner and Stillman Shepherd, straight from the family farm in Ganges Township. ¶ John Nies was the oldest son of Dirk John and Ikien Nies who had immigrated to Fillmore Township from Holland in 1852. The father died in 1853 and the four sons carried on. John wrote later that the leader of the Dutch colony, the Reverend A. C. Van Raalte, "preached a powerful sermon, explaining carefully the causes of the war," and the young men "became convinced it was their duty to go. It became a cause to them."[6] ¶ William T. Kimsey, 21, who had lived at Saugatuck off and on beginning in 1855, returned to his old home in Waterloo, Indiana, and, accompanied by his younger brother, John M., enlisted on September 25, 1861, in Co. K of the 44th Indiana Infantry. Although both were printers by trade, having founded a newspaper in DeKalb County, Indiana, they both enlisted as musicians and were soon part of the regimental band. Their father was an Indiana doctor, but their grandfather had come to America from England as part of the British army during the Revolutionary War. He found his sympathies were on the side of the colonists, and he visited General George Washington who gave him an officer's commission in the Continental Army.

FORMER PLAYMATES ENLIST TOGETHER

Many of the men signing up to fight for the Union were lifelong friends. In the 1840s less than 100 people, some accounts say less than 50, actually lived in the area that would be Saugatuck Village. There were three young children, James G. Butler, son of Allegan County's first settlers, whose mother died in 1842; Clara Brown, a year younger than James, whose family moved in with the Butlers to help care for the children after Eliza Butler's death; and Charles C. Billings, who was born in 1843, son of the local stage driver, whose family lived nearby on Butler Street. ¶ James Butler enlisted in the 3rd Michigan Cavalry on September 2, 1861, at Grand Rapids and came to Saugatuck with a recruiting team. One of the first men he enlisted was his childhood friend, Charles C. Billings, who paused only long enough to marry Clara Brown before signing up on

C. BILLINGS
FRONT 9

1861
1862
1863
1864
1865
AFTER THE WAR

29

September 6. Even before the unit was mustered-in Butler was promoted to the rank of commissary sergeant. ¶ Other enlistees in the 3rd Michigan Cavalry, Co. A., included Albert H. Fenn, 18, son of Elam A. Fenn, the founder of Fennville; Sergeant James G. Butler, 21, son of William G. Butler, the founder of Saugatuck; Joshua C. Young, 26, an engineer from Manlius Township; George W. Smith, 20, a teamster who later worked for the Douglas Basket Factory; Seth Winn, 21, from the family farm in Ganges; James K. Dole, 17, a Saugatuck "jobber"; Kneeland Graves, 34, a Saugatuck teamster; Solomon Stanton, 30, a Saugatuck blacksmith; Jacob Heringa, 21, later a Saugatuck sawmill worker; David White, 28, a Saugatuck raftsman; John Beers, 44, of Saugatuck; Frederick Edwards, 23, of Saugatuck; Isaac Wilson, a Saugatuck lumberman who enlisted as second lieutenant in Co. A; Freeman Ross, 33, an engineer working at Singapore; James Algers, 27, of Saugatuck; Theodore "Frederick" Kleeman, 32, who owned a tavern in Saugatuck; William McCormick, 21, son of James McCormick, one of the first settlers in Manlius Township who had arrived in 1837; Edward Pheelan, 40, of Saugatuck; Edward Slocum, 30, a Manlius Township hotel keeper; Robert W. Helmer, 35, a Saugatuck Township sawyer; and John Priest, a Saugatuck blacksmith who missed the recruiters in Saugatuck and traveled to Bloomingdale to enlist.

GUARDING A STEAMER

Early enlistees were already under fire. William H. Parrish, with the 6th Michigan Infantry, was encamped at Baltimore when his company received an assignment to guard a steamer attempting to run to Washington with hay and grain, probably for the vast number of cavalry horses encamped at the capital. On October 27, 1861 Parrish wrote to his brother:

> Orders were received to detail seventy men to guard the steamship Columbia to Washington. Co. G got the preference, started from camp 1/2 past 8 o'clock, got onboard, started from the wharf at 1/2 past 10 . . . . started for the Potomac which we reached at dusk, continued up the river until about 12 o'clock when we anchored until daylight. Started on at half past 7.

1861

1862

1863

1864

1865

AFTER THE WAR

30

We were stopped by a federal blockade fleet and told that the Rebels had erected Batteries just above so that there was no passing . . . . We lay at anchor until 8 o'clock at night the rebels had fired six shots into the steam ship Pawnee, injuring her considerable. There were also 30 boats including steamers, barques, schooners and sloops in sight, which the fleet had stopped thinking it unsafe to run up. We started at 8 o'clock up the river. We had persuaded the Capt. of the boat to go up. We ran up about 3 miles . . . when I saw the flash of a gun . . . it was soon followed by another and another until they numbered 24. 3 of our men were not seen, when they were looked for they were found in the hay half scared to death. None of the shots took effect. We stayed in Washington until last night . . . We went off the boat and drilled some. The soldiers there looked as though they never saw drilling before. We did not know what it meant until the officer told our lieutenant we were the best drilled Co. he had seen.[7]

FLOCKING TO THE 13TH

From October 1 to 12, 1861, a series of rallies was held at Ganges for enlistment in Co. B, 13th Michigan Infantry. Enlistees included the following men, all Ganges Township farmers or farm laborers, most from family farms: Corporal John H. Baldwin, 24; William B. Chase, 32; Wagoner Israel Bensinger, 26; James W. Billings, 16 (in 1862 his father, Walter, would enlist in the Calvary); William Gould, 23; David Hyett, 21; Richard Purdy, 32; George F. Warner, 23; Corporal Joseph Miller, 24; William O. Allen, 31; VanSlycke Clark, 34; Robert Meldrum, 24; Musician Edward Breen, 16; Cyril Le Duc, 29; and Edson Amidon. Other area enlistees: Sergeant Dewitt C. Kenyon, 34, who enlisted at Ganges, but was actually a resident of Barry County; Second Lieutenant Jacob G. Fry, 32, of Glenn, a veteran of the Mexican War; Samuel Stillson, 27, a Saugatuck Township farmer; Sergeant Spencer Banks, 28, of Pier Cove; A. C. L. Gillespie from Saugatuck Township; Daniel Lee, 27, later a bridge tender at Douglas; and John Stillson, 21, a farm laborer on the Philetus Purdy farm in Saugatuck Township. ¶ The same month recruiters for Co. I, 13th Michigan Infantry began their work at Saugatuck. Enlistees included: Second Lieutenant Peter Van Arsdale, 27, who enlisted at

1861
1862
1863
1864
1865
AFTER THE WAR

31

Saugatuck but was a resident of Kalamazoo County; Peter H. Billings, 28, from the Fennville area Billings family; Mordant D. Loomis, 21; William A. Upson, 22, the brother of Lewis Upson who had married Elizabeth, the daughter of Douglas founders Lucinda and William F. Dutcher; Edward J. Stow, 39, of Manlius Township; Charles L. Bard of Saugatuck; Henry Holt, 23, a Kalamazoo River fisherman; Sergeant George M. Rowe, 22; Amos Dunning, 26, a Saugatuck Township carpenter and John Knight, 21, of Saugatuck. ¶ In a second push for enlistment in the 13th Michigan Infantry, Co. B held a rally at Ganges in December, 1861, those enlisting included: Henry B. Oliver, a Saugatuck Township farmer; Austin Foote, 28, a Ganges farm laborer; James Scrimger, 34, a Mexican war veteran from New Casco, later Glenn; Edward Penfold, Ganges farmer; Musician Franklin W. Martin, 17, a laborer boarding with Saugatuck fisherman George Shriver; Charles E. McCarty, 27, later a Clyde Township farmer; Lewis Bell, Ganges Township farm laborer; John Claffy, 33, a Saugatuck Township farmer; Frank May; and Adam Miller, a Ganges farmer . The first captain of Co. B was George B. Force of Gun Plain. ¶ Later in December, recruiters for Co. I, 13th Michigan Infantry hit Saugatuck again. New enlistees included Ezekial Niles, 55, who had recently arrived in Saugatuck Township from Clinton County; Leander Ballard, 42, a farmer who enlisted at Ganges; John A. McClair, 30, a day laborer who was living in Allegan in 1860; William Joslyn, 18; and Orrin P. Kingsbury, 32, a Ganges Township farmer. The first captain of Co. I was Henry C. Stoughton of Otsego.

"TELL ME WHO GETS YOUR WOOD . . ."

In the patriotic fervor of the moment many young men enlisted with their friends, and lived to have second thoughts, especially those who left behind wives and children. James M. Ducumb of the 29th Indiana Infantry wrote his young wife from camp in Hardin County, Kentucky, on November 20, 1861:

You stated in your last letter that you was a very unhappy woman because of my absence, you will please
bear in mind that you are not the only lonesome person. What under the sun can I do for you now? Going
into the war was as unexpected to me as it was to you.
If everything could have been foreseen things might
have turned out different. I wish you to tell me how
you get money to buy Clothing and groceries up to
this time. Also where you got Corn enough to fatten
the hogs because the hogs ought to have at least 40
bu. of corn, also tell me if you have been able to get
the cellar closed . . . . I want you to answer these ques-
tions as they come. I want you to tell me who gets
your wood and how you have managed your affairs.[8]

Physician-turned-wagoner John P. Parrish, who had enlisted to serve with his son, William Henry, in the 6th
Michigan Infantry, found that his efforts to safeguard his
son had paid off. He wrote his wife on December 7, 1861,
from Baltimore:

William Henry has been sick two weeks with the
lung fever. He got cold and had to march on the expedition that we are on. He was very sick for a week
that I had to take care of him nights and walk by the
side of the ambulance day times to give him medicine
and drink and fix his bed . . . . I had no medicine for
him. I had to depend on the regimental surgeon for
medicine. He is quite comfortable now the fever is
broke . . . . He will be up in a few days I think. You
need not worry about him for I am allowed to be with
him and to take care of him in a good room in a first
rate place. There was some 10 or 12 sick and lazy that
came back at the same time. I had charge of the rest
of the sick. One poor fellow . . . had the same disease
that William did. He rode in the same ambulance
four days and on Sunday night got on the steamer to
come to Baltimore with us, but on Monday morning
at 1/2 past 8 he died.[9]

Nearly three years later, when he was pondering re-enlist-
ment (he decided against it), Parrish wrote,

If I had known how long it would have been [not seeing his wife and children] perhaps I should not have
gone with William and then he would have never
lived through his dreadful sickness, at least that is
the opinion of those that were there at the time. I say,
as I have before, I am glad I went.[10]

HURRAH FOR THE VOLUNTEERS!

They come, they come, the sturdy and strong
With hearts that know no fears;
Behold the march of the mortal throng,
And hark to their thundering cheers.
Ha! The Eagle screams and the bayonet gleams!
Hurrah for the volunteers!

They come from the forest, the shop and the plow,
The free-born pioneers;
And you hear the Northman's solemn vow,
As the cloud of battle nears.
Ha! The Eagle screams and the bayonet gleams!
Hurrah for the volunteers!

They form and file at stern command,
As the rebel boat appears;
And the rifle aimed with steady hand,
Cries, "Death to the mutineers!"
Ha! The Eagle screams and the bayonet gleams!
Hurrah for the volunteers!

Come then, brave men, from the Land of Lakes,
With steady step and cheers,
Our country calls, as the Union breaks,
On the Northwest pioneers!
Ha! The Eagle screams and the bayonet gleams!
Hurrah for the volunteers!

Kalamazoo Gazette
July 26, 1861

1862

IN 1861 BOTH SIDES WERE JUST BEGINNING TO collect and train soldiers. The few engagements had been largely unstructured affairs, fought by green troops that were unschooled and inclined to bolt. As 1862 opened, the high command was just starting to create a comprehensive battle plan and the troops were becoming more proficient. Still the majority of the fighting men on both sides had not yet been in battle or "seen the elephant" as it was expressed in the jargon of the day.

THE 8TH RECLAIMS A CORNER OF SOUTH CAROLINA

On the first day of January, 1862, the 8th Michigan Infantry launched a successful attack on fortifications near Port Royal Ferry, South Carolina. Supported by fire from gunboats on the river, the regiment located and eliminated a masked battery in the woods near the ferry landing. They planted the first American flag on the mainland of South Carolina since the state seceded. Skirmishers would have included Corporal Owen Cook, son of the Saugatuck physician, Dr. James B. Cook; Quincy Lamoreux, a lumberman from the New Richmond area, and John Langan.

A CIVILIAN FIGHTS IN THE WEST

At some point in the beginning years of the war, Frederick H. May of Douglas left Michigan for Southern Illinois where he worked toward the completion of the Northern Missouri Railway, a much needed supply line for the Union army. In later years he was often spoken of as a "war hero," although he never served in the military, and was sometimes given the courtesy title of "Colonel." His obituary in a New Jersey newspaper tells the story this way:

> During the War of Rebellion he was active in aiding the Government transportation of troops and in keeping the railroads open when menaced by rebel guerillas. Once when ordered by "bushwhackers" to pull down the American flag in a railroad camp, he refused, and the leader, pulling a pistol, gave him five minutes to decide. Every half minute the guerilla called time, but when four and one-half minutes had expired a man who supplied the railroad camp with meat (he was also a friend of the leaders of the "bushwhackers") arrived out of breath and persuaded the leader to spare Mr. May, as his meat account for that week had not been settled.[1]

May was the widower of Mary Ann, the eldest daughter of Douglas founder William F. Dutcher. It was May who drew the first map of the Village of Douglas and named the town after his birthplace, Douglas, the capital of the Isle of Man, located in the Irish Sea between Scotland and Ireland. After the war, May became one of the investors

ENGRAVING: GALLANT CHARGE OF THE 8TH MICHIGAN AT ROYAL FERRY PL. 8

F. H. MAY FRONT 10

36

in the river boat Ira Chaffee, built in 1867 at Allegan. In 1869 he was hired as manager of the Allegan and Holland Railroad, later a part of the Michigan Lake Shore Railroad Company. May Station, a small watering station south of Holland in northern Fillmore Township, was named for him. He later moved to New Jersey and was president and general manager of the American Rapid Telegraph Company. He died in New Jersey in 1908 at the age of 82.

"SLAVERY SHOULD BE SWEPT FROM THE LAND."

On January 18, 1862, Governor Blair approved an act to re-organize the state militia, fearing that Great Britain might enter the war on the side of the south. A joint Legislative resolution was also approved which stated that while Michigan did not object to the burdens of fighting for the Union it felt that these burdens "should be lightened as far as possible, by confiscating to the largest extent, the property of all insurrectionists; and that as between the institution of slavery and the maintenance of the Federal Government, Michigan does not hesitate to say, that in such exigency, slavery should be swept from the land and our country maintained." A few Democrats in both houses opposed the resolution. ¶ The average Union soldier voiced few feelings for or against slavery. Studies of Civil War correspondence have shown that it was not a major topic in letters home. John P. Parrish, serving with the 6th Michigan Infantry in Louisiana where he had come in contact with many freed or runaway slaves, was one of the few deep thinkers on this subject. He wrote his wife in June of 1863:

> I think that the great beast, the dragon that thought to change laws, times and seasons speaking great smelling words and giving out that he himself was some great one, is losing some of his power and dominion . . . . God suffered the devil to lead on his coworkers (that is the Rebs) to think that they were some great ones in order that the institution of Slavery might fall of itself. For it never could sustain itself as long as it did if it had not been held up by us of the north. And now we are getting paid off for our share in upholding this outrageous sin against God

1861
1862
1863
1864
1865
AFTER THE WAR

37

J. P. PARRISH
FRONT II

and man in fighting to divest it of its power over
destinies of this Nation and my wish and prayers
are that God will thoroughly purge us of this sin
Nationally and individually.[2]

But deep thinkers in the trenches were not common. Parrish goes on to comment:

> Since writing this last page I have read it to Mr.
> Stringham of Co. E and I asked him what he
> thought of those sentiments. He said that they were
> about right. then again I read them to others of our
> Co. and they did not think much of it. But I find
> that the ones that will hoot at such ideas are those
> that do not admit of an overruling power in the des-
> tinies of nations. But all those that are strictly moral
> or of a religious turn think that I have expressed
> their views exactly. Therefore I feel encouraged that
> my views are supported by all right thinking men.

THE 6TH THWARTS A GENERAL

In January of 1862, the 6th Michigan Infantry was still stationed in Baltimore but made occasional forays into the
Virginia countryside. In a letter written January 26, 1862,
William Henry Parrish describes one futile effort and some
foraging that led to a scene:

> We started on the evening of the 13th. We went on
> board the Steamer Georgia and the next morning we
> found ourselves in the river Pocomok which emp-
> ties into Chesapeake Bay. We stopped at Newton
> Marshes for Oakhall the 17th where we expected to
> find the Rebels but they run. We stayed there a few
> days which time the boys occupied . . . picking up
> chickens turkeys and geese . . . .We then marched to
> Drommondtown . . . While there the General saw
> one of the 6th with a turkey. He asked him where he
> got it, the soldier told him of course that he bought
> it. The next day the General found that the soldier
> had stole it, so he was going to shoot him. He said
> he knew who it was if he could see him again. So he
> had the 6th brought out in rank and he proceeded to
> examine and such gobbling you never heard I'll bet.
> He finally picked Charles Knight, that Swan Creek
> chap, as the man but they told him that that man
> was sick in his tent all day. So he had to leave with-
> out his man, the boys gobbling, cooing, squealing,
> bleating, etc. Some of the officers said he would have
> a nice time shooting one of the 6th.[3]

Alfred C. Wallin, second lieutenant with Co. G, 6th Michigan Infantry, served for less than a year before resigning his commission. His resignation was approved January 23, 1862. From the regiment's winter quarters in Baltimore *Allegan Journal* correspondent George H. Harris explained in the January 27, 1862, issue that Wallin's decision was "owing to the inactivity here, and the unfavorable prospects of this command ever getting into any active engagement, and not willing to remain the recipient of the bounties of a magnanimous government, without an opportunity to render in return a just equivalent, and wishing to continue his studies at Ann Arbor, after matured reflection, concluded to resign his commission in the army." He must have changed his mind quickly for he was recommissioned February 1, 1862. The 6th left Baltimore by steamboat on February 22, 1862, for Baton Rouge, Louisiana.

THE 13TH INFANTRY HEADS FOR THE FRONT

On January 17, 1862, the 13th Michigan Infantry mustered-in at Kalamazoo. Former U.S. Senator Charles E. Stuart had organized the regiment recruiting from the western part of the state, but resigned his commission as colonel on January 27 and was replaced by Michael Shoemaker of Jackson. There were 925 officers and men on the rolls at the mustering in. County records show that more than 300 men served with the 13th Michigan Infantry from Allegan County and about 70 of these were from the Saugatuck-Ganges area.¶ Private A. C. L. Gillespie of Saugatuck Township had only a brief military career. He was deemed unable to make the trip and was left behind in a Kalamazoo hospital.

INCIDENT NEAR NEW MADRID

The 2nd Michigan Cavalry arrived in St. Louis and went by transport to Commerce, then over land to New Madrid, "where we first met the rebels and here our first fight took place" on March 13, 1862. John Nies wrote later:

> This fight took place between the fortifications on Island #10 and our forces at Madrid to which place the rebels retreated. One of their shells came over

1861

1862

1863

1864

1865

AFTER THE WAR

39

intact and was picked up by one of the boys who proceeded to open it and getting too near the fire, it exploded, and after the smoke had cleared away not a vestige of him was to be found.[4]

"NOT A BUSH OR TREE LEFT" AT SHILOH

The Battle of Shiloh or Pittsburgh Landing, Tennessee, began at dawn on April 6, 1862. Private James M. Ducomb of the 29th Indiana Infantry, whose descendants later lived in Saugatuck, wrote his wife on April 17, 1862:

> The Secesh took our men wholly by surprise, that is Grant's Forces. Our generals was not expecting an attack and . . . if it had not been for our Gunboats on the Tennessee River Grant's Forces would have all been killed and taken prisoners before Buells Forces could have arrived to assist them. The fight commenced on Sunday morning about 4 o'clock April the 6th /62 and ended the next day about Four o'clock. . . . If it had not been for the Timber there would have been a great many more men killed on both Sides and probably the Battle would not have lasted as long if it had been Cleared land. The fight was an awful one. The Secesh fought like Bull dogs. They were druged [drugged?] with all the Powder & whiskey they wanted. This they do to make them fight hard & not fear Danger. The Majority of the wounded were sent to their respective States where they belong to be Cured up. They were sent by Boatloads. . . I feel thankful that I am Still alive.[5]

The Confederates were finally forced to withdraw to Corinth but Union losses during the two days totaled nearly 14,000 men. The 13th Michigan Infantry, which had been delayed in crossing the river, arrived from Nashville "in the gathering dusk" on the second day of fighting. The 2nd Michigan Cavalry was also sent but John Nies later explained "We arrived too late to take part in the battle of Shiloh. One thing I noticed was that the bark on the trees was so badly riddled with bullets."[6] ¶ A month later Will and Scott Eddy camped on the battleground on their way back to their regiment, the 44th Indiana Infantry, after a furlough. Scott reported: "It had been a forest and not a bush left. Trees a foot through cut off 20 or 30 foot from ground. Wagons, caissons, cannon, all over. Some sight!"[7] ¶ The war was also

1861

1862

1863

1864

1865

AFTER THE WAR

40

one of ideologies. A Flint clergyman who arrived to tend to the spiritual needs of the 13th Michigan Infantry just after the Battle at Shiloh wrote in a letter dated April 17, 1862, and printed in the *Allegan Journal:*

> The enemy have shown themselves fierce and determined and the struggle is far greater than we are wont to believe at the North. I had a conversation with a Secession prisoner who remained to take care of the wounded whom they had been compelled to leave on the ground in their retreat. He advocated the war on their part by saying they were like our fathers in the time of the Revolution. I feel sure that we have got a desperate and determined foe to encounter and many of our brave men must yet perish.

THE SIEGE OF CORINTH

In April, 1862, under command of Major General Henry W. Halleck, the Union forces in the West began to advance slowly on Corinth, Mississippi. Private Scott W. Eddy of the 44th Indiana Infantry later sized up the situation in his autobiography:

> Bragg didn't want to fight and Hallack [sic] was a coward. Tom Crittenden wanted to pick ten thousand men, guaranteed to take Bragg's army. Could have done it . . . . Well, one night the rebels got all their music going. We thought must be 50 bands. We knew they were evacuating. Hallack never did a thing. Next morning we went into Corinth. Our Colonel Reed was the first man in – just room for one wagon in the road. The timber had been felled on both sides of the road, limbs cut off and sharpened.[8]

Confederates, under General Pierre G. T. Beauregard, evacuated Corinth on May 30. Occupying forces included the 13th Michigan Infantry, Battery B of the 1st Michigan Light Artillery, and the 1st Michigan Engineers and Mechanics.

WITH THE 6TH AT NEW ORLEANS

The first day of May, 1862, Union troops, including the 6th Michigan Infantry, occupied New Orleans a few days after naval forces commanded by Flag Officer David Farragut had run past the Confederate forts below the city and decimated the Confederate navy which had been guarding the Mississippi River delta. The 6th was landed at Black Bay in the rear of Fort St. Phillips with the intention of attacking but discovered that the fort, along with Fort Jackson, had surrendered. The regiment reboarded the boats and landed on May 2 at New Orleans. Lieutenant Alfred Wallin of Co. G described their reception for the Allegan newspaper:

> We were ordered to clear the dock of the dense crowd which had collected; but from whose stony lips not a syllable of welcome had come; not a single waving handkerchief; not a gesture of greeting in all that grim sea of humanity. Stark led the way and took command of half the men; I the other half. We drew up in single file on the edge of the dock; brought the men to an armed port, and moved slowly upon the silent, reluctant, yet receding crowd. We made way for the regiment and they came in shore, loaded their guns with ball, and took up the line of march for their commodious quarters in the house built by our Government, but which has of late been converted to the use of the rebels. There are about 5,000 Union troops here, besides a corps of French citizens who aid in keeping the city quiet. But I have no doubt that in the event of an attack they would aid the rebels.[9]

On May 16, 1862, part of the 6th Michigan Infantry headed up the river from New Orleans. As one private wrote:

> No one dreamed that we were to penetrate an enemy's country four hundred miles, without anything in the shape of a gunboat or even cannon for our protection . . . . We passed towns and cities, the inhabitants of which had no higher wish than to destroy us. They might easily have done so, but they were deceived as to the character of two schooners we had in tow, taking them for two of those dreadful mortar boats, which were so warningly effective at Fort Jackson and Fort Phillips. The schooners were, in fact, a couple of coal ships entirely unarmed and commanded by a couple of skippers who devoutly thanked their stars, every time a bend or bluff was passed without a broadside from the enemy.

1861
1862
1863
1864
1865
AFTER THE WAR

42

BIRD'S EYE VIEW
OF ACTION AT
NEW ORLEANS
PL. 9

About 50 miles from Vicksburg, at a settlement named Grand Gulf, a field battery of four guns opened fire on the boat:

> The gunners worked their guns with great rapid-
> ity, but not with remarkable accuracy of aim. Our
> surprise was complete. The men and officers obey-
> ing the inſtinct of self preservation rushed to the
> side of the boat fartheſt from the batteries, which
> of course came near capsizing our balloon like craft,
> and rendering her utterly unmanageable. One wheel
> was out of water while the other was half buried and
> in full motion. In this shape we turned round . . .
> thereby doubling the length of time which we would
> have been under fire had we kept the boat trimmed
> . . . our guns were not loaded and all expected to be
> out of the reach of their balls before ammunition
> could be procured and the pieces charged . . . . The
> gun boat we relied upon for protection . . . was out of
> sight and hearing. . . When the boat careened over
> and in the hotteſt of the fire, the Sergeant [Hare
> of Otsego] seized a musket and drove a crowd of
> negroes and boat hands from their hiding place in
> the lower part of the ship to the other side, thereby
> aiding in doing the only practical thing left us, viz.:
> trimming ship. After doing this, he with two other
> soldiers worked vigorously at supplying the furnaces
> with fuel, from which the panic ſtricken deck hands
> had fled in terror.[10]

But William Henry Parrish, who had been ill earlier in the war with pneumonia, was not with them. He could not recover totally from the effects of his earlier illness compounded by the southern heat and received a discharge for disability on April 12, 1862, at the hospital on Ship Island in the Mississippi. While he was ſtill in transit home his father, who remained on duty as a cook for the hospital, wrote the family in Michigan on May 9, 1862:

> Tell William Henry that the ship Eliza and Elias
> is to have ſteam pumps on board in a few days and
> ſtart again for Boſton. He ſtarted the 7th on board
> of her for home. She ran aground, sprung a leak and
> they had to come back. There were 6 of the Michi-
> gan 6 Regt. on her that had discharges and the same
> 6 are all on the Idaho with 28 or thereabouts of other

1861

1862

1863

1864

1865

AFTER THE WAR

43

Regiments that have been discharged from service
. . . . I hear the knowing ones saying that there will
be 2 or more heavy battles, one in the east and one in
the west and if our troops conquer it will just about
finish the war. I should hope that it would.[11]

BANISHED TO THE SWAMP NEAR BATON ROUGE

The 6th Michigan Infantry, after three months of wandering around the south, finally moved into its semi-perma-
nent quarters at Baton Rouge, Louisiana on May 29, 1862.
Shortly after they settled in, Colonel T. S. Clark, acting
on behalf of Brigadier General Thomas Williams who was
then in command of the troops at Baton Rouge, ordered
the 6th to camp into the nearby swampy woods and surrender the barracks to the 9th Connecticut Infantry which
had just arrived. The plan seemed doubly unfair because the
Connecticut men had tents, while the men from Michigan
did not and they were not allowed to use the tents that the
eastern soldiers were not using after they moved into the
barracks. The Michigan officers protested and were placed
under arrest for refusing to obey an order and sent to New
Orleans for trial. ¶ Lieutenant Alfred C. Wallin of Co. G,
who had earlier briefly resigned his commission to protest
the inactivity of winter quarters, resigned again on July 1,
1862. This time he did not reconsider. In December of 1862,
Wallin visited Allegan and the editor wrote afterwards that
the former lieutenant "designed to enter the legal profession.
. . . 'Alf.' looks in the best of health."[12] ¶ The 6th remained
under such field officers as it could scrape up, until General
Williams was killed in a skirmish August 5, and the western
theater commander, General Benjamin F. Butler, released
the imprisoned officers. Williams was a West Point gradu-
ate, the son of John R. Williams mayor of Detroit, and had
served with distinction during the Mexican War. His actions were attributed to his dislike of volunteer soldiers.

MEANWHILE BACK IN VIRGINIA

At Fair Oaks, Virginia (or Seven Pines) Union General
George B. McClellan had placed forces both north and
south of the Chickahominy River while he waited for re-

1861

1862

1863

1864

1865

AFTER THE WAR

44

inforcements. On May 31, 1862, Confederate General Joseph E. Johnston attacked south of the flooded river, but
McClellan managed to get one division across the river,
on shaky bridges and over swampy bottom lands, and the
Union line held. Johnston was seriously wounded and was
succeeded on June 1 by Robert E. Lee, who withdrew his
troops to Richmond. ¶ The 3rd Infantry was among the
Michigan troops active in the battle. Nelson T. Davis, a
Ganges farmer, and John Simkins of Saugatuck were killed
in action. Corporal Edwin R. Goble of Van Buren County,
who had enlisted at Saugatuck, was wounded and died a
month later in a Philadelphia hospital. Two other area men
fighting with the 3rd Infantry were wounded. Alfred M.
Gardner, a Saugatuck Township farm laborer, was discharged from the service on December 31, 1862, because of
his wounds suffered at Fair Oaks. Perry Goshorn, one of
four Goshorn brothers who farmed in the vicinity of Goshorn Lake was hospitalized but returned to action in time
to be wounded a second time at the Battle of Groveton,
Virginia, on August 29, 1862.

AFTER THE
BATTLE OF
FAIR OAKS
PL. 10

1861
1862
1863
1864
1865
AFTER THE WAR
45

SAUGATUCK MAN HELPS CAPTURE A SAILING SHIP
The Atlantic shore continued to be a contest between
Southern blockade runners attempting to get supplies into
the ports and cotton bales out, and the U. S. Navy which
worked hard at preventing the traffic. On June 3, 1862, the
U. S. bark, Gem of the Sea with Saugatuck-area sailor William G. Edgcomb aboard, captured the schooner Mary
Stewart while she was attempting to run the blockade near
the mouth of the Santee River off Georgetown, South Carolina. ¶ According to the official report "All the crew had
deserted her in their boat and made the best of their way for
the shore a short time previous to our boarding her."[13] The
schooner was sent to New York with her cargo of salt, soda,
paper, soap, mackerel, castor oil, tea and alum to be adjudi-
cated as a prize of war. The victory was especially sweet because the boat had formerly been owned by William Aiken,
Governor of South Carolina. Between December of 1861
and October of 1863, the Gem of the Sea, classified as a sail-

ing bark, captured or destroyed 14 southern-sympathizing sailing craft which tried to run the blockade in the south Atlantic. ¶ After the war, Edgcomb was master of several steam vessels at Saugatuck, and served for 10 years as justice of the peace.

PRIVATE BELTON "YIELDS TO THE TRAITORS"

Recruits were finding out that war was a great deal less enjoyable than it had seemed when they signed up back home. On June 18, 1862, Private Charles P. Belton of the 1st Michigan Infantry deserted at Gaines Mill, Virginia. The reorganized 1st Michigan Infantry had the same officers as the one that had trained to be part of the first soldiers called to war, the three months regiment. Then the new regiment left Michigan on September 16, 1861, and spent the winter encamped at Annapolis Junction, Maryland, while guarding the Washington and Baltimore Railroad. Then the 1st Michigan moved to Fortress Monroe, "attracting much notice by its fine military appearance and excellent discipline, while its stylish dress parades became a matter of notoriety." It participated in the aborted Peninsula Campaign and Belton bolted before, or during, the first battle. He was 33, a farmer from Cheshire Township, and had enlisted in Co. K on July 13, 1861, one of the first enlistees from western Allegan County. To add to the irony, Belton had written a letter to the *Allegan Journal* on March 23, 1862, from Fortress Monroe where the regiment was stationed which said in part:

> We are sick and tired of the policy of inactivity which has governed army movements so long . . . all our Michigan boys are anxious to fight in this Department as they are in every other Department of the Army. The officers and men in this Regiment I am sure will do their part. – We feel anxious to try. We might have been placed in the Fortress, but Col. Robinson and the rest of our gallant officers had rather face the enemy on the field than to live in inglorious ease in any fort. I will warrant that the noble sons of Michigan will never yield to the traitors while they can draw a sword or fire a gun.[14]

THE 9TH SURRENDERS AT MURFREESBORO

On July 13, 1862, six companies of the 9th Michigan Infantry were attacked at Murfreesboro, Tennessee, by a much larger Confederate cavalry force commanded by Nathan Bedford Forrest. After heavy fighting, the commander of the Michigan companies, Lieutenant Colonel John G. Parkhurst of Coldwater, felt that he had to surrender "or suffer my little force to be cut up alive." One of those captured was Elijah Guy Lyman, later a Casco Township farmer. After only two days in custody he was paroled and in August was exchanged. ¶ As the Battle of Murfreesboro progressed the 2nd Michigan Cavalry remained on the alert. John Nies later wrote:

> We lined up in battle line, there were two to a line. They [the Confederates] left but placed a cannon in the center of the bridge and we captured a few. That night we stood attention at our horses' heads all night. I tied my horse to my boot leg and during the night as our army were using rockets to signal and these rockets made a great deal of noise, my horse became frightened and carried me off by my boot, dragging me through the mud.[15]

THE 6TH INFANTRY AT BATON ROUGE

On August 5, 1862, the 6th Michigan Infantry which was on the banks of the Mississippi near Baton Rouge, had what E. J. Wheelock describes in a letter written on August 6 as:

> . . . one of the most eventful days in the history of the Michigan 6th Regiment of Infantry. At 4 ½ o'clock A.M. the Rebels opened fire on our entire line of pickets, driving them in in 15 minutes with slight loss. Our Regiment came immediately to the rescue. Six companies were supported by Nims' battery. Co.'s A, F, C, and D were supported by the 21st Indiana battery. The 7th Maine and 14th Indiana disgraced themselves by breaking and running on the second rally of the enemy . . . After the fight had been in progress about an hour I got my musket ready and started for the field but the smoke was so thick that I could not tell our men from theirs. Before I had gone 20 rods I found myself in the Rebel ranks. The smoke was so thick that they did not no-

tice me. As luck would have it they were ordered to charge on our Battery. This gave me a chance to get out and reach our own ranks, although it was a critical position to be placed in. [16]

Frank B. Seymour, a Clyde Township farmer, who had worn his corporal's stripe for less than a month, was wounded during the battle. He recovered in time to accept a promotion to sergeant in December. Wheelock reported that Charles Symonds was also slightly wounded "but will be able for duty in 3 or 4 days." ¶ After the battle, the 6th Michigan Infantry was commended by General Butler "for the gallant behavior of its officers and men." The unit, fighting by detachments rather than as a regiment, "prevented the enemy from flanking our right" and "handsomely held in check the enemy's advance." The 6th Michigan also captured the flag of the 9th Louisiana and sent it back to Governor Blair "to be placed with the archives of the State."

MORE UNITS READIED FOR THE FIELD

Recruitment continued through July and into August for the 4th Michigan Cavalry. Benjamin D. Pritchard, an Allegan lawyer, was attempting to enlist an entire company, with plans to be captain of that company. Shortly afterwards, his former law partner, Judge William B. Williams, resigned his judgeship and raised a company for the 5th Michigan Cavalry. Both companies were almost entirely men from Allegan County. ¶ At the same time. recruiters for the 19th Michigan Infantry visited Allegan County on August 11, 1862, and signed several men from the Fennville area including: Henry L. Blakeslee, 24, the first settler in Fennville; Milo Barker, 28, a Manlius Township day laborer; James Billings, 19, from the family farm in Clyde Township; Charles E. Reynolds of Clyde Township; Timothy Daggett, 18, of Otsego, later a resident of Saugatuck; Jacob Gunsaul, 22, of Ganges, and William Watson of Clyde, who later lived in New Casco. Elisha B. Bassett, an Allegan lawyer, enlisted as second lieutenant of Co. B. ¶ From August 12 to 20, there was a rally in the Saugatuck and Ganges area for enlistment in the 5th Michigan Cavalry. New

H. BLAKESLEE
FRONT 12

recruits included Quartermaster Lawrence Crosby, 27, of Saugatuck; First Sergeant George Lonsbury, 33, an Allegan photographer who later owned a farm in the Fennville area; William Powell, 27, of Saugatuck; Nathan Slayter, 28, of Dudleyville (later part of Douglas), a hand in the Wade sawmill; First Lieutenant George N. Dutcher, 28, son of Douglas founder William F. Dutcher; Bugler George N. Gardner, 18, a Ganges farmer; David Taylor, 23, a Ganges farmer; Elliot Chase, 22, a Saugatuck Township farmer; John Hill, 22, a Saugatuck laborer; Lewis Hirner, 30, a Saugatuck Township farmer; Samuel Shaver, 24, a Saugatuck hostler; Teamster Anthony Slack, 24, a Heath Township farmer who would later live in Douglas; Henry Werner, 33, a Saugatuck Township farm laborer; Corporal William White, 25, a worker at the Wallin tannery in Saugatuck Township; Thomas Collier, 22, a worker in the Helmer sawmill and Cornelius Gavin, 28, of Saugatuck. The company reported as ready at Detroit on August 23, 1862. ¶ The 19th Michigan Infantry completed the recruitment process and headed for training camp. On August 11, Henry Blakeslee, the first person to actually live in what would later be Fennville, enlisted in Co. B, 19th Michigan Infantry, leaving behind his 17-year-old wife, Irene, the daughter of Fennville founder, Elam Fenn, and a two-month-old daughter. Henry and two friends, Milo Barker of Manlius Township and James Billings of Clyde Township, began their training at Camp Wilcox at Dowagiac. He wrote home August 25, 1862, describing their tent:

> There is 23 boys that sleep in the same tent, our heads on the outside and our feet towards the middle, it brings our feet just as close together as they can be pushed and of course, we being so close together we cannot rest so well, we being all cramped up . . . We have speaking and singing, story telling in our tent in the evening. [17]

BATTLE CONTINUES IN VIRGINIA

On August 29, 1862, at Groveton, Virginia, in an action sometimes called the second battle of Bull Run or Manassas, Lee defeated the disorganized Union Army of Virginia which had been formed August 12 under Major General John Pope and included the 1st, 2nd, 3rd, 4th, 5th, 7th, 8th, and 16th Michigan Infantry and the 1st Michigan Cavalry. Perry Goshorn and Albert Hamlin, serving with the 3rd Michigan Infantry were wounded. It was Goshorn's second wound in three months. Both were discharged for disability in mid-November. ¶ At Antietam Creek, near Sharpsburg, Maryland, the North, under General George B. McClellan, caught up with the Army of Northern Virginia on September 17, 1862. There was no decisive victory and the losses were heavy on both sides. This battle has been called the bloodiest single day of the war. Lee withdrew to Virginia over the next two days. Michigan regiments on the field included the 1st, 4th, 7th, 8th, 16th and 17th Infantry which suffered more than 350 casualties in the one day battle. Area men on the line would have included Owen Cook, Quincy Lamoreaux and John Langan with the 8th and Bugler Frank Fisher with the 17th Infantry.

NEW TROOPS HEAD SOUTH

The 4th Michigan Cavalry was mustered into federal service on August 29, 1862, at Detroit and left for Louisville, Kentucky on September 26, armed, mounted and equipped. It was commanded by Colonel Robert H. G. Minty of Detroit, previously with the 2nd and 3rd Michigan Cavalry units. Benjamin D. Pritchard, an Allegan lawyer, was captain of Co. L, made up almost entirely of Allegan County men. On their way from Allegan to Kalamazoo, the men were greeted by the people of Plainwell with " a generous outpouring by them of those things which minister to the material man." At Kalamazoo where they had to go to board the train, Judge Henry H. Booth provided a "sumptuous dinner" to the entire company. According to a letter from Pritchard, printed in the *Allegan Journal* issue of September 1, 1862:

> Our Regiment is full to overflowing. One compa-
> ny has been sent away and I understand there are
> 3 more companies raised for the Regiment which

cannot be accepted . . . . The boys break into military life with the same spirit which characterized their enlistment. . . . I think it will be the crack regiment of the State. I have seen several who have not seen its equal yet.

At the training camp in Detroit they were just "across the fence" from Co. I of the 5th Michigan Cavalry, headed by Pritchard's old law partner, William B. Williams. ¶ During the first week of September, 1862, Captain Williams, visit-

AREA MEN SERVED ON
HORSEBACK AND EARLY

An unusually large percentage of Saugatuck area troops served in the horse units of the army.. Of 289 total area men in all services, 119 (41 percent) served in cavalry units; 147 (51 percent) in infantry units. By comparison, in all Northern armies combined, less than 20 percent of those enlisted served in the cavalry. In addition there were 18 Saugatuck-area men in the U. S. Navy, 4 sharpshooters, one in the engineers and mechanics corps, and one in a light artillery battery. ¶ The Saugatuck area also had three men who served in the regular Army. James Gibson of Douglas enlisted in the 1st U. S. Cavalry in October of 1846 and served until 1871, a 25-year career of duty. Alonzo Greenhalgh of Saugatuck enlisted as a private in the 7th U. S. Infantry on October 5, 1864 and served until his discharge October 5, 1867. Louis A. Hare, also of Saugatuck served in the 16th U. S. Infantry from July 23, 1861 to April 5, 1865. ¶ The area had men in most regiments formed in Michigan with particularly high concentrations in the 13th Michigan Infantry where there were 73, including Co. I which was almost entirely lakeshore residents and the 3rd Michigan Cavalry, where 43 men served, including several officers.. ¶ And they signed up early in the war, when the patriotic fervor and indignation was at its height. Fifty-three percent of the total number of recruits enlisted in 1861, anxious that the war would be finished before they got into it. Twenty-two percent of the total number enlisted in 1862; 9 percent in 1863 (when many were predicting that the war would be over soon); 11 percent in 1864 and 9 percent in 1865. ¶ Of the men who enlisted from the Saugatuck area in 1861, 36 percent re-enlisted when their first tour of duty was over, including five soldiers who were discharged for illness or disability and, after a period of healing at home, later re-enlisted. This figure becomes more impressive when the nearly half (48 percent) of men who were no longer available to re-enlist are removed from the equation. These are soldiers who either died in the war, were discharged for illness or disability, or discharged for some other reason. (e.g., court martial, under age). Of the soldiers who enlisted in 1861 and were still able to serve, only 18, (just over 13 percent) chose not to re-enlist. ¶ In Company B, 13th Michigan Infantry, which would be typical, of 41 men from the Saugatuck area who enlisted in 1861, when it came time to re-enlist, 15 signed on for another tour of duty, four had been killed in action or died of disease, 21 had been discharged for illness or wounds, and one had deserted.

1861
1862
1863
1864
1865
AFTER THE WAR

51

ing Allegan from Detroit where his 5th Michigan Cavalry company was in training, accepted "splendid swords, sashes and belts" as a present from the "Lake Shore towns" for himself and First Lieutenant George N. Dutcher, who remained with the troops in Detroit. The presentation speech was made by F. B. Wallin of Saugatuck and described by the Allegan newspaper editor as "extremely felicitious." [18]

¶ After they arrived at training camp, Captain Williams wrote to the Allegan newspaper to express "gratitude to the ladies of Gunplain for their kindness to us on our way to Detroit in supplying us not only with a bountiful breakfast but also an ample store for our way." And to the ladies of Ganges who had provided 100 Testaments he wrote:

> They were received by us not only as a token of their kind regards but also of their anxious care and solicitude in our behalf and will be treasured by us not only in their behalf, but also for the doctrines and principles therein enunciated. [19]

The 5th Michigan Cavalry had first been styled the 1st Michigan Mounted Rifles. The original authority called for them to be armed "with repeating rifles and a brace of pistols each, but no swords." The unit was mustered at Detroit on August 30, 1862, but its departure was delayed waiting for arms and equipment. Private William H. Rockwell of Trowbridge Township, who was serving as cook for Company I, wrote home on October 1, 1862: "Guns came and was refused so we will have to wait to have them made." [20]

¶ Private Henry Avery told later how a Saugatuck enlistee helped the 5th Cavalry pass the hours and days spent waiting for traveling orders:

> One source of amusement at Detroit was John Hill, whom we called 'Beauty' from his queer comical expressions of face. He would take a banjo which he could play well and getting on a dry goods box would play and sing comic songs by the hour . . . this same John Hill could take a Spencer or revolver and furnish just as good a time for the rebels to dance by, keeping time with "Hang Jeff Davis on a Sour Apple Tree." [21]

"IF THEIR CHILDREN COULD BE EDUCATED . . . "

On September 17, 1862, John P. Parrish of the 6th Michigan Infantry took time out from his job as cook in a Louisiana military hospital to write a multi-page letter home. In it he described the former slaves who had attached themselves to the regiment:

> There is not much sugar cane raised here, but up the river further they make it the main crop. I should say by what I saw when I was up to Baton Rouge, and the negroes say that. That was what they had to work at mostly when they were at home with olemassa up the river. They are an ignorant worthless set of human beings, they don't think of doing anything only just as you set them at work and then see that they do it, and then tell them the next thing to do, and so on through the whole day, but this is the way that they have been used to doing and they don't think of any other way, so I suppose that they are not so much to blame. I suppose if any of us had been raised in that way we would do the same thing as they do. I think that the most of them if they could be educated and could have the liberty of having their ways that the difference in their appearance and actions would be immense, and then to think of the difference and the improvement if their children and children's children could be educated. I think that they would be full as smart and full as knowing as those that say that they have no souls and are nothing but an improved race of baboons or large monkey.[22]

1861
1862
1863
1864
1865
AFTER THE WAR

53

DISEASE

Disease and illness killed nearly twice as many soldiers in the Civil War as died on the battlefield or of wounds sustained in battle. This was especially true in regiments made up largely of farm boys who had not been exposed to "childhood" diseases like measles, mumps and chickenpox or the even more dangerous small pox, typhoid fever and scarlet fever. ¶ A total of 14,753 Michigan soldiers died during the war. Of these 2,798 were killed on the battlefield, 1,650 died later of wounds sustained in battle, 768 died as the result of other causes (accidents, drowning, etc.) and 9,537 died of disease. ¶ Northern boys suffered from swamp-bred diseases like malaria, that were more common down south than in Michigan, but they were also simply prostrated by high temperatures in the southern summer, which compounded the dehydration caused by diarrhea and similar illnesses. ¶ In addition there were dangers northerners seldom thought about. One day the men of the 44th Indiana Infantry were forced to wait for boats to take them across the Tennessee River and Private Scott Eddy later reported, "There were copperhead snakes and tarantulas. We did not dare sit down until the ground was perfectly clean."

WOUNDS AND DISEASE FINISH THE WAR FOR SOME

But the war was already over for some soldiers. On September 9, 1862, Amos B. Cook, of the 2ⁿᵈ Michigan Cavalry, while waiting for the action to begin at Corinth, Mississippi, received a discharge for disability. He had enlisted on September 25, 1861, at Grand Rapids and had been hampered, almost his entire military career by illness. His discharge describes his disabilities as "phthisis pulmonolis and chronic diarrhea." With the discharge in his pocket he started for home and got as far as Chelsea, near Ann Arbor, where he became so ill that he was taken in by a local family. He died at their house on November 17, 1862. Cook was the eldest son of Dr. James B. Cook who had opened a practice in Saugatuck in 1859. At the time of Amos' death, a second Cook son, Asa Owen, was on campaign with the 8ᵗʰ Michigan Infantry and had just survived the Battle of Antietam. ¶ In a two day battle at Corinth, Mississippi, on October 3 and 4, the Union Army of the Mississipi turned back Confederate regiments which were attempting to move north to assist General Braxton Bragg in Kentucky. Corporal Angus Fraser, a Ganges farmer, fighting with Battery C, 1st Michigan Light Artillery, was wounded by a shell. Others in the action would have included Second Lieutenant James G. Butler and more than 20 area men who served with the 3ʳᵈ Michigan Cavalry.

"I HAVE NEVER DONE ANYTHING THAT IS AS HARD AS SOLDIERING."

Henry Blakeslee and the 19ᵗʰ Michigan Infantry finished their training at Dowagiac and headed for Kentucky, making much of the journey on foot. He wrote his wife on October 27, 1862:

> I am now a ways from you, we are marching all most every day. The first day we left Covington, we started in the afternoon and marched 10 miles and stopped at Florence over night, the next day we marched 20 miles and camped at Crittington [Crittenden], the next day we marched 14 miles and camped in the woods, we slept out of doors in the open air, the next day we marched 18 miles and camped at Falmouth, and there we staid two or three days and

then we marched 16 miles, the next day we marched
14 miles and today we started for Lexington, we only
marched six miles when we received orders to halt
and so we pitched our tents and here we are two
miles from Paris. We averaged 50 pounds to each
man . . . You do not know anything about the war
in Michigan, although I have not seen much, I have
seen enough to satisfy me. I have never done anything that is as hard as soldiering . . . .When you
write tell me about the weather, did you think about
my birthday, the 11th of Oct? I was 24.[23]

The 19th Michigan Infantry finally reached Lexington,
Kentucky, after a march of about 100 miles. Henry Blakeslee
wrote his wife on October 29, 1862:

Yesterday we passed through some of the prettiest
farming country I ever see, the people in Lexington
seem glad to see us, not long ago the south passed
through and took everything they could lay their
hands on, they are tired of them, and appear to be
glad to see us. We hope to keep still and keep in the
ranks, going along, but the rebels run around like
sheep.[24]

MOUNTS FOR THE CAVALRY

The Allegan Journal, for November 12, 1862, carried an advertisement that read:

CAVALRY HORSES FOR SALE — The under-
signed has 1/2 dozen fine Cavalry Horses for sale
and is ready to furnish to any parties having contracts with the Government. Timothy S. Coates
Saugatuck, Allegan Co., Mich Nov. 12, 1862

Timothy S. Coates was one of Allegan County's pioneer
settlers. He ran a blacksmith shop and tavern at Richmond
in Manlius Township, had been the first supervisor of Pine
Plains Township, and, from April, 1853, to March, 1860,
was keeper of the lighthouse at the mouth of the Kalamazoo River. He had six sons. Five of the six sons were vessel
captains on the Great Lakes. Although Timothy lived on
Butler Street in downtown Saugatuck, he must have had at
least a small farm, where he raised the horses he was offering for sale. ¶ His advertisement may have been in response
to an ad from the *Detroit Advertiser*, which appeared in a

1861
1862
1863
1864
1865
AFTER THE WAR

55

September, 1862, *Allegan Journal,* announcing the letting of contracts for the purchase of 2,000 horses. It specified,

> The horses must be sound in all particulars, from 15 to 10 hands high, not less than four nor more than nine years of age, color to be bays, browns, blacks, or sorrels, good square trotters, bridle wise and of size sufficient for the purposes above named.

Reuben Sewers Sr., a Saugatuck fisherman, had something to do with procuring horses for the army. His 1939 obituary states, "Although not old enough to enlist in the Civil War he recalled its horrors of burying dead solders and horses and often hid horses for the Union army while soldiers hid in the tunnels."[25]

ACCIDENTS, BUSHWHACKERS MAKE DEATH TOLL RISE

As in modern armies, accidents and unexpected actions also took their toll on the volunteers. Ira F. Austin of the 4th Michigan Cavalry died on November 17, 1862 of injuries from falling off a horse at New Albany, Indiana. He was buried at the National Cemetery, New Albany. He was from Ganges and had enlisted in Co. L at Allegan, on July 21, 1862 at the age of 26. ¶ Andrew T. Foot of the 4th Michigan Cavalry was shot through the thigh by some bushwhackers on November 27, 1862. He later died at Nashville and was buried in the National Cemetery there. Foot was a United Brethren clergyman from Ganges Township and, although fondly remembered for his spiritual guidance, had enlisted as a cavalry soldier, not a chaplain. He was 34.

MORE HORSEMEN ON THE WAY FROM MICHIGAN

In November and December of 1862, Elisha Mix, 44, of Manlius began efforts to raise Co. F for the 8th Michigan Cavalry expecting to be captain. Mix had come to Allegan County in 1853 with Elam A. Fenn who founded Fennville. Enlistees included Quartermaster Sergeant Homer Manvel, 21, of Saugatuck; John A. Kinney, 23, of Saugatuck; Joseph B. Morris, 24, of Ganges; Elisha T. H. Walker, 21, a Clyde Township farmer; Richard A. Follett, 27, of Casco

1861

1862

1863

1864

1865

AFTER THE WAR

56

Township and Walter Billings, 44, a farmer from Peach Belt, Ganges Township. ¶ The new Spencer Repeating Rifles for the 5th Michigan Cavalry arrived at Detroit the first week in December, and the *Advertiser and Tribune* described them as "the neatest weapon we have ever seen." The rifles could discharge eight cartridges without reloading and cost $40 each. The men also received .44 caliber Colt Army Revolvers. The regiment (still known, as least unofficially, as the First Michigan Mounted Rifles) left for Washington with 1,144 officers and men. They arrived in the city on December 9 and went into camp on East Capitol Hill. ¶ The 6th Michigan Cavalry, under the command of Colonel George Gray, an Irish-born Grand Rapids attorney, and Lieutenant Colonel Russell Alger marched to the Grand Rapids depot on the moonlit evening of December 10, 1862, to embark for Washington. Although they were still only partly armed, they were fully dressed and well-mounted. Horses proved so abundant that the mounts of each company were chosen by color, Co. A was mounted on bays, Co. B on browns, Co. C on grays, Co. E on blacks, etc. The regiment made a fine appearance when they arrived in Washington D. C. on December 15 and went into camp atop Meridian Hill. On December 12, a provisional cavalry brigade consisting of the 5th and 6th Michigan Cavalry was formed in Washington. Colonel Joseph T. Copeland of Pontiac, formerly lieutenant colonel of the 1st Michigan Cavalry, was promoted to Brigadier General and placed in command.

SPENCER RIFLE
PL. II

1861
1862
1863
1864
1865
AFTER THE WAR

57

THE 4TH CAVALRY SEARCHES FOR MORGAN

The members of the 4th Michigan Cavalry were occupying their time searching for Confederate Captain John Morgan and his cavalry men who carried on a sort of guerrilla warfare, taking prisoners and destroying railroads and tunnels. The 4th was camped near Lebanon, Kentucky, known to be a stronghold of the guerrillas. In a letter to the *Allegan Journal*, dated December 19, 1862, a 4th Michigan Cavalry soldier, relates the search for Morgan and his men:

We got up . . . a little before daylight and started on the Lebanon pike, four abreast; and as the sun was just rising we turned a curve in the road and saw about 100 of Morgan's men sitting on their horses some 40 rods ahead. It was then, as fast as our horses could carry us for some six miles and I saw the 4th Kentucky Cavalry dashing across the fields to head them, I thought there was some prospect; but alas, they disappeared like a flock of young quails, not a feather to be seen.[26]

He also reports that food is difficult to find "for the people have been totally robbed of the last mouthful by the two invading armies; for what one has not taken, the other has." Morgan would be captured in June 1863, but escaped from the Ohio Penitentiary four months later and continued his disruption of the Union efforts until he was killed during a surprise raid in Greenville, Tennessee in September 1864.

BUILDING BRIDGES IN VIRGINIA

VOLUNTEERS
CROSSING
THE
RAPPAHANNOCK
PL. 12

In early December engineers attempting to lay a pontoon bridge across the Rappahannock River near Fredericksburg, Virginia, were being harassed by snipers firing from the other side. The situation was described by Color Sergeant Daniel G. Crotty of the 3rd Michigan Infantry:

> The enemy's sharp-shooters are making sad havoc among the pontoon builders, for they are firing from the houses in the city at our men. Something must be done to remedy this, and a detail is made from the gallant Seventh Mich. Infantry to cross and clean out the rebel sharp-shooters. Those few who crossed in those open boats have earned for themselves a crown of glory, and that little party will be remembered as long as their country will last, for performing one of the most daring feats of the war . . . . They have a very poor way of defending them selves, but they still keep on, and are about to land, when the house skulkers pour their deadly lead among the devoted band. They strive to keep a foothold and commence firing. Some more troops are crossing in boats to reinforce. . . .We have a foothold now, and the bridges are quickly built.[27]

Men measured the scenery comparing it to home. William Rockwell writing home during a trek through Virginia not-

1861
1862
1863
1864
1865
AFTER THE WAR

ed, "The Rappahannock is not wider than the Kalamazoo, but very rapid and probably deeper. The water is muddy. There is not much left of the city."[28] The attack on Fredericksburg began December 13, 1862, but did not succeed. After suffering 12,700 casualties (killed and wounded), the Union army recrossed the Rappahannock and returned to their camps to regroup.

WILLIAM HENRY PARRISH RE-ENLISTS

Back home, William Henry Parrish, formerly of the 6th Michigan Infantry, who had been discharged because of continuing illness, was itching to get back into the fight. His father, John P. Parrish, who had enlisted in the same company to watch over his son, was still serving with the 6th in Louisiana. William was joined by his 17-year-old brother, Ira, who either lied about his age or had his mother's permission. It is likely that William planned to provide his younger brother with the same sort of care that his father had given him when they served together in the 6th. Whatever the impetus for the action, on December 16, 1862, they enlisted in the 8th Michigan Cavalry, were mustered in and left for Kentucky where both became so ill that they were confined to the hospital. Eventually, they were released, although William Henry continued to work at the hospital as a clerk in the surgeon's office. He wrote home, "Pretty good place too. Do not have to go into battle and being naturally cowardly it suits me." [29]

Once he was out of the hospital, his younger brother, Ira, seemed to enjoy the adventure. He wrote his mother:

> We left our camp last night making four weeks time that we were on the march without our tents and sleeping on the ground with nothing but the canopy for a roof . . . . A soldier's life is the life to live. It is so exciting. Let a man lay down to sleep and maby he will sleep five minutes and maby all night, but he is just as apt to have to get up in two or three hours and march all night. And maby he will march 40 or 50 miles before daylight. I have marched 35 miles in 3 hours, but it was the greatest time running horses I ever saw. [30]

1861
1862
1863
1864
1865
AFTER THE WAR

59

THE 5TH CAVALRY STILL IN WASHINGTON

During their stay in Washington, drilling daily with the 5th Michigan Cavalry, soldiers were allowed to go into the country with permission but could not go into the city without a pass, part of an effort to safeguard the city from rebel spies. Private Henry Avery later described one trip. He and a friend had asked for a pass to go into town and buy some stamps:

> When we met the patrol. Halt! Order! Arms! was the command of the guard; your passes sir, to us. I pulled it out of my pocket, gave it to the sergeant who glanced it over. Fall in guards, forward march; we were under arrest; the pass was dated wrong and we went to prison and were greeted with 'Fresh fish! Fresh fish,' from the rascals who ought never to see the outside of prison bars. We were taken to an upper room to await examination. During the day as I was looking out on the street, I saw a man from our regiment passing whom I hailed and told him to tell Captain Williams where we were, and in an hour or two Lieutenant Dutcher's white horse was seen coming and we were soon free to go to camp.[31]

G. N. DUTCHER
FRONT 13

In addition to his position as first lieutenant of Co. I, George N. Dutcher of Douglas was spending some of his spare time serving on the regimental court martial panel as Judge Advocate. ¶ Four months after organization, the 5th Michigan Cavalry was finally paid for their services. Captain Williams wrote home proudly:

> We today mustered for pay and Co. I mustered 72 privates, 14 non-commissioned officers, 2 farriers and blacksmiths, 1 saddler, 1 waggoner and 2 teamsters – all present at muster – not a man in the hospital and not a man that did not answer to his name. We were mustered by Capt. Smith of the regular army. He paid us a very fine compliment as a company, he said, "72 privates, every man present, I never saw that before and I have mustered for pay over 100,000 men."[32]

NEWS FROM RELATIVES

Henry Blakeslee of the 19th Michigan Infantry, celebrating Christmas at Nicholsville, Kentucky, wrote his wife, Irene, news of her brother, Albert H. Fenn, serving with the 3rd Michigan Cavalry:

> The second Mich. cavalry are here and I saw one of the soldiers that was well acquainted with Albert, he said he camped beside his Regt. quite a while, said he was a first rate fellow, and was generally pretty healthy. The reason you do not get more letters and more regularly is because there [they're] on a march. The second Mich. have gone off on a 80 day scout now . . . they have gone where teams cannot go. One of the soldiers told me they have gone to tear up a railroad between Richmond, Virginia, and Mobile, Alabama and they say they are after Morgan. He is a hard bird to catch. He was here before we came and stole a great many of the best horses, but the south thinks its alright, but if one of our boys gets a chicken, which they did last night, they make a fuss about it.[33]

A COSTLY BATTLE AT STONE'S RIVER

With winter rapidly closing in on them, it was important that Union control of the fertile lower middle Tennessee River valley be established. As the two armies began to jockey for positions for a major engagement at Stone's River near Murfreesboro, Tennessee, there was intermittent skirmishing throughout the day. On December 29, 1862, John M. Loughry of Co. L, 4th Michigan Cavalry was killed in some of this action. Loughry was a Heath Township farmer who had enlisted on July 21, 1862, at the age of 38. ¶ By the end of the day, the Northern soldiers, under command of General William S. Rosecrans, had located the enemy in position in front of Murfreesboro. Partly as a subterfuge and partly to escape the cold, many Confederate men were dressed in Union clothing, adding to the confusion. ¶ On the last day of the year, Confederate General Braxton Bragg attacked and nearly routed the Army of the Cumberland at Stone's River, Tennessee. Captain W. G. Eaton of Co. I of the 13th Michigan Infantry wrote on January 4, 1863:

> The Battle Field before Murfreesboro, Tennessee: The 13th Mich. has just passed through one of the hardest contested battles of the war. Col. Shoemaker is deserving of all credit for the coolness and firmness with which he handled the Regiment and the

BATTLE OF
STONE'S RIVER
PL. 13

1861
1862
1863
1864
1865
AFTER THE WAR

61

officers and men are deserving the highest praise for their steadiness under fire and the manner in which they repulsed the enemy.[34]

Eaton also sends a list of Co. I casualties, including Mordant D. Loomis. "wounded – since died" and Harry Holt "wounded slightly" with a gunshot wound to the left elbow. In Co. B the wounded included Cyril Le Duc, a Ganges Township farmer, who was transferred to the Veteran Reserve Corps on his release from the hospital; Joseph Miller, who received a gunshot wound to the right hip and carried the ball in his body until his death in 1905; Freeland Gray of Ganges, and John Wynn of Co. C, who received three separate wounds in the battle (in the shoulder, the side and the head), but continued in the service until the end of the war. The 13th Michigan Infantry lost a third of the force it took into the battle. Also participating in the Battle at Stone's River were the 9th, 10th, 11th, and 21st Michigan Infantry and the 4th Michigan Cavalry. ¶ Scott Eddy, then of the 44th Indiana Infantry, describes his day:

> Was ordered . . . to go and reinforce General Johnson who had been surprised early in the morning and routed. We got right into a nest. Marched across a large cleared place about 100 acres. Got over a fence into woods. The Rebels, 8 deep, marching around us, ordered back over fence and to lie down. Jonny Coogan got hit before he got back. I was looking through 3rd crack of fence. Saw Coogan getting over the fence blood running over his face. I thought time I got down. The lft. [lieutenant] had told me to get down. I went to slide down. The ball struck me. I grunted and straightened up, lft said, "Are you hit?" I said yes. Jont's head was on my right heel. [Jont was his elder brother, Jonathan Pratt Eddy.] The lft told him to help me off the field. Jont and a musician took me back . . . . We found Dr. back in a cedar grove. I laid down on a big brick and they made three cuts and stuck the nippers in to get the ball. Strapped cotton on with court plaster . . . . I got in sight of General Hospital. A line of Rebel Cavalry came up took the hospital. Piled everything up and was going to burn it. A Rebel doctor got a

gun sash on and ordered them away. And a line of
our boys came up and gave them a volley and away
they went.[35]

After waiting on the ground outside the amputating tent
most of the night in the rain, Eddy was ordered to go by ambulance to Nashville, 30 miles away, where he made contact
with his brother, Will, who was working in the hospital.
Scott wrote later, "He came to see me and made arrange-
ments to move me . . . and before I touched a bed stripped
and had a bath. Had a nice clean white cot bed. That is
all that saved my life." ¶ But the contest was not yet over.
The Union troops celebrated the new year with a three-day
battle that forced the Confederates out of Murfreesboro,
Tennessee. On the field of battle were the 9th, 10th, 11th, 13th,
and 21st Michigan Infantry and the 4th Michigan Cavalry.

1861

1862

1863

1864

1865

AFTER THE WAR

ALLEGAN COUNTY DRAFTEES CALLED TO REPORT

On March 3, 1863, Congress passed the conscription act which provided for the drafting, with certain exceptions, of "all able bodied male citizens of the United States and persons of foreign birth who shall have declared on oath their intention to become citizens" between the ages of 20 and 45, with unmarried men given precedent. ¶ In the operation that began in October-November, 1863, a total of 6,383 Michigan men were drafted. Of these, according to the Annual Report of the Adjutant General of the State of Michigan for the year 1863, 261 were delivered to the Grand Rapids induction center, 643 furnished substitutes (of whom 43 deserted before reaching Grand Rapids), 1,626 paid a $300 commutation fee, 2,130 were exempted for various reasons and 1,069 simply failed to report. ¶ Warren Prentice, who had settled onto a Saugatuck Township farm after a career at sea, and afterwards as a sailor on the Great Lakes, was drafted into the 4th Michigan Cavalry. He wrote later in his autobiography: "As soon as I commenced farming the Civil War commenced. I did not go at first for I thought perhaps it would not be necessary, but finally I went in 1863 and in February 1864 I got the catarrh stuck on me, and it has kept me company ever since." (Catarrh is an old word for respiratory inflammation and its resultant congestion.) ¶ Warren Pratt traveled to the regiment with Prentice but deserted at Louisville, Kentucky on December 26, 1864. He was drafted from Saugatuck Township, but had given his address as Richmond (in Manlius Township) on December 13, 1862 when he applied for a marriage license to wed Alice Prindle of Schoolcraft. ¶ A man could be exempted from the draft for physical or mental disability, if he was the only son of infirm parents, if he had dependent children under 12,

W. PRENTICE BACK 34

if two brothers were already serving, or if he had been convicted of a felony. Thirteen Michigan men claimed exemptions from the draft because they were already serving in the Army, however, previous service did not necessarily cause one to be exempt from the draft. James Reeve of Clyde Township served three distinct tours of duty during the Civil War, the last one as the result of the draft. ¶ A drafted man could also send a substitute, which was worthwhile if he could find a substitute for less than the $300 commutation fee. In August, 1864, replacements for the depleted 8th Michigan Cavalry included James B. Rhodes who enlisted as a substitute for Henry L. Lathrop; Jacob Boas who enlisted as a substitute for James Williams, who ran a fruit farm near Douglas, and Charles W. Holmes who enlisted for one year as a substitute for Great Lakes Captain A. H. Coates of Saugatuck. Also entering service in August was Arthur Allen, 18, of Cheshire who went as a substitute for draftee James W. Allen and was assigned to the 1st Michigan Colored Infantry. ¶ Forty-five men were drafted in Allegan County to fill out the 1863 quota, and 33 of these (73 percent) were reported "delivered at the barracks." Many counties had a much lower participation rate. In the same draft only 72 of 173 (41 percent) of the men drafted from St. Clair County made it to training camp and 64 of 127 (50 percent) from Macomb County. ¶ Of the total of 6,383 men in the first Michigan draft, 1,626 paid the $300 commutation fee and added $487,800 to the state treasury. These monies were largely used to pay bounties for voluntary enlistees and men who re-enlisted.

1863

AFTER THE DISASTROUS RESULTS at Fredericks-burg, Virginia, the Northern troops had moved back across the Rappahannock River and were again in a holding pattern. On January 1, 1863, the Emancipation Proclamation, issued by President Lincoln freed "all persons held as slaves within any State or designated part of a State the people whereof shall then be in rebellion against the United States."

VISITING PRESIDENT LINCOLN

The regiments that would become the Michigan Cavalry Brigade had remained in camp near the capital, with only occasional forays into the countryside. The January 5, 1863, issue of the *Allegan Journal* carried a report of a visit to the President:

> The 5th and 6th Michigan Cavalry are now encamped near Washington City, about one mile from the Capitol, eastward. The officers of the 5th, in company with Hon. F. W. Kellogg, recently paid a visit to the President, Heads of the different Departments, &c. Their reception, throughout, was a very marked and flattering one. President Lincoln remarked that in Michigan soldiers seemed to be born ready made.

Captain J. H. Kidd of the 6th Michigan Cavalry, in writing about the visit later in his "recollections," noted that the President was "spare, haggard and bent . . . yet a strikingly handsome man." After "perfunctory" handshakes all around, he attempted to escape back to his work, only to be stopped by Congressman Kellogg who announced that the new unit was made up of "Wolverines," and that they were on the track of "Jeb" Stuart, whom they propose to pursue and capture. " 'Gentlemen,' said the President, with a twinkle of the eye, and the first and only indication of humor that he gave, 'I can assure you that it would give me much greater pleasure to see Jeb Stuart in captivity than it has given me to see you,' and with a bow and smile he vanished.¹

Shortly afterwards, the 6th Michigan Cavalry went into winter quarters at Baltimore, Maryland. George H. Harris of Saugatuck describes some of the rumors circulating among the thousands of troops camped in the Washington area in a letter to the *Allegan Journal* dated January 15:

> Madame rumor is as busy as ever, and her votaries employ their time in circulating all sort of reports which are listened to and sometimes believed; one story in particular which I hope may prove to be true is being circulated around camp, that we will be discharged within the next forty days; -- well, perhaps we may, but I doubt it very much. another report

1861

1862

1863

1864

1865

AFTER THE WAR

66

> which if true is of considerable importance to us;
> is that this Regiment will be called back to Michi-
> gan to defend Detroit against the menacing attitude
> of England; that fortifications are being erected by
> the British authorities across the river in Windsor,
> with the design to shell Detroit; now I wish that you
> would enlighten me on this very important point.[2]

There were many southern sympathizers among the residents of Washington and the surrounding countryside.
Shortly after the cavalry first arrived in the area, a spring,
which served as a source of water for the Union soldiers, was
poisoned and several men died. When it happened a second
time, the perpetrator was caught, tied to a tree and shot.
Private William H. Rockwell of the 5th Michigan Cavalry
wrote home, January 4, 1863: "I saw the bullet holes in the
tree that went through him."[3]

"I AM GLAD THAT YOU ENJOY YOURSELF SO WELL"
Young couples found wartime separation hard. It was especially difficult for Henry Blakeslee who had left his young
wife, Irene, and their infant, Hattie, in the care of her parents, Elam and Mary Jane Fenn in Manlius Township.
Boarding with the Fenns was 21-year-old James Reeve, who
is described on the 1860 census as a sawyer, probably in the
Fenn sawmill. He had enlisted in the 3rd Michigan Infantry
in May of 1861, but was discharged for disability on August
7, 1862, and would have been returning to Allegan County
about the time Blakeslee left for the service. On January
21, the young husband nervously responded to a letter from
home with:

> I hear that you and Jim enjoy your selfs first rate, I
> am glad that you enjoy yourself so well, and I hope
> you allways will, but I hope you will not run off with
> him, for I would like to see my darling once more.
> . . . I expect the reason Jim takes so much notice of
> Hattie so as to get in your good graces . . . and that
> shall be the last I see of you. Ha, ha.[4]

SAUGATUCK SOLDIERS' SOCIETY GIVES A CONCERT
Friends and family back home were doing their part to support the Michigan soldiers and the war effort. The January
27, 1863, issue of the *Allegan Journal* carried this notice:

1861 1862 1863 1864 1865 AFTER THE WAR

67

> The Soldiers Society of Saugatuck will give a prom-
> enade concert and supper at the Newark House in
> Saugatuck on Jan 27th. All are invited to attend.
>
> J. F. Geer Sec'y

The Soldiers Society was a local wing of the Michigan Soldier's Relief Association, which raised funds to aid Michigan soldiers as they carried out their service. With these
funds the association bought bedding for use by Michigan
men in hospitals, established a "home" in Washington
where men passing through could find shelter for a night
"without being thrown in the bad associations of the city,"
and sent supplies to individual soldiers and units. Their 1864
annual report notes that they had distributed "9 reams of
paper, 3000 envelopes, 53 barrels crackers, 102 dozen cans
condensed milk, 49 3/8 dozen cans prepared beef, 41 dozen
cans of chicken, 23 boxes lemons, 5 barrels sugar, 70 gal-
lons whiskey, 1654 lbs. tobacco, 7 barrels pickles, 5 barrels
onions, 40 boxes herring and 4 firkins butter."[5] ¶ Money for
all of these projects was donated by organizations and individuals and raised through the holding of tableaux, socials,
oyster suppers, calico balls, ice cream parties and sanitary
festivals on the home front. Records from the Michigan
Soldier's Relief Association show that the profit from the
concert in Saugatuck described above was $33. It was con-
veyed to them by Samuel Johnson, the brother of sawmill
owner O. R. Johnson. Samuel lived on the hill in Saugatuck
in the large square house (later Frolic Resort) which still
stands on Allegan Street. It was identical to the house built
by his brother just off Butler Street downtown that was later
owned by Captain R. C. Brittain.

FIGHTING WOULD CHANGE THEIR NOTIONS
The Emancipation Proclamation was not universally
hailed, even by citizens of the North. William Orr wrote to
his family, in a letter dated February 8, 1863:

> I hope that the war will end without too much more
> fighting . . . . I am afraid that the excitement that
> is getting up in the north is going to prolong, for
> so long as the south can get encouragement from
> the north they will keep up the war. I do wish that

the north could become united, set aside all party feelings and try and help us save the glorious old union for I do think there has been men enuf killed and crippled . . . . There is no use to talk about compromising with the secesh, for that they want us to acknowledge their independence and the soldiers opinion on that is we will fight them as long as there is one of us left before we will do that. Why not go to work and help put down the rebellion and stop their howling about the president and his proclamation . . . . I wish all the men that is opposed to the proclamation had to come and fight, they would soon change their notions.[6]

MURDER IN MISSISSIPPI

By this stage of the war, Saugatuck and Ganges area soldiers were spread from the Atlantic to the Mississippi river. On January 28, 1863, Jacob Heringa, a corporal with the 3rd Michigan Cavalry, records in his diary one day of action at the Coldwater River near Panola, Mississippi:

One man of Company I was killed. Rebel loss not known. Crossing the Coldwater river we moved on towards Helena. The man of Co. I that was killed was first wounded and afterwards murdered treacherously. After this the Colonel commanding gave the order to burn and destroy everything but the dwelling houses. This order was heartily responded to. Sawmills, tanneries and barns were laid in ashes without interruption all along the road. Rebels afterward captured say that during all this daring raid the Rebel General Chalmer with 5000 Cavalry was close to our heels all the time, but was afraid to attack us.[7]

A FLAG CAUSES PROBLEMS

Unhappy with the inaction of wintertime, on February 8, 1863, the men of the 5th Michigan Cavalry were pleased to receive orders for their first assignment, which was to scout along a Virginia road searching for the enemy. ¶ While the men were still in Detroit, the women of Allegan County had sent Co. I a handsome, handmade red and white guidon, a swallow-tailed banner which served as a rallying point during battle. The flag was definitely non-regulation, being much larger than the average guidon and included a heavy gold fringe. It also bore silk appliqued lettering

1861

1862

1863

1864

1865

AFTER THE WAR

70

that spelled out: "Company I, First Michigan Mounted Rifles." The flag was graciously accepted by the company and a resolution carried in the December 8, 1862, issue of the *Allegan Journal* promised "That we will remember the beautiful donors (God bless them) in the fire and smoke of battle" and that "we will use our best endeavors to protect it through the perils of the battle-field and return it to them at the termination of this rebellion unsullied." ¶ It was with this flag that they headed out on February 8 (or it might have been a similar expedition on February 26). Captain Williams recalled afterwards that after "a noisy little skirmish," the men galloped back to their own lines. The men in camp, nervous over the sounds of firing, saw horsemen bearing down on them carrying a flag similar to one of the current Confederate battle flags and opened fire on their own troops. Fortunately, communication was established and the identity of the troops was confirmed in time to prevent injury. However, Captain Williams quietly retired the ornate flag and acquired a regulation guidon for the balance of the war. The flag which had been presented by the Allegan County ladies was later discovered in a trunk in the home of Williams' granddaughter, and, in 1955, was given to the Allegan County Historical Society. It was on display at their museum in the old jail in downtown Allegan until 2000 when it was formally transferred to the Civil War flag collection in the Michigan capitol.

RECRUITING: "COME IN OUT OF THE DRAFT"

Because of the loss of fighting men through battles, by desertions and to disease, all regiments required frequent replenishment and the inactivity of winter was prime time for recruiting activities. In the February 27, 1863, issue the *Allegan Journal* announced:

> Lieutenant Col. Moyers and Quartermaster James G. Butler, of the 3rd Michigan Cavalry are at home on a brief furlough. These brave and gallant officers are in the best of health and in good spirits and have fought nobly for our country's cause. A grateful people welcome them home even for a brief period with loud acclamation. The people of Allegan County

appreciate their services to our common country and those of the many gallant spirits who have gone from Old Allegan to protect the old Flag from the onslaught of traitors.

The newspaper related the purpose for their visit two paragraphs later on the same page:

CAVALRYMEN WANTED — Lieut. Col. Moyers and Lieut. Butler are at home on recruiting service for a brief period for the old and gallant Mich. 3ᵈ Cavalry, one of the best regiments in the service. We understand that they want 400 men to fill up the regiment to its full standard, and would like to have 40 from Allegan Co. Young horsemen of Allegan, attention. Come in out of the draft.

ON CAMPAIGN WITH LORD WYNDHAM

Near the end of February, 1863, Sir Percy Wynham, a self-styled British "Lord," was given command of a portion of the 5ᵗʰ and 6ᵗʰ Michigan Cavalry regiments and left the encampment at Washington, D. C., to try to capture or curtail the Mosby Rangers, a loosely organized group of Confederate guerrillas. He ordered that the tents be left behind and each man carry three days of cooked rations and 40 rounds of ammunition. Captain James H. Kidd of the 6ᵗʰ Michigan Cavalry, Co. E, later wrote:

Sir Percy Wyndham was an Englishman, an alleged lord. But lord or son of a lord, his capacity as a cavalry officer was not great . . . . He seemed bent on killing as many horses as possible, not to mention the men. The fact was the newspapers were in the habit of reporting that Colonel or General so-and-so had made a forced march of so many miles in so many hours, and it is probable that "Sir Percy" was in search of some more of that kind of cheap renown. It was a safe pastime, harmless to the enemy and not dangerous to himself, through hurtful to horse-flesh. [8]

They were gone six days, mostly in the rain. George Dutcher later claimed in his application for pension that this interlude with Wyndham was the start of his health problems later on, "When I first discovered the rheumatism coming on it was from aches and severe pains in my muscles after sleeping on ground and exposed to storms and long hard marches, but most especially on the Percy Wyndham raid when we had no fires or tents. I was sent back to camp from Falmouth with rheumatism by the Surgeon in charge. I have had the Rheumatism ever since only worse as years pass." Other sources note that Wyndham was a showman who enjoyed orating to his troops on the march in an effort to boost morale. By the time Wyndham was relieved of command in March after he was nearly captured by some of Mosby's guerrillas near Fairfax, they all considered him "a big bag of wind." [9] The new commander was General Julius Stahel, a Hungarian immigrant.

1861

1862

1863

1864

1865

AFTER THE WAR

72

HOSPITALS AND MEDICINE

If a soldier received a wound in an arm or a leg, that limb could be removed. Not much could be done for a soldier who was struck in the body. He was sent to the hospital and either his body fought the infection, gangrene, or peritonitis and survived, or he died. ¶ Bullets and other foreign matter left in the body created chronic infections that caused death, sometimes many years later. One unusual example was Nahum Gilbert of Otsego, a veteran of the 1st Michigan Cavalry who lent his name to the first GAR post in Saugatuck. He had been wounded at Gettysburg in July of 1863. After his death 26 years later, on December 28, 1889, it was discovered that the minie ball had lodged in the spinal column between the second and third vertebra. It was encysted within the membranes of the spinal cord, lying against the back of the spinal canal, but not imbedded in the bone. Although he had been paralyzed for a time when it had first occurred he had lived an active life, serving variously as postmaster of Otsego, Allegan County Clerk, and was in his second term as Register of Deeds when he died. The editor of the Lake Shore Commercial of Saugatuck wrote, "The ball, a minnie conical shaped, was not corroded, and it is regarded by the physicians here as a most remarkable fact that a man could carry a minnie ball for over 26 years encysted within the membranes of the spinal cord and be able to walk about and attend to business." ¶ Joseph Miller of Ganges, a veteran of the 13th Michigan Infantry, had a similar experience. He died in Ganges on May 18, 1905, from infection or gangrene caused by a minie ball that had struck him during the battle of Stone's River, December 31, 1862, 43 years earlier. His daughter, Lizzie (Miller) Wightman, wrote: "Gangrene set in in Pa's right foot, both had been sore for a long time, one had been sore for about 4 years, I believe." He was born in Rochester, New York, moved to Michigan with his parents, spent his boyhood days on the farm in Ganges." His obituary spoke of the "intense suffering" caused by that type of wound. He was 68 years old. ¶ James Hibberdine observed before he signed up in 1864, that many soldiers even if they survive the war are "ruined for life." He added, "Very few that return from the south sick ever wholly recover." The rigors of

BLAKESLEE'S "BRUSH WITH THE ENEMY"

The possibility of real action was getting closer for Henry Blakeslee. After a march of nearly 100 miles the 19ᵗʰ Michigan Infantry was "In camp 10 miles from Franklin" in Tennessee. He wrote home February 22, 1863:

> We are the right wing of Rosecrans army and I should not wonder if we had a brush with the enemy before long, the enemy picketts are only 10 miles from us, and we are advancing in slowly, we have orders this morning not to get a great ways from camp for there was reb guerillas scouting around and they would take us prisoners. [10]

---

long days of marching and sleeping on cold hard ground were believed to cause kidney problems and a steady stream of pension applications would later blame the cold and dampness for their rheumatism. ¶ More men died in the camps than on the battlefield. In most hospitals sickness was dealt with in much the same way as injuries. Ira Parrish of the 8ᵗʰ Michigan Cavalry, himself the son of a physician, wrote home on August 10, 1863 from the Post Hospital at Hickmon Bridge, Kentucky, where he had been confined by illness:

> *There is fifteen men in this ward with me and there is only three men taking medicine. I have not taken any. They don't cure folks here by giving them medicine, but by taking care of them or let them get well of their own accord:*

Others felt that Army hospitals, with the close quarters and unsanitary conditions, were only a last resort. Soldiers with money would sometimes seek out nursing in a private home when they were ill or wounded. Even in the South, residents were receptive to nursing a soldier, especially if he was willing to pay for it, and the hospitals were so overcrowded and overworked that permission for the

arrangement was usually readily available. ¶ Henry Bird, Jr., of the 141st Illinois Infantry, who later ran a drug store in Douglas, contracted what he called "typhoid pneumonia" on the way to duty in Kentucky Because he belonged to the Masons, a fraternal organization, he was placed in a Masonic hospital in Columbus, Ohio. Bird later credited the Masons with his eventual recovery. ¶ Private Henry Blakeslee of the 19ᵗʰ Michigan Infantry wrote home from Kentucky December 19, 1862:

> *I enjoy good health, and have for sometime, but war is hard on the soldiers, there was another one died yesterday out of our company, some of us boys dig graves allmost every day. The Hospitals are full of sick ones and they have gone to private houses, some of them. If I am sick I shall go to a private house for if I go into a Hospital I am afraid I never shall come out alive.*

Blakeslee did not come out alive. He was killed in action at Thompson's Station, March 6, 1863.

73

On March 5, 1863, ten days after Private Henry Blakeslee's letter to his wife, his unit, the 19th Michigan Infantry, while on a reconnaissance mission, was virtually wiped out when it ran into three brigades and a battery of Confederate forces at Thompson's Station, (or Spring Hill) Tennessee. Four separate times with fixed bayonets, they charged down the hill at the enemy, but they could not push them back. In the last Confederate rush, the colors of the 19th Michigan were captured. At that point, nearly surrounded, and with ammunition practically exhausted, the 19th Michigan threw down its weapons and surrendered. The regiment went into the fight with 512 men and suffered losses of 457, including 345 who were listed as missing and presumed captured. Two members of Co. B, including Henry Blakeslee, were killed.

Private Judson L. Austin, wrote in a letter published in the *Allegan Journal*, April 20, 1863:

> This is the most dreadful letter I ever tried to write in my life. I tell you it comes hard for me to send the news home. But it must be done by someone and while you read this, thank God from the bottom of your heart that there is someone left to tell the sad fate of the others. Sad, sad indeed that men should meet to shoot and kill each other in this kind of style .... Henry Blakesly, [sic] a fine young man, but this could not stop the fatal ball. It passed through his breast in such a spot as to cause instant death. He leaves a young wife and child to mourn his loss.[11]

Another eye witness later told the family that Henry had fired and was partially hidden behind a tree reloading, when the fatal shot struck. A small pocket Bible that he had carried throughout the war was returned to Michigan, and is still owned by the family in Fennville. Blakeslee had written his wife on January 24:

> Keep up good courage darling, pray for me, that my life may be spared and that I can see your smiling face again, bring up our little daughter in the way she should go, do not let your love spoil her .... If I never come home again you can have what little property I have and I guess, my father, R. Blakeslee,

will help you sometime I hope. Do not be discouraged because I write this but I have never spoke about it before and thought I might as well now as ever.[12]

James Billings, the son of early Clyde Township farmer Charles T. Billings, who had enlisted with Blakeslee and served by his side, was wounded in the wrist in the same action and sent to the rear in an ambulance. Billings was discharged for disability on April 16, 1863.

It was the regiment's first full-scale battle and emotions ran high. Private Timothy Daggett of Co. B was considered one of the wild frontier lads. Judson L. Austin of Cheshire Township wrote to his wife:

T. DAGGETT
FRONT 15

> There is one boy in our co. that is going home on furlow of 20 days. His name is Timothy Daget. [sic] His parents live near Otsego. Tim has been sick for some time and is very low but the Doc thinks he is able to go home. I hope he will stand the journey and get home safe and then stay there until he is able to stand it again if he ever gets so again. Tim is a rough wicked boy but has a heart like an ox. Makes a good soldier. He is the one that shot the Reb at Springhill after we had surrendered. I hope he will get home and get well so he may live to mend some of his evil ways and live to do good in the world in another shape from soldiering.[13]

Daggett served until his discharge on June 30, 1865, the last of his service in the 17th Regular Veterans Reserve Corps. On his return to Michigan he moved to Saugatuck. ¶ Prisoners taken at Thompson's Station included Daggett, Milo Barker of Manlius, and Jacob Gunsaul, a Ganges farmer, who was corporal of Co. B. They were marched 75 miles from Thompson's Station to Tullahoma, Tennessee, where they traveled in open cattle cars to prison facilities in Richmond, Virginia.

THE REBELS GET THE REST OF THE 19TH

The surviving remnant of the 19th Michigan Infantry, along with Co. D which had not been at Thompson's Station when most of the regiment was captured on March 5, was assigned to guard the railroad bridge over the Little Harpeth River, two miles south of Brentwood. There they had a wooden stockade for their protection. As dawn broke on the morning of March 25 they found the fortification surrounded by Confederate soldiers under the personal command of Brigadier General Nathan B. Forrest. After only a token attack, those within the fort surrendered. The 2nd Michigan Cavalry was in the vicinity and John Nies later wrote:

J. NIES
FRONT 16

> The enemy was in our rear for the purpose of burning up the railroad which they did quite successfully. They captured the guard that was stationed at the bridge, made up of remnants of four regiments, including what was left of the 19th infantry. They took them captive with everything they had and then burned the bridge, and demolished the telegraph line . . . Gen. Grainger . . . dispatched relief at double-quick-time, they arrived too late, for the rebels had been gone about an hour. Then we gave chase, as fast as our horses could run, and overtook their rearguard after a two-mile run. The rebels fled so rapidly that they left behind all their plunder. The road for three miles was strewed with blankets, shirts, guns, in short, everything . . . .We intended to surround them but they just then received reinforcements and threatened to surround us. Being outnumbered we fled and escaped the best we could.[14]

The newly captured members of the 19th Michigan Infantry traveled the same route to incarceration in Richmond prisons that the earlier prisoners had followed, they frequently found the names of their comrades written in the prisons when they stopped on their way to Virginia. The two parts of the regiment were eventually reunited and all of the enlisted men were exchanged and shipped north by the end of April, the officers followed on May 31. Those captured at Brentwood included William Watson, a 37-year-old Clyde Township farmer who had left behind a wife and two small children when he enlisted. He was exchanged in April and sent back to Michigan where he died at New Casco (later Glenn) in June of 1863 from disease contracted in Confederate prisons.

THE MICHIGAN MILITARY DRAFT BEGINS

Although there was nothing in Michigan to rival the draft riots of New York City, draftees proved to be more reluctant and less trustworthy in training camps than volunteers. Camps were sometimes fenced and guarded to keep them there. J. E. Babbitt of Co. F of the 8th Michigan Cavalry wrote the *Allegan Journal* on February 24, 1863:

> It may be a wonder to you and our friends how we should be at the Detroit Barracks and the Reg't at Mt. Clemens; I will explain: The Adjutant General telegraphed last Saturday to the Col. of the 8th Reg't Michigan Cavalry to send the best company in his regiment to Detroit to guard the drafted men. In less than one hour from the receipt of the telegram our company received orders to report at the Barrack on Monday, Feb. 23. The drafted men and substitutes are coming in. There are about three hundred now in camp.

THE MICHIGAN CAVALRY BRIGADE

A new horse unit was forming. On March 2, 1863, the 7th Michigan Cavalry was added to the provisional cavalry brigade that had been formed from the 5th and 6th Michigan Cavalry in December, 1862. In June of 1863, the 1st Michigan Cavalry rounded out the brigade, popularly known as the Michigan Cavalry Brigade, or Wolverine Brigade. The 1st Michigan Cavalry had gained a reputation as a well-trained and dependable mounted unit, especially formidable during a sabre charge, although they were also armed with Burnside carbines. The 5th Cavalry had been equipped with the Spencer repeating rifles. The 6th Cavalry had a combination of Spencer breech-loading rifles and Burnside breech-loading carbines. Nearly all cavalry men also carried one or more Colt revolvers. The 5th and 6th regiments fought primarily dismounted using their repeating rifles to good advantage, while each fourth man held four horses, his own and those belonging to three comrades, out of action but ready to mount at a moment's notice. Command of this unit would be given to newly promoted Brigadier General George A. Custer on the eve of the Battle of Gettysburg. ¶ With thousands of armed men in close prox-

CAVALRY AT GETTYSBURG PL. 14

imity, there were occasional mistakes and acts of dangerous horseplay. On March 27, 1863, David Taylor of the 5th Michigan Cavalry died at the regiment's camp in Washington, D.C., from wounds received from the accidental discharge of a pistol. According to James Henry Avery, who later described his wartime service, one day while they were camped near Washington a comrade:

> . . . was in the tent of Sergeant Martin Baldwin of Allegan talking some bantering talk, when he picked up a revolver and cocking it, pointed it at Baldwin's head saying, "I will shoot you." Baldwin raised up his hand and pushed it away, which caused it to be discharged, the ball passing out the tent and piercing the abdomen of Corporal Taylor who was leaning against a bale of hay, causing his death in a few days.[15]

Taylor, whose parents Dennis and Harriet Taylor farmed in Ganges Township, was buried in the Military Asylum Cemetery, Washington, D. C., although a tombstone was also erected in his honor in Taylor Cemetery, Ganges. Avery identifies the gun's owner as Lewis Hirner of Ganges, who would die at the Battle of Yellow Tavern on June 11, 1864. However, the April 20, 1863, issue of the *Allegan Journal*, attributes the mistake to Corporal Herman Garvelink and notes "Garvelink has been placed under arrest."

ENCOUNTER AT ALDIE

While encamped near Washington, small parties were frequently sent on forays to the countryside. Lieutenant Samuel Harris later wrote about an incident that occurred on April 20, 1863:

> Early in the spring we were sent out on a raid to Ashby's Gap by way of Leesburg, Aldie, Middleberg, Upperville and Paris which is within a few miles of the Gap. As we neared Paris I was placed in command of the advance. Lieutenant George N. Dutcher had command of the advanced guard. He was a short distance ahead of me. As he entered Paris he was fired on by men in the houses. He held his own until I came to his assistance with my command, when we drove the rebels and bushwhack-

ers out of the houses and up the mountain. Lieut. Dutcher was wounded by being shot through his hand. I bound it up with my handkerchief and sent him back to our surgeon.[16]

In his pension papers, Dutcher described his assailants as members of "Fitzhuger's cavalry" (i.e. that segment of J.E.B. Stuart's cavalry under the direct command of Brigadier General Fitzhugh Lee, a nephew of Robert E. Lee). Dutcher suffered a saber cut on the left hand and at the same time a gun shot wound to the left hand. He was granted leave and reported to the Marine Hospital in Chicago to have his wounds dressed and to recuperate. ¶ It was an especially poor time for Dutcher to be wounded because he had just been promoted. On April 17, 1863, Private William H. Rockwell of Trowbridge Township wrote home to his family from "Camp near Fairfax": "Capt. W. B. Williams is home on a furlow of twenty days. We are commanded by Lieutenant Dutcher. He makes a good commander."[17] ¶ Less lucky than Dutcher, Kneeland Graves of the 3rd Michigan Cavalry was killed by guerrillas near Jackson, Tennessee, on April 25, 1863. He was buried at the National Cemetery, Corinth, Mississippi. Graves, described on the 1860 Saugatuck census as a teamster, was born in New York State and enlisted September 1, 1861, at Saugatuck at the age of 34.

THE 3RD INFANTRY AT CHANCELLORSVILLE

The 3rd Michigan Infantry saw action at Chancellorsville, Virginia, near the Rapidan River. George W. Bailey chronicled the four day battle in his diary:

> Friday, May 1: Clear and warm. Called up at five this morning, cooked and ate our breakfast . . . Came up to the front of the lines at noon, considerable firing in the front.

> Saturday, May 2: Clear and hot. Advanced one mile when we met the enemy. Patrick H. Doran Co. F, was killed and several of the regiment were wounded. The enemy drove the 11th corps. and flanked us on the right.

> Sunday, May 3: Clear and warm. Battle is raging still . . . . Our division made a charge last night and several of our boys were wounded and quite a number are missing.

> Monday, May 4: Clear most of the day – a little rain in the afternoon. Not much fighting today, the enemy still holds the battlefield.[18]

The Union artillery slipped to the rear after dark on May 5; the rest of the Army followed. ¶ Calvin Hall was missing in action on the third day of fighting and presumed taken prisoner. He returned to his regiment October 31, 1863, and fought to the close of the war.

"THREE YEARS OF SOLDIERING WILL SATISFY ME."
The term of service for men who had enlisted for three years at the very beginning of the war was getting close to the expiration date and there was a considerable push to get them to re-enlist. On May 14, 1863, the men of the 3rd Michigan Cavalry heard the details of a new plan that offered a $50 bounty and a 30-day furlough to any soldier who would enlist for more than the original term of his service. In July, Freeman Ross, who had been an engineer at a Singapore mill when he enlisted, along with Ezra Whaley became the first in the 3rd Cavalry to leave on the coveted furlough. ¶ However, George W. Bailey of the 3rd Michigan Infantry was unmoved by a similar pep talk. He wrote in his diary, September 21, 1863: "Great excitement in the camp about enlisting in the Veterans Corps. Most all of the boys are going to enlist for three years more in the cavalry and artillery. It may be a big thing, but *I for one can't see it.* Three years of soldiering will satisfy me."[19] His determination would do him little good. When his three years were up he was incarcerated in a Southern prison. ¶ To sweeten the pot and hang onto trained men many communities and states offered bounties to men who re-enlisted. It was sometimes a difficult decision. John P. Parrish, serving in the hospital pharmacy with the 6th Michigan Infantry in Port Hudson, Louisiana, decided against re-enlisting, but wrote home:

> I suppose if I had re-enlisted and sent the certificate home I could have drawn one of those two hundred

1861
1862
1863
1864
1865
AFTER THE WAR
80

dollar bountys that Pine Plains [Township] raised, with the State and County bountys raised the pile up to four and a half or five hundred dollars and had a furlough to come home in a few days to stay thirty five days in the State. But then the having to leave would be worse than all the rest.[20]

CAPTURING THE FLAG

On May 22, 1863, the 4th Michigan Cavalry captured the flag of the 1st Alabama Cavalry at Middleton, Tennessee. The regiment presented it to the State of Michigan "as additional evidence of our attachment to the beautiful State we so proudly call our own and their devotion to the cause of our common country, and we respectfully request that said flag be placed among the State archives as a memento of the service rendered by the 4th Michigan cavalry in the suppression of this wicked rebellion . . . that while we deprecate the existence of the unnatural strife now going on between the different States in this Union we will not cry 'Hold, enough!' until every rebel flag is either in safe keeping or trampled in the dust; that we know no friends except the friends of the old flag; no enemies except its enemies."

BREWING BEER FOR THE WOUNDED

Scott Eddy of the 44th Indiana Infantry, who had taken a ball in his hip on December 31, 1862, at Nashville was sent early in the spring to a convalescent camp. He later wrote:

That was fun. Went to the Regiment every day. Two of us got a beer receipt [recipe] made a half barrel. Took it down on the path that led to the spring. Lots of foreigners. When they went for water they took beer. A good deal of foam. At noon we went to camp with $21.60. Sold the receipt and went to the Regiment.[21]

On May 28 when his wound still had not healed properly he was discharged for disability and left for home.

THE 6TH INFANTRY IN THE SOUTH

The 6th Michigan Infantry was part of the brigade which was ordered to take Port Hudson, a Rebel stronghold on a bluff overlooking the Mississippi River between Baton Rouge and Vicksburg. Attempts to storm the fort in late

1861
1862
1863
1864
1865
AFTER THE WAR

81

May failed, and soldiers settled in for a siege. Parts of the 6th encamped a mile to the rear of the fortress and were stationed daily in rifle pits around the fort where they served as sharpshooters, picking off any Confederate soldier foolish enough to show himself. The fort was under bombardment by Federal gunboats on the river and shells exploding prematurely were an added peril. "We were actually more afraid of them than of the Confederate guns," one soldier wrote. ¶ A second assault was attempted and failed on June 14. At some point in these proceedings, John Rollins of the 6th Michigan Infantry was wounded in action and removed to the hospital at Baton Rouge, Louisiana. ¶ On July 8, a force of Northern cavalry arrived at Port Hudson with the news that Vicksburg had surrendered on the 4th of July. Negotiations were opened. A soldier later wrote, "Toward evening the Federal forces with banners flying and bands playing, marched in through the sally ports and took possession. The Confederates stacked their arms and marched at our command." [22]

THE 8TH CAVALRY HEADS FOR MT. STERLING

The 8th Michigan Cavalry was in camp at Hickman Bridge, Kentucky, when it received orders to march day and night to Mt. Sterling. The lieutenant of Co. F later reported to the *Allegan Journal*:

> On Tuesday morning [June 16] we started at three o'clock to overhaul the Rebels which was accomplished about six o'clock P.M. after marching thirty miles, the last four on the run. When we came up to them quite a smart firing was kept up for about an hour when the devils broke for the mountains leaving horses, baggage and a great many arms laying around loose. We took about fifty prisoners and seventy horses, besides killing some fifteen or twenty of the enemy and wounding about as many more.

GEN. E. MIX
FRONT 17

> Major Mix [Elijah Mix of Manlius Township] was in command of the third battalion always on hand and it seemed as though in the right place every time. He had been in the saddle averaging sixteen hours a day for ten days to the time of the battle but if you

1861
1862
1863
1864
1865
AFTER THE WAR

had seen him you would not have thought him very tired; he had an eye on every move that was made . . . . Company F, the Allegan boys made the first and only charge that was made and here let me say their friends will never be ashamed of them for they went in with a will and a cheer that showed there was not a coward or slink among them—When we got to the bridge over the Triplet River it was all in flames, but the boys were not discouraged at that, they charged down a steep bank into the river and across up the bank . . . Company F was complimented by the General and detailed as his body guard and to guard the provisions during the night; the next day we returned to camp without losing a man and but a very few horses. [23]

THE ROAD TO GETTYSBURG

On June 28, 1863, Lieutenant George Armstrong Custer of Ohio, often claimed by Michigan because he had spent time with relatives in Monroe, was appointed brigadier general. His promotion was precipitous. One day he was a lieutenant assigned as an aide on the staff of General Alfred Pleasanton, the next day he was appointed brigadier general, jumping completely over the ranks of captain, major and colonel. Custer was immediately given command of the Michigan Cavalry Brigade, replacing General Joseph T. Copeland. He rushed to meet his new brigade and finally succeeded in gathering them all together just outside of Littlestown, Pennsyvania, six and a half miles from Hanover, where they camped for the night of June 29, 1863. ¶ As Southern forces moved northward into Pennsylvania, the cavalry, under General J. E. B. Stuart, was separated from the main body of the army under General Robert E. Lee. At Hanover, Pennsylvania, six miles north of what would be known as the Mason-Dixon line, townspeople reported that they had been treated rudely by the Confederate soldiers who had passed through, and the Union troops were greeted enthusiastically with flowers and good things to eat. They did not stop in Hanover when they arrived but scooped up pies and cool drinks from their saddles. As the last of the column, largely the 5th New York Cavalry, reached the town about 10

1861

1862

1863

1864

1865

AFTER THE WAR

83

1861

1862

1863

1864

1865

AFTER THE WAR

a.m. they were charged by a Rebel brigade, and a full scale battle broke out in the streets. According to the Allegan newspaper the battle raged for "several hours" and resulted in "the slaughter of some 40 Rebels, 75 prisoners and the capture of several battle-flags." Remaining Confederate soldiers retreated to the shelter of cannon on nearby bluffs. ¶ The 5th Michigan Cavalry was between Hanover and Littletown when it received orders to "dismount to fight action front." Private J. H. Avery noted later:

> As this was our first order of the kind, and came so suddenly, we were somewhat flustered, officers and men, but we were quickly in line, leaving every fourth man to care for the horses. The line advanced in good style, met the rebs, and after a short time beat them back, when we mounted and followed on a charge through Hanover. [24]

Captain George N. Dutcher of Co. I was wounded. According to an account written by Private Hiram Ellis in the July 27, 1863, *Allegan Journal*, Dutcher "fell badly wounded but still cheering on his men until carried off the field." Official government documents record that the incident occurred at Littletown, June 30, but in later pension applications Dutcher describes the date and place as July 2 at Gettysburg, perhaps hoping that a more recognized battle might draw additional sympathy for his request. He described the wound as "a gunshot wound through his right groin, the ball passing entirely through from front to back." Other records note that the ball had also perforated the intestine. For this wound he was treated at a hospital set up at Hanover in the Pleasant Hill Hotel, one that became very busy as a result of the battle beginning the next day at Gettysburg. ¶ Gettysburg is 14 miles northwest of Hanover. The incidents at Hanover and Littletown on June 30 proved important to subsequent events at Gettysburg. By delaying Stuart and his cavalry units, Lee was forced into the fight the next day without full knowledge of the placement of troops in the field. Knowledge that contact with his cavalry prior to engagement might have brought him. After the attack at Hanover, the 5th Michigan Cavalry remounted and "pursued the Rebel Cavalry until we were within 17 miles of Harrisburg, but did not succeed in overtaking their column." [25]

MICHIGAN AND THE BATTLE OF GETTYSBURG

The battlefield at Gettysburg was filled with men from Michigan. In addition to the Michigan Cavalry Brigade, (1st, 5th, 6th, and 7th Michigan Cavalry) the battle included the 1st, 3rd, 4th, 5th, and 7th Michigan Infantry. Major Noah H. Ferry of the 5th Michigan Cavalry, son of the Reverend William M. Ferry, the founder of Grand Haven, was killed on July 3. Hiram Ellis of the 5th Michigan Cavalry describes their work:

> We were engaged two days in the Battle at Gettysburg, on the extreme right. Gen. Gregg with his Cav. being reported on the extreme left. The enemy massed itself against Gen. Hancock's corps several times. Upon such occasions, our Cavalry made the most desperate charges into the Rebel Infantry and Cavalry combined, strongly posted amongst woods and behind stone-walls and succeeded in driving them back and taking many prisoners. The boys from Allegan County, did their duty in the bravest manner and many were their hairbreadth escapes, but space does not allow me to particularize. [26]

During the thick of the battle at Gettysburg on July 3, Private William H. Dunn of the 5th Michigan Cavalry rescued Major L. S. Trowbridge who was unhorsed. Private James H. Avery later wrote:

WM. H. DUNN
FRONT 19

> It was during this desperate fight that Major Trowbridge of the fifth had his horse shot under him, and being likely to be taken prisoner, Billy Dunn of Company I, gave him his horse, and was himself taken prisoner. Just before dark, when the regiment was in line of battle, Billy came to us having succeeded in escaping from the johnnies, all right. [27]

Further activities were described by Private Hiram Ellis, 5th Michigan Cavalry, in the July 27, 1863, *Allegan Journal*:

> The 4th of July we celebrated by passing around to the rear of Lee's army and attacking a train of wagons in the mountains, taking 1600 prisoners, 200 of

whom were officers. We destroyed the train which was over 7 miles long and numbered 580 wagons. Our loss was 2 men. It took us all night to complete the job.

On July 8, the Michigan Brigade caught up with Stuart's cavalry near Boonsborough, Maryland. William Rockwell of the 5th Michigan Cavalry wrote home in a letter dated July 9:

> Yesterday was one of the hardest Cavalry fights of the war. I was on the battlefield from 8 in the morning till 8 at night with the balls and shells, grape and canister shot flying like hail all around me. I got my middle finger wounded a little, but not to bother me much. This is the eighth fight we have had with the Rebs and have whipped them every time. It was a horrible sight to see the miserable rebs lay mangled and wounded all over the ground. They fight desperately. They attacked us for we hold the gap in the Mountains. We drove them about two miles, took eleven of their cannon. They was so hard up for shells some of their cannon was loaded with stones. Our General said in the morning he did not expect to drive them. If he could hold them in check till the infantry got along it was all he expected us to do. In the evening he came to us and said we done bully and ordered some regiments close by to give us three cheers. [28]

Following the battle at Gettysburg, the 5th Michigan Cavalry moved quickly southward. Private Avery describes their sergeant, William C. Weeks, as "a short, wiry, fiery man, always at the front, and ready to punish slinkers, but a good comrade and jolly companion." After Gettysburg the regiment headed south with four long, steady days of marching and skirmishing. Avery later wrote:

> The boys were so sleepy it was impossible for them to keep their eyes open. Once, when we halted for a few minutes, Sergeant Weeks got off his horse and sat down and getting asleep, his horse went off without him and left him to walk. [29]

"THE REBS WILL SOON GIVE UP"

The 5th Michigan Cavalry returned to camp in Virginia. After Gettysburg, even though the battle was largely indecisive, the Rebels had "won" on the first day, there was a feeling that the Confederate army was on the run, and the end was getting near. In mid-August William Rockwell wrote from camp near Falmouth:

> It is one year today that I enlisted and at that time I did not think it possible that the war would last till this time and some of our boys is foolish enough to think the war is no nigher the end than when we enlisted. But if we watch the progress of the war we must know that the war can't last much longer for they are almost starved out from the best information we can get. There was three rebs swam the river last night and gave themselves up to our pickets. They say they believe the rebs will soon give up. [30]

CAPTAIN DUTCHER AND THE KNIGHTS OF THE GOLDEN CIRCLE

Captain George N. Dutcher of the 5th Michigan Cavalry was allowed a 20 day leave of absence to go to Chicago while he recuperated from the groin wound he suffered at the Battle of Hanover on June 30. Not part of the military record, but an oral tradition in the family and mentioned in his obituary, is his service while he was recuperating in Chicago. According to the obituary he was "attached to the Invalid Corps, which consisted of partially disabled soldiers fit for garrison duty, who were usefully employed in guarding the rebel prisoners confined at Camp Douglas, Chicago. . . .While so attached, Captain Dutcher did some very creditable things in connection with the Knights of the Golden Circle expose . . . "[31] ¶ The Knights of the Golden Circle was a group of Southern sympathizers in the free States which planned to free the Confederate prisoners at Camp Douglas and, joined by Canadian refugees, Missouri bushwhackers and members of the Knights, they would move the theater of war from the south to the center of the Union. A preliminary plan was foiled in August of 1863, and an even more elaborate effort (which many have discounted as more bluff than reality) was discovered and thwarted in November of 1864. Dutcher was in Chicago at least as late as August 31, 1863, when a doctor at Chicago's Marine Hospital, sent a statement to the regiment in Washington

1861

1862

1863

1864

1865

AFTER THE WAR

87

that Dutcher's "wound is still unhealed." ¶ After a little longer in Chicago and a visit to his mother and other family at Douglas, Dutcher headed back to his regiment. In the September 14, 1863, issue of the *Allegan Journal*, the editor wrote: "Capt. G. N. Dutcher passed through town this morning en route for his regiment on the Rappahannock. His anxiety to be again in the field hastened his departure although still suffering from the severe wound received at Gettysburg." ¶ Immediately after Gettysburg, recruitment began for the 10th Michigan Cavalry with Thaddeus Foote of Grand Rapids as colonel and Luther S. Trowbridge of Detroit as lieutenant colonel. William H. Dunn of Ganges, who had saved Trowbridge at Gettysburg, was named second lieutenant of Co. D. Enlistment was slow and the regiment was not mustered until November 18. It eventually included William Dunn's younger brother, 17-year-old Leonidas H. Dunn, and 29-year-old George E. Dunn who was a sash and door maker from Ganges. Henry Hannibal Goodrich, son of Ganges doctor, Chauncey B. Goodrich, enlisted in Co. D as a corporal, but in 1864 was discharged to accept a promotion as second lieutenant in the U. S. Colored Artillery.

MEANWHILE IN THE WEST

On July 12, 1863, the 3rd Michigan Cavalry was on its way to Jackson, Tennessee, when it struck the enemy's pickets near the Forked Deer River. After the bridge was fortified the action began and was described in the August 3, *Allegan Journal*:

> The Colonel [Gilbert Moyers of Allegan] dismounted his entire regiment and sent them forward to the right, left and front, and opened upon the enemy with a howitzer (there are two belonging to this regiment) forcing him back gradually until he reached a commanding position under cover of a wood which he held stubbornly, until at length Capt. Nugent charged across an open field when he fled in confusion. At this time the 3rd Michigan were remounted and the 2d Iowa were brought forward for a charge upon the enemy, the former led by Col. Moyers and the latter by Col. Hatch. These preparations occa-

sioned by a moment's delay, after which our brave soldiers might be seen going at full speed, yelling like so many demons; the gallant Colonels at the head of their respective columns which moved parallel with each other on different streets.

Captain Elisha Mix, Co. F of the 8th Michigan Cavalry first saw active duty in July during the pursuit and capture of Confederate General John H. Morgan and the remnants of his raiders at Buffington Island (New Lisbon), Ohio. Action began on July 2 in Kentucky and proceeded through Indiana and into Ohio with numerous clashes along the way. Morgan was finally captured on July 26. Involved in the operation were the 25th Michigan Infantry, the 8th and 9th Michigan Cavalry, the 1st Michigan Sharpshooters and Battery L of the Michigan Light Artillery.

A STAB AT "FRESH MEAT FOR SUPPER"

Despite the grimness of the war there were lighter moments. A comrade in the 13th Michigan Infantry, John McCline, later wrote of an incident involving Private Joseph Sinclair of Saugatuck that occurred on the way to Franklin, Tennessee, early in September, 1863:

> He was a reckless, dare devil and always ready for anything going. The command had halted for a brief spell on a slight rise along the pike, and several fine shoats were noticed grazing in the corner of the fence opposite our wagon. "Oh, boys," Joe exclaimed, "Here is a chance to get some fresh meat for supper." And we with one accord said: "Yes, Joe, get him!" He fixed his bayonet and alighted from his seat in the wagon and creeping up cautiously with the intention of running him through back of the right shoulder, he made a quick dart; but the pig was quicker and got away without a scratch. Joe's stab was such a vigorous one that he went headlong, gun and all, into a heap, to the intense amusement of all in the wagon.[32]

Sinclair was discharged "by order" at Washington, D.C., on June 8, 1865. After the war he returned to Allegan County. The 1870 census shows him working in a Saugatuck Village sawmill. He died September 26, 1884, and is buried in Riverside Cemetery, Saugatuck.

1861 1862 1863 1864 1865 AFTER THE WAR

89

FILLING OUT THE RANKS

As fighting and disease continued to diminish the ranks, such officers as could be spared left the battlefields to come home and beat the bushes for men to fill the spaces created in the ranks. The two intrepid recruiters from the 3rd Michigan Cavalry, after two visits to Michigan, were making progress. On August 17, the *Allegan Journal* reported that Colonel Moyers had the 40 men sought from Allegan County and Lieutenant Butler was in Paw Paw, Van Buren County, where he is "meeting with much success." On August 22, 1863, Order 2026 granted Butler and 50 men transportation from Cairo, Illinois to Memphis, Tennessee to join the regiment. ¶ According to the diary kept by Corporal Jacob Heringa, the new men arrived on August 24. On that day he wrote, "We were pleasantly surprised today with the appearance of 30 recruits direct from Michigan. they join Comp. A. These again will swell our numbers to seventy-five men." Later after he had put the men through two days of drilling he declared, "They drill remarkably well for new beginners."[33] ¶ The August 17, 1863, Allegan newspaper reported: "O. D. Squire of Ganges, a member of Co. L, Mich. 4th Cavalry, has returned from the Army on a furlough having been injured by a wagon running over him. May he soon recover." This would appear to be Jonathan D. Squier (or Squire or Squires, even the family disagreed over the spelling of the name) of Pier Cove, who had enlisted August 14, 1862, at Allegan. ¶ To add to the attrition in the ranks caused by battle and disease, some trained soldiers were about to be lost to their regiments through the expiration of their terms of service. In some States old units died and were replaced by new regiments. In Michigan there was a serious effort to renew the old regiments with frequent additions of fresh troops. Counties that could not provide enough enlistees, according to an allotment system, had to revert to the draft to fill the open spots. The editor of the *Allegan Journal* enthused in the September 7, 1863, issue:

> Sergeant P. A. Pullman of Co. B of the 19th Michigan Infantry is in town recruiting. He wants 25 men to fill up the Company that represents Allegan

County in that Regiment. Let us fill up its ranks
—our brothers in the field appeal to us to come
down and help them; let not the appeal be in vain.
There never was a better time to enlist. Let us fill up
our quota from this County and avoid the draft; but
there is no time for delay, it must be done at once or
the draft will be upon us.

DRAFT BECOMES A REALITY

The first draft list was published in the Allegan newspaper
in July, 1863. It is reproduced below. Service records could
be located only for the names in italics. Many who were
drafted bought substitutes, were released from the obliga-
tion because of age or disability, or simply refused to answer
the summons.

SAUGATUCK TOWNSHIP

Edmond H. Fogg
John Bacon
Warren W. Pratt
Gustave Augustin
Nelson Helmes
MortimerVanElkenburgh
Isaac Herman
Alfred N. Gardner
Peter Samoyn
William Randall
James Wilcox
Nelson A. Berra
Dennis Dorgan
Madison Raplee

GANGES TOWNSHIP

Frederick Plummer
Sylvester Sweeny
John Townsend
Warner Prentice
James Wescott
Nathaniel J. Clark
Wm. H. Sutherland
Almond W. Clark
J. H. Barden
William Hill

Madison Raplee, whose name appears on the draft list, was
refused as an enlistee early in the war. He might have had
some physical ailment, or he might have been rejected as a
new father; his son, Elmon, was born on January 7, 1862.
On October 31, 1863, Raplee tried again and was mustered
immediately into the 4th Michigan Cavalry. He wasn't even
allowed to return home to say good-bye to his family. When
she was informed of the circumstances, his wife Eliza, with
19-month-old Elmon, tried desperately to catch the train
for a farewell meeting but she was unsuccessful. She never
saw him again. After training, he joined his regiment on
February 18, 1864, at Nashville, Tennessee, where he died

1861 1862 1863 1864 1865 AFTER THE WAR

from complications of the measles ("inflammation of the brochea" according to his military records), "on or about March 27, 1864." He was buried in the National Cemetery at Nashville.

AID AND COMFORT FOR THE SOLDIER

A private serving with Co. A, 3rd Michigan Cavalry, at that time camped near Corinth, Mississippi, wrote in a letter dated September 14, 1863, and published in the October 5, 1863, issue of the *Allegan Journal*, that many of the regiment were ill, at least partially as a result of "the baneful effects of this wretched Corinth water and the oppressive heat of the climate." He reports that Dr. Hoy of Saugatuck "has been detailed to take their charge. He is a worthy and kind hearted man." William T. Hoy was born in Spain in 1818 and moved to Ohio with his family about 1821 and to Allegan County in 1855. On the 1860 census, he is described as a farmer in Lee Township. Shortly afterwards he moved to Saugatuck. Military records indicate that he did not enroll in the service as a doctor, but he seems to have served in that capacity. A letter in the April 18, 1864, *Allegan Journal* noted that "he is now a clerk in the Overton hospital – a post for which he is well qualified." He returned to Saugatuck after the war and the 1870 census shows him as a "physician" although he is never included in historical lists of doctors that served the community. ¶ On the local scene, there was a big push to get Soldier's Aid chapters and young people's groups to send portable foodstuffs to the soldiers, as well as sewing kits, books and other items to relieve the body and mind. In the September 14, 1863, *Allegan Journal* there is a notice that Sergeant George Harris of Co. G of the 6th Michigan Infantry, "will be happy to convey to the Company any articles which their friends in this County would desire to send. In this time of abundance let us not forget our brothers in the field. Dry your peaches, your plums, your apples, your pears and your green corn and sent it down to the boys, you can hardly imagine how good it will taste down there." In August a shipment was dispatched to the 3rd Michigan Cavalry which included dried fruits, dried beef, butter, farina, wines, jellies and jams, three barrels of dried apples and onions, two kegs of eggs, one half barrel of pickles and $141 in currency.

OHIO RENEGADE DESCRIBED IN 1863 LETTER

Although many letters survive that were sent from the soldiers to loved ones at home, no letters could be uncovered that were written from Saugatuck to the men in the field. One letter written October 18, 1863, from a Saugatuck man to relatives, speaks not of the military engagements of the war, but of an Ohio politician. John P. Hanchett, an investor (and later master) of the sternwheel riverboat, Comet, which had been built at Saugatuck in 1863, wrote his aunt:

> I think some of going down to Ohio on a visit next winter. I am glad Ohio did not disgrace herself by making a Governor of that traitor Vallanddigham or as some have it more appropriately Villain damn man. I feared he would deceive many by pretending to be a great friend to soldiers. He proposed to raise the soldiers pay and to pay them in gold just to break down the Government as he knew paying them all in gold would be impossible and that of course would make the rebellion a success.[34]

Clement L. Vallandigham was a conservative Democrat, a member of the House of Representatives from Ohio, who opposed the federal government's prosecution of the Civil War and hindered their efforts where he could. He began a campaign for governor of Ohio, but was so vocal in his opposition to the war that he was arrested on May 5 and banished to the Confederacy. To show their outrage, Ohio Democrats actually nominated him as their gubernatorial candidate. He left the Confederate States in June and shipped to Bermuda and then Canada, which he used as a campaign base. However, he lost the October election as Hanchett notes in his letter.

FEDERAL HORSES PROVE TOO SMART IN TENNESSEE

While the 8th Michigan Cavalry was camped near Oak Springs, Tennessee, northeast of Chattanooga, a portion of the regiment was ordered into nearby Cleveland, to collect

1861

1862

1863

1864

1865

AFTER THE WAR

93

such Confederate property as they could find. In a letter back home, Colonel Elisha Mix described what happened next in the November 16, 1863, issue of the *Allegan Journal*:

> Everything went finely until the morning of the 18ᵗʰ about 6 o'clock in the morning – the rebels about 17 hundred ſtrong, attacked our pickets on three sides of town and drove them in. Capt. Babbitt had about 20 horses saddled at the time with him in the center of the town. To horse was sounded and he dashed into about three hundred rebels, driving them out of the town and across the Railroad, when the rebels unmasked a Battery of three guns at ten rods diſtant, with grape and caniſter, killing ten of his horses and wounding 4 men; this gave time for all his horses to be saddled which saved the command . . . . They next tried to flank our boys, but Federal horses were too smart for them in a race of two miles, and then it was fight and run for eleven miles, over fences and across the Hiwassee River, where they held the fort until reinforcements came to their assiſtance.

During the fight, Mix added, Co. F, largely Allegan County men,

> . . . was forgotten by the Field officer of the day and were cut off from the command. They had continual fighting with the rebel skirmishers for three days and nights, traveling in meantime, over one hundred miles, and arrived within two miles of Loudon [southweſt of Knoxville, Tennessee] at day light the morning of the 4ᵗʰ day.

ALONG THE CHICKAMAUGA

Colonel Joshua Culver of Paw Paw, commanding the 13ᵗʰ Michigan Infantry in September of 1863, reported:

BATTLE OF
CHICKAMAUGA
PL. 19

> On the afternoon of the 18ᵗʰ the regiment was ordered to deploy as skirmishers along the Chickamauga to the right of Lee and Gordon's Mills, where we were warmly engaged by the enemy's skirmishers who were supported by a seƈtion of artillery. We held this position until about 12 M., when we were recalled to join our brigade and division that had been moved about one mile to the left . . . .We executed the movement on the double-quick, with the thermometer 90 degrees above. The battle was raging furiously on our front and flank; we formed

our lines under the enemy's fire and were immediately ordered to charge the exultant rebels who were forcing back a part of the brigade. The charge was executed in a hand-some manner, and checked their advance but at a fearful sacrifice of life . . . " [35]

In a letter from Chattanooga dated September 19, 1863, E. H. Porter, of the 4th Michigan Cavalry, wrote:

> After a long, dirty, rough and tedious march I am here at last in Chattanooga . . . . we have been 3 days in coming 30 miles over the mountains. Oh, dear! If we didn't have rough traveling over the mountains . . . . Some places we could look down from the road on which we were 400 feet perpendicular into the Tennessee river . . . .This was on what is called 'Look out Mountain" – rightly named . . . . Our Brigade train started out with rations yesterday and went out only six miles and were ordered back. They could distinctly hear the rifle firing and the cannoneering. Report has just come into Chattanooga that in yesterday's fight our Brigade lost between four and five hundred men. Capt. Pritchard is very badly wounded in the arm, and has had two pieces of bone taken out . . . . It is expected that one of the greatest battles of the war will be fought here within a few days . . . orders have just come in for the Brigade Commissary and myself to get 5 days rations and move to the front and issue them to-night. I shall go and will probably be up all night. [36]

In this day's fighting at Chickamauga, Georgia, about 12 miles south of Chattanooga, John H. Baldwin, suffered a gunshot wound to his left hand and David Hyett, was reported missing in action. Both men were with Co. B, 13th Michigan Infantry. Batteries A and D of the 1st Michigan Light Artillery were overrun with the loss of all but two of their guns. Louis A. Hare of the 16th U. S. Infantry was taken prisoner. ¶ September 20, 1863, the second day at Chickamauga, was near disaster for the North, but the Union army finally managed to pull back to Chattanooga where they were penned up. Private A. B. Case of the 13th Michigan Infantry described the scene in a letter to his wife which was printed in the October 5, 1863, issue of the *Allegan Journal*:

1861 1862 1863 1864 1865 AFTER THE WAR

95

We are lying behind the breast-works listening to one of the most terrific engagements in our life which has been fought in this war. Our men stand nobly to the work – the rebels appear to use their utmost endeavors to turn our flank, but as yet, they have not succeeded . . . . Six o'clock PM, we are driven back three miles."

The following day Private Case added:

We have just come in; I was cut off with Co. A, and came in by Mountain road . . . We drove the enemy, report says, and are now in position at Roseville, in front five miles from here. I am now drawing rations for the men and am going to join them this afternoon. We are receiving reinforcements very rapidly and will come out victorious in the end.

The 13th Michigan Infantry spent September 22 fortifying Chattanooga. The following day, Private John H. Stephens wrote his mother:

It is all still so far to day, but the rebs are trying to surround us and in that case will compel us to eat our own rations. We have a strong position and can thrash them if they will only try to whip us in our fortifications . . . the rebs have all our hospitals and lots of men. The boys have been up 5 nights and are stiff and sore . . . Nearly the whole southern army is here.[37]

The 13th went into action with 217 men and 107 of these were reported killed, wounded or missing. Also active at Chickamauga were the 2nd and 4th Michigan Cavalry and the 9th and 11th Michigan Infantry. ¶ Local men lost from the 13th Michigan Infantry included William O. Allen and Lewis Bell, both of Ganges, who were taken prisoners. Wounded soldiers included Daniel Lee of Ganges with a wound in the right arm, he was discharged December 24 for disability and later tended the draw bridge between Saugatuck and Douglas; Samuel Stillson, a Saugatuck Township farmer, wounded in the right forearm; and First Sergeant Charles L. Bard of Saugatuck who was wounded in the right side.

PLATES

PLATE 1 | *A traveling artist drew this picture of the sawmill owned by H. D. Moore in 1858. At the right of the picture Moore's Creek, from Goshorn Lake, enters the Kalamazoo River. The large building near the top of the hill in the center of the picture may be the old Reformed church.*

PLATE 2 | *This sketch of Saugatuck appeared on an 1864 wall map of Allegan County. The paddlewheel steamer at right is said to be the Comet. The Congregational Church, built in 1860, is prominent on the hill, center.*

PLATE 3 | *A substantial lighthouse was built in 1858 to replace one which had toppled into the Kalamazoo River. This picture was taken in the 1880s and shows the George Baker family and friends. Later turned into a summer cottage the building stood until demolished by a tornado in April of 1956.*

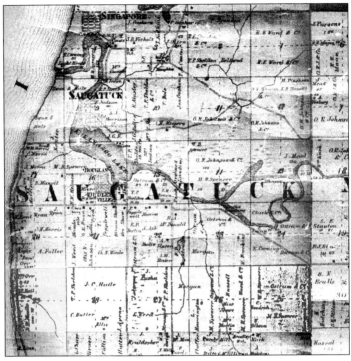

PLATE 4 | *The 1864 wall map shows four communities in the northwest quarter of Saugatuck Township. Singapore at the northernmost bend of the Kalamazoo River near its mouth; Saugatuck, on the north end of Kalamazoo Lake; and Douglas and Dudleyville, separated by a single street, on the south side of the river.*

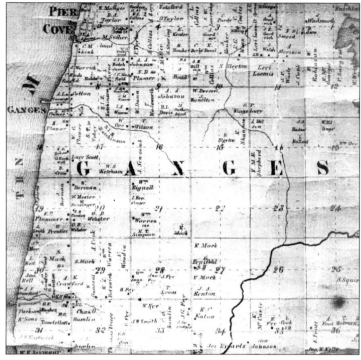

PLATE 5 | *The 1864 wall map shows Pier Cove in the northwestern corner of Ganges Township, with Ganges located at the site of what was sometimes called Plummerville. In the southwestern corner of the township the settlement known as Crawford's Corners, which would later be Glenn, is just beginning.*

For the Allegan Journal.

Union Meeting at Newark.

A National mass meeting of the citizens of Saugatuck and vincinity was held at the Morrison Hall on Monday evening, April 29.

Levi Loomis, of Ganges, was called to the chair and J. G. Butler elected Secretary.

Messrs. Geo. Harris, F. B. Wallin, E. Mix and Nelson Wade were chosen as a Committee on Resolutions, who reported the following which were unanimously adopted.

WHEREAS, A portion of our country is in open rebellion against the Government and with arms are opposing the constituted authorities and bidding defiance to the Laws: therefore

Resolved, That we cannot admit the right of Secession, for it involves our own destruction, or in other words secession is rebellion, and as such should be put down by all the powers of the Federal Government.

Resolved, That like our forefathers we pledge our lives, our fortunes, and our sacred honor to sustain inviolate the Union and Constitution purchased by their blood.

Patriotic speeches were made by F. B. Wallin and F. B. Stockbridge of Saugatuck. Hon. G. Moyers of Allegan, followed by the presentation of an Enrollment list, and the names of twenty of the audience were immediately subscribed. After a few national songs from the glee Club, the meeting adjourned, giving 3 cheers for the volunteers, 3 for Gen. Scott, and 3 for the Union. LEVI LOOMIS, *Pres't*

JAMES G. BUTLER, *Sec'y*

PLATE 6 | *Just 17 days after the first shot was fired at Fort Sumter, a meeting was held at Saugatuck supporting the war, and giving Saugatuck-area men their first chance to join up "to sustain inviolate the Union and Constitution."*

PLATE 7 | *The Union meeting was held in Morrison's Hall, the upper floor of Morrison's general store (arrow), which was located near the intersection of Butler and Culver Streets in Saugatuck. It burned in 1879.*

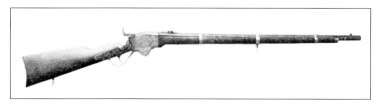

103

PLATE 8 | *Spencer Breech-Loading Repeating Rifle*

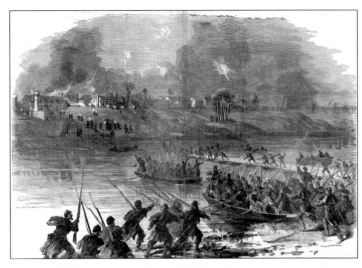

PLATE 9 | *Volunteers from the 7th Michigan Infantry crossing the Rappahannock to drive off Confederate sharpshooters who were delaying work on the pontoon bridge, December 11, 1862.*

1 | 13 | Mich.

Mordant D Loomis

Priv., Co. D, 13 Reg't Michigan Inf.

Age 21 years.

Appears on Co. Muster-out Roll, dated

Washington D.C. June 1, 1865.

Muster-out to date ...., 186 .

Last paid to ...., 186 .

Clothing account:

Last settled ...., 186 ; drawn since $......100

Due soldier $......100; due U.S. $......100

Am't for cloth'g in kind or money adv'd $......100

Due U.S. for arms, equipments, &c., $......100

Bounty paid, $......100; due, $......100.

Remarks: Killed in battle at Stone River Tenn Dec 31 62

Book mark: ....

Hilton

(361) Copyist.

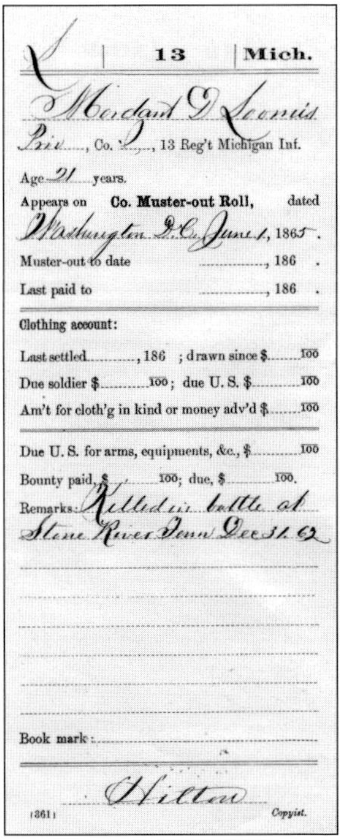

PLATE 10 | *Muster-out roll from the military record of Mordant D. Loomis of the 13th Michigan Infantry, which shows that he was killed at Stone River, Tennessee, December 31, 1862.*

PLATE 11 | *The decisive charge of the Battle of Stone's River, Tennessee, on January 2, 1863. Here Union soldiers are depicted capturing the flag of the 26th Tennessee Infantry.*

PLATE 12 | *The Saugatuck House (then known as the Newark House) on Butler Street was the scene of a "promenade concert and supper" to raise funds for the Michigan Soldier's Relief Association in 1863 Built in the 1850s it was Saugatuck's earliest hotel and continued in business until 1913 when it was razed to make way for Parrish's drug store.*

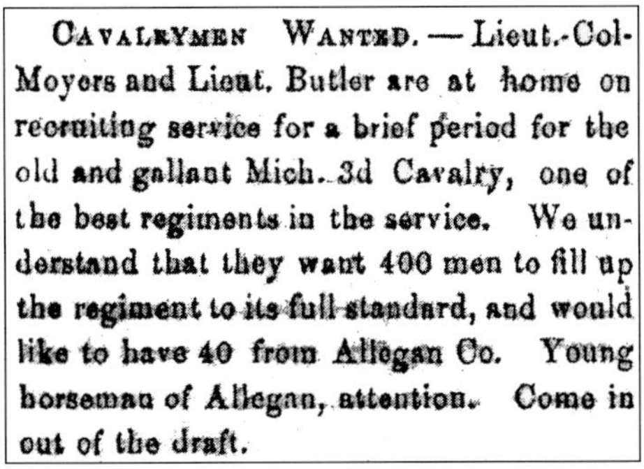

CAVALRYMEN WANTED. — Lieut.-Col·
Moyers and Lieut. Butler are at home on
recruiting service for a brief period for the
old and gallant Mich. 3d Cavalry, one of
the best regiments in the service. We understand that they want 400 men to fill up
the regiment to its full standard, and would
like to have 40 from Allegan Co. Young
horsemen of Allegan, attention. Come in
out of the draft.

PLATE 13 | *A recruiting ad from the February 27,
1863, issue of the* Allegan Journal.

PLATE 14 | *Although they rode horses into battle cavalry units often fought
dismounted. Each fourth man held his own and three other horses just out of
battle range, but ready to be mounted at a moment's notice. This engraving
depicts the cavalry at Gettysburg.*

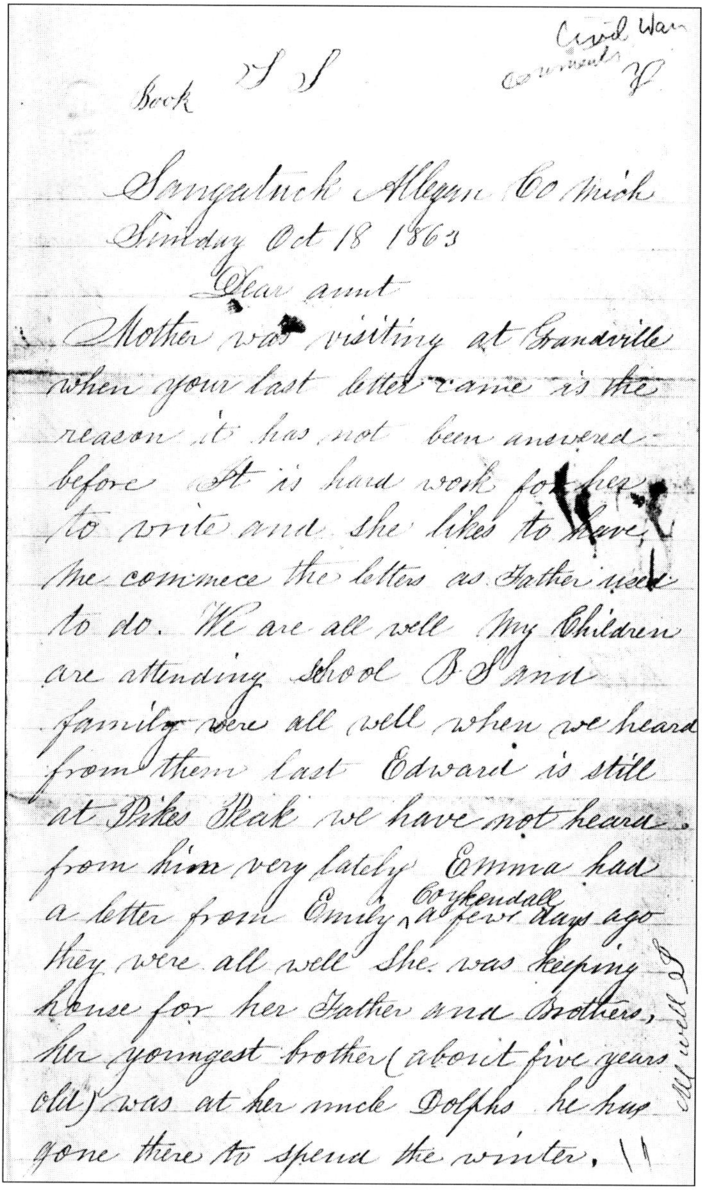

Book *S S*

Civil War comments

Saugatuck Allegan Co Mich
Sunday Oct 18 1863
Dear aunt
Mother was visiting at Grandville when your last letter came is the reason it has not been answered before It is hard work for her to write and she likes to have me commence the letters as Father used to do. We are all well My Children are attending School B S and family were all well when we heard from them last Edward is still at Pikes Peak we have not heard from him very lately Emma had a letter from Emily Coykendall a few days ago they were all well She was keeping house for her Father and Brothers, her youngest brother (about five years old) was at her uncle Dolphs he has gone there to spend the winter. \\

107

PLATE 15 | *Page one of the only letter discovered that was written in Saugatuck during the years of the Civil War. The writer, J. P. Hanchett was a steamboat investor.*

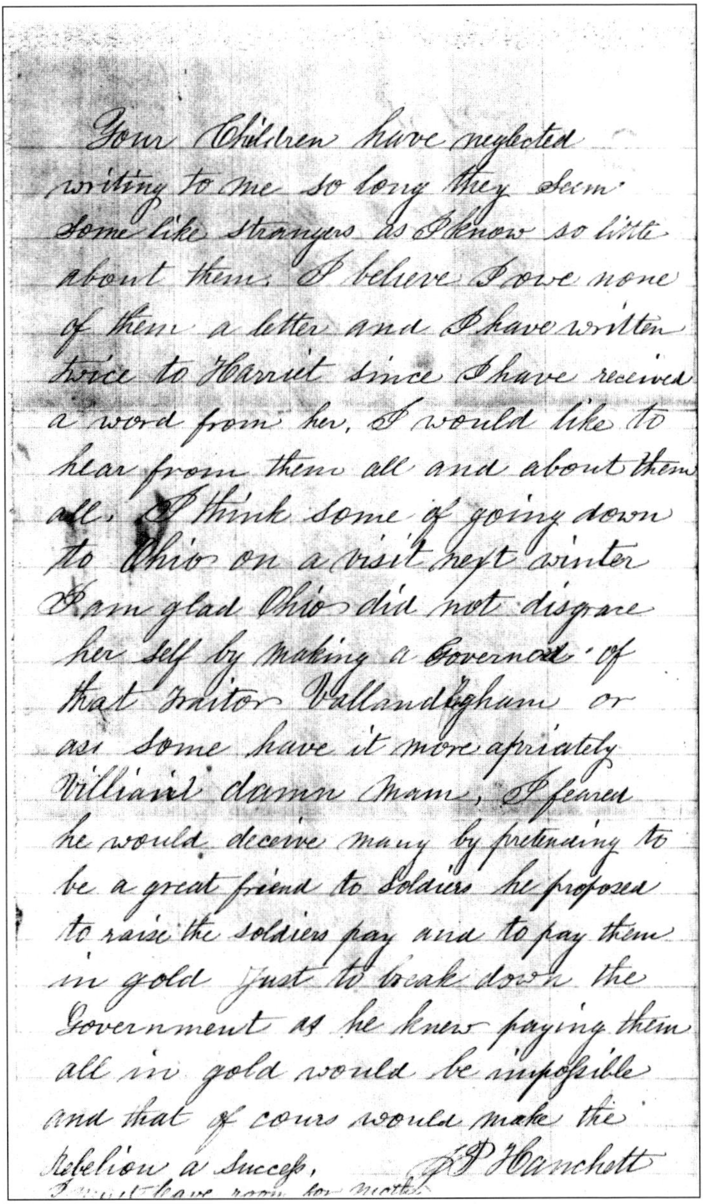

Your Children have neglected writing to me so long they seem some like strangers as I know so little about them. I believe I owe none of them a letter and I have written twice to Harriet since I have received a word from her, I would like to hear from them all and about them all. I think some of going down to Ohio on a visit next winter I am glad Ohio did not disgrace her self by making a Governor of that traitor Vallandigham or as some have it more apriately Villiant damn Mam; I feared he would deceive many by pretending to be a great friend to Soldiers he proposed to raise the soldiers pay and to pay them in gold just to break down the Government as he knew paying them all in gold would be impofsible and that of cours would make the rebelion a Succefs. P Hanchett

I must have room for more

PLATE 16 | *Page two of the Hanchett letter.*

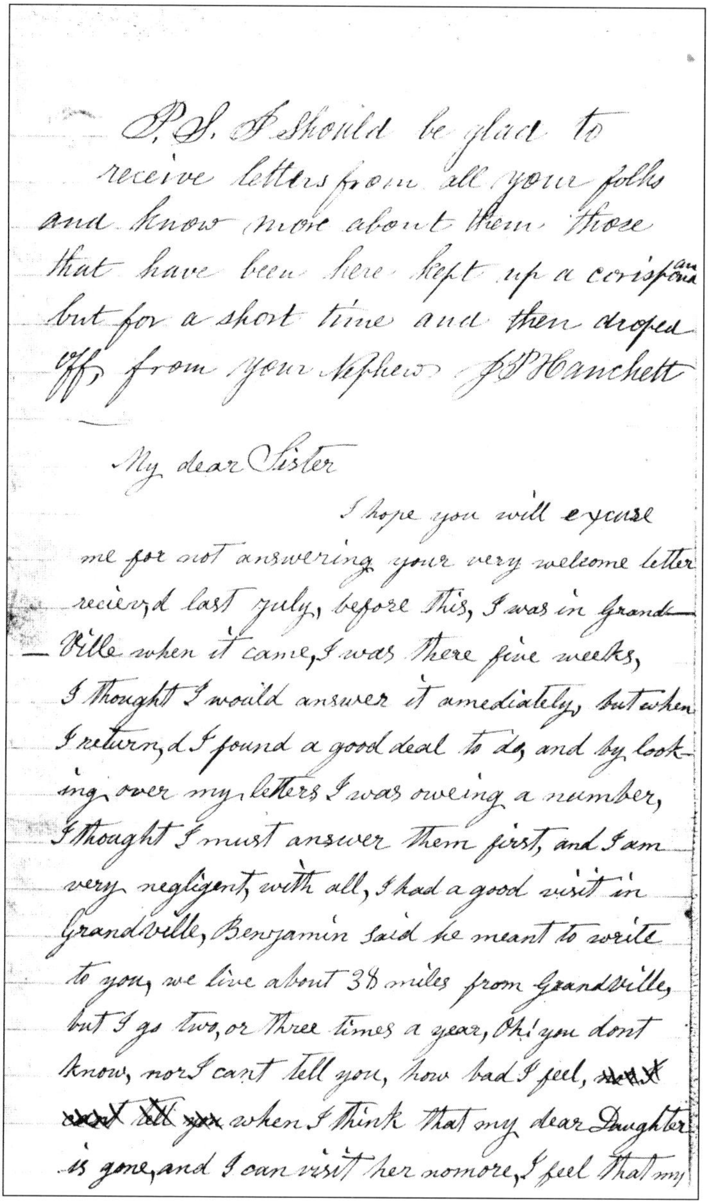

P.S. I should be glad to receive letters from all your folks and know more about them those that have been here kept up a corispond⁻an but for a short time and then droped off, from your Nephew J.P. Hanchett

My dear Sister

I hope you will excuse me for not answering your very welcome letter reciev'd last July, before this, I was in Grand- Ville when it came, I was there five weeks, I thought I would answer it amediately, but when I return'd I found a good deal to do, and by look- ing over my letters I was oweing a number, I thought I must answer them first, and I am very negligent, with all, I had a good visit in Grandville, Benjamin said he meant to write to you, we live about 38 miles from Grandville, but I go two, or three times a year, Oh! you dont know, nor I cant tell you, how bad I feel, ～～～ ～～～ ～～ when I think that my dear Daughter is gone, and I can visit her nomore, I feel that my

PLATE 17 | *Page three of the Hanchett letter.*

109

Family is leaveing me fast, I feel very lonly, but I try to feel submiss, and that it is all right, the Lord knows what is good for us, better then we do, and we aught not to murmur, it is now over 6 years since Edward went away, and I think it very doubtful whether I ever see him again, but it gives me great satisfaction to hear from him, I feel that I am growing old fast, and have but a short time to stay, and I hope that we shall all so live, that we shall meet in a hapier world, where sin and sorrow never comes, where we shall part nomore, I am very glad you and Laura live where you can see eachother often, Oh! how I do wish I could see you, and your Children, pleas give my love to Alvira and her family, and to all of your Children when you see them, Now I will tell you about my teeth, I think a great deal of them, (as you say) but my under teeth have always bothered me a great deal, my food gits under them, and more espeecially if I eat any thing with seeds in, and my under gums are sore, a good deal of the time, I am very glad you have got some, I think you will git used to them, and like them, I think mine help me very much about talking, it is hard work to talk without them, I presume your under ones will always trouble you some, I think I have not heard from Phebe since last may, they were all well then, I recieved a letter from Laura, last August, they were all well, I have sent Laura a Photograph picture and I calculate to send you one as soon as I can git some more taken, you wrote that Lorette had lost her two little Girls, I feel to sympathise with her, and should like very much to see her, how many children has she left, now I must close and send it to office, good bye, this from your affectionate Sister write again soon

Rebecca Hanchet

PLATE 18 | *The final page of the Hanchett letter.*

PLATE 19 | *Union loss was heavy at the Battle of Chickamauga, Georgia, September 19-20, 1863. In this old engraving the headquarters staff survey the field. General William S. Rosecrans is second from left*

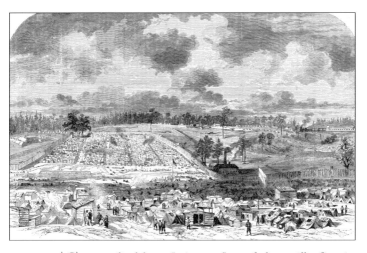

PLATE 20 | *The great Confederate "prison pen" at Andersonville, Georgia, where up to 33,000 prisoners were held with no furnished shelter, and no water or sewage facilities other than that offered by a small stream that trickled through the compound. Of 45,613 who were incarcerated in the pen for varying periods, 12, 912 died.*

PLATE 21 | *Only the fringe and fragments of the bottom two stripes were left of the flag of the 1st Michigan Sharpshooters when it was raised at the courthouse following the capture of Petersburg. The ribbons which list the battles that the regiment participated in were added to the pole before the Grand Review at the end of the war. Also visible in the picture is some netting applied to the ribbons and fragments in the 1960s in an attempt to stabilize the fabric.*

GLORY! GLORY!
SURRENDER OF LEE !
His Army Disbanded !

PLATE 22 | *The* Allegan Journal *joyfully announced Lee's surrender.*

PLATE 23 | *The Flag of Truce*

PLATE 24 | *Union soldiers sharing their rations with Confederate soldiers after Lee's surrender.*

PLATE 25 | *Over 1,500 people, mostly Union soldiers freed from southern prisons, lost their lives when a boiler exploded aboard the overcrowded steamboat Sultana as it moved northward on the Mississippi River on April 27, 1865.*

PLATE 26 | *After Confederate President Jefferson Davis, was caught trying to flee wearing a woman's cloak, the Northern political cartoonists redrew and exaggerated the scene.*

115

PLATE 27 | *Jefferson Davis entering an ambulance after his capture to be transported to a northern prison. One of the guards depicted here would be Sergeant Levi Tuttle of Saugatuck.*

PLATE 28 | *To celebrate the conclusion of the war the military units of the Union armies paraded down Pennsylvania Avenue in review for two days, May 23 and 24, 1865.*

(Confederate.

P | 7 | Texas.

A. Plummer

Pvt Co K, 7 Regt. Texas Inf

Residence Allegan Co. Michigan

Appears on a

Roll of Prisoners of War

of furloughed and detailed men, Confederate States Army, commanded by —, surrendered at New Orleans, La., by General E. K. Smith, C. S. A., to Maj. Gen. E. R. S. Canby, U. S. A., May 26, 1865, and paroled at Shreveport, La., June 15, 1865.

Roll dated Shreveport, La., June 15, 1865.

Number of roll:
127

(639b) Copyist.

1302

Plummer. A

Co. K, 7 Texas Infantry.

(Gregg's Reg't Texas Inf.)

Part of Bailey's Consol'd Reg't Inf., Oct., '62, to Jan., '63.
Became Cos. B and C, Granbury's Consol'd Texas Brig., about April 9, 1865.

(Confederate.)

Private Private

CARD NUMBERS.

4422/456

Number of medical cards herein 0
Number of personal papers herein 0

Book Mark:

See also

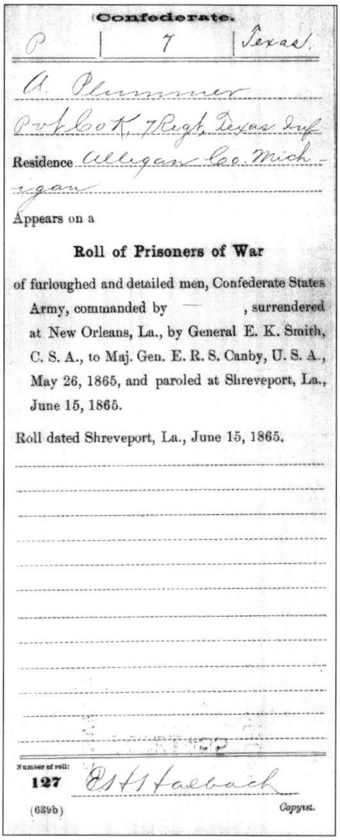

PLATE 29 | *The prisoner of war roll from the Confederate military record of A. Plummer, Allegan Co., Michigan, shows that he was surrendered at New Orleans on May 26, 1865.*

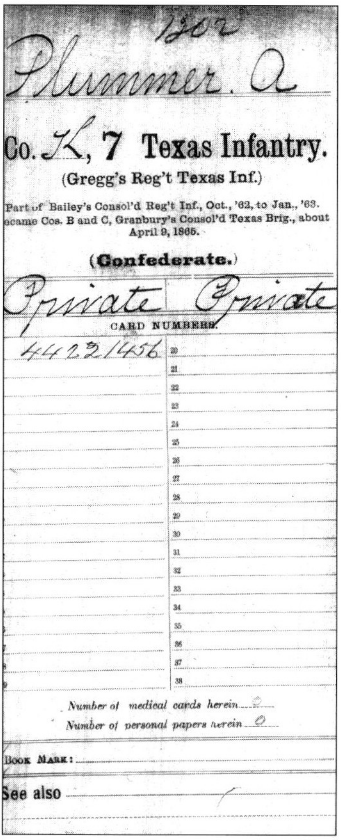

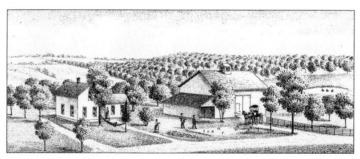

PLATE 30 | *When Andrew Plummer finally returned to Michigan it was a great surprise for his family who had thought him dead. In this 1892 engraving the Plummer family is shown on their 100 acre farm, with a croquet game on the front lawn.*

PLATE 31 |*Walter Billings with his horse, Billy, and his dog, Watchie my Son,
went on frequent forays after the war to visit his offspring in the West.*

118

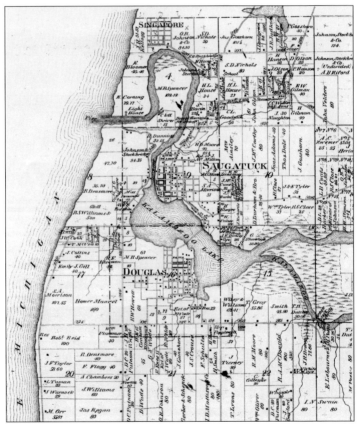

PLATE 32 |*By the time this 1873 map was drawn Singapore was a thriving
lumber town, both Saugatuck and Douglas had incorporated as villages, and
piers had been constructed to protect the mouth of the Kalamazoo River.*

PLATE 33 |*Reunions were a favorite pastime after the war. This ribbon commemorates the Allegan County Soldiers and Sailors Association, 14th annual reunion, held at Saugatuck in 1893.*

PLATE 34 │ *A monument honoring the "Defenders of Our Nation, 1861–1865" was erected on the courthouse lawn in Allegan in 1904.*

106. Decoration Day 1907 at Ganges, Mich.
The Soldiers Monument.

PLATE 35 | *Civil War veterans gather on Decoration Day, 1907, the year after dedication of the Civil War monument in Taylor Cemetery, Ganges. Major William H. Dunn is visible on horseback at the far right.*

121

PLATE 36 | *May Wightman Winne of Ganges with the tombstone of her great-grandfather Madison Raplee in the National Cemetery at Nashville. The family had searched for the gravesite since the war, but was unable to locate it because the name was misspelled both on the cemetery records and the stone.*

PLATE 37 | *The Ganges band leads the parade from the Ganges Methodist Episcopal Church to the cemetery on Decoration Day, 1907. The old Ganges Union School is visible in the background.*

122

PLATE 38 | *The Ganges band on the way to the cemetery, probably before 1890.*

PLATE 39 | *An equestrian statue of General George A. Custer, dedicated in Monroe, Michigan, in 1910.*

PLATE 40 | *A parade of veterans on Butler Street about 1923. William T. Kimsey, former drum major of the 44th Indiana Infantry, leads the march.*

PLAYED WAR-TIME MUSIC

—Photo by Perrey

William H. Hannen, Fort Wayne, and William T. Kimsey, Douglas, Mich., fifer and drummer in the Forty-fourth Indiana regiment, who played the old war music at the regimental reunion in Fort Wayne, Thursday, and gave it the spirit of '61.

PLATE 41 | *William T. Kimsey at the age of 93.*

Claimed By Death

William T. Kimsey.

Wm. Kimsey Dies At The Age Of 93

Veteran Who Helped To Nominate Lincoln Is Heart Attack Victim.

William Thomas Kimsey, 93-year-old veteran of the Civil War, who came to this city last week from his home in Douglas, Mich., to attend the annual reunion of the Forty-fourth Infantry Thursday, died suddenly of chronic myocarditis Sunday at 9:30 a.m. at the home of a nephew, Thomas W. Stuart, 1434 Stophlet Street, where he was visiting.

The body was sent to Douglas this morning from Klaehn Sons' Funeral Parlors and was accompanied by Mr. Stuart and William H. Hannen, aged 86, 1101 Lake Avenue, who played a fife in the regiment in which Mr. Kimsey was a drummer.

Mr. Kimsey was stricken while talking to relatives at the nephew's home and died a few minutes later. Dr. Walter E. Kruse, deputy coroner, investigated the case. The deceased planned to return to his home this week.

Mr. Kimsey had the distinction of having been a delegate to the National Republican Convention in Chicago in 1864 at which Abraham Lincoln was nominated for President. For many years he had been a newspaper editor. He is said to have established the first newspapers at Auburn, Waterloo, Saugatuck, Mich., and Douglas, Mich.

The deceased veteran often recalled that while he resided at Auburn he walked to Fort Wayne to see the first railroad train he ever had seen. The drum which the aged veteran had carried with the Forty-fourth Indiana Volunteer Infantry during the Civil War was brought with him to the reunion here.

Surviving besides the nephew here are a stepson, Robert B. Minier, of Chicago; two great-grandchildren and several nieces and nephews.

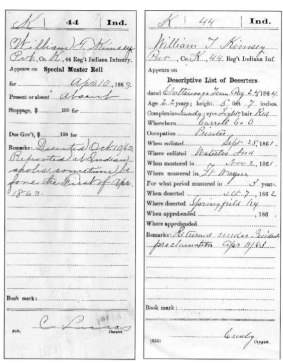

PLATE 43 | *Red-headed drummer William T. Kimsey appeared on a list of deserters when he left the 44th Indiana Infantry without permission in October of 1862. He returned the following April under a blanket amnesty offered by President Lincoln to soldiers who returned to their units.*

PLATE 44 | *A company from the 44th Indiana Infantry, the young man with the drum on the far left may be William T. Kimsey, later a printer in Douglas.*

PLATE 45 | *Saugatuck's Silver Cornet band in front of the bandstand that stood in the northwest corner of the village square about 1910.*

CAPTURED: SWEET POTATOES, ONIONS AND REBELS

The editor of the *Allegan Journal*, D. C. Henderson, tired of merely reporting the war and enlisted to join it. He served in Co. I, 3rd Michigan Cavalry, which was well covered from then on. In a letter dated September 23, 1863, from camp near Corinth, Mississippi, he wrote about a raid carried on at Bear Creek, beyond Iuka, Mississippi, by Isaac Wilson, a Saugatuck lumberman:

> Our battery of artillery consisting of two howitzers and 20 men was commanded by the brave and intrepid Lieut. Ike Wilson so well known to the lumbermen of the towns of Heath, Watson and Allegan. Ike's battery smoked out a band of bushwhackers and made them skedaddle most beautifully. Having so accomplished their purposes our boys returned after an absence of two days with their haversacks well filled with top onions and red peppers and in the best of health and spirits having all partaken of the celebrated springs of Iuka. [38]

On the next raid, the company captured eight Rebels, 500 sides of leather and returned with haversacks well filled with sweet potatoes and green corn.

THE 5TH CAVALRY IN VIRGINIA

A favorite trick of the Rebels was to invade the Federal camps suddenly in the night or early morning when the men were not prepared to fight. Near James City, Virginia, the camp of the 5th Michigan Cavalry was attacked on October 10, 1863, and several prisoners were taken. According to a comrade, Sergeants William White of Saugatuck and William C. Weeks of Allegan "did not have time to mount their horses, so struck out on a run with the rebs after them. Coming to a fence, they jumped over just as the foremost rebs asked White to surrender. Instead of doing so, however, he picked up a rail and knocked Mr. Reb. on the head, and they got away all safe." [39] They were luckier than one man who paused long enough to grab the frying pan in which he was cooking his breakfast. He was captured and died in a southern prison. Shortly after this event,

WM. WHITE
FRONT 20

White was promoted to master sergeant. ¶ The next day, the 5th Michigan Cavalry, the 1st Vermont Cavalry, and the 1st Michigan Cavalry, under the direct command of General George A. Custer, continued the march to the Rappahannock River, with the 6th and 7th Michigan Cavalry regiments bringing up the rear and skirmishing steadily with Confederate horsemen. When Custer reached the depot at Brandy Station, he realized that he was rapidly being hemmed in. After a brief conference with General Pleasanton, who had passed through enemy lines to effect the meeting, it was decided that they should press forward toward the river. Custer was reported to have inquired loudly, "Boys of Michigan, there are some people between us and home. I'm going home. Who else goes?" Custer wrote later, "It required but a glance at the countenances of the men

DESERTERS

There were several points in military service when a recruit was likely to decide that a soldier's life was not for him and simply run away from it. ¶ The first was when the regiment shipped out to the war. Many of the new soldiers had never been out of their home county before and just the adventure of going across the state to a training camp was enough for some. ¶ William Powell of Saugatuck, who had enlisted in Co. I of the 5th Michigan Cavalry August 13, 1862, deserted less than a month later on September 11. A letter in the Allegan Journal, dated September 26, 1862, has an asterisk after his name, noting that he was one of three who deserted the company on their journey to training camp in Detroit. ¶ After training at Kalamazoo, the 13th Michigan Infantry boarded a train for Nashville on February 12, 1862. Vanslycke Clark, who had enlisted at Ganges on October 12, 1861, missed the train and

has no further military record. ¶ The second point when desertion was common was at or before a soldier's first engagement with the enemy when the fear that he would die in the service became a distinct possibility. Early in the war, at Bull Run near Washington and at Shiloh in the west, there was a mass exodus to the rear. Company commanders found it impossible to stem the tide. ¶ On June 18, 1862, Charles P. Belton of the 1st Michigan Infantry deserted at Gaines Mill, Virginia, before or during his first battle. He was 33, a farmer from Cheshire Township, and had enlisted in Company K, July 13, 1861, one of the first enlistees from western Allegan County. ¶ During the siege of Corinth, Mississippi, on May 10, 1862, George W. Smith of Co. A, 3rd Michigan Cavalry was recorded as a deserter. Smith must not only have returned, but done very well eventually in his military career. In the March 12, 1866, issue of the Allegan to enable me to read the settled determination with which they undertook the task before them." They pushed onward while the recently formed Michigan Brigade band played a lively edition of "Yankee Doodle." ¶ Not to be outdone by Custer, a mere brigade commander, General Judson Kilpatrick, in command of the division, led the charge personally. According to an October 26, 1863, *Allegan Journal* account, he did it "with reckless gallantry." One of the victims of the Battle of Brandy Station was Captain George N. Dutcher of Douglas, formerly captain of Co. I of the 5th Michigan Cavalry, who was plagued by his unhealed wound sustained the day before Gettysburg. He had been serving as a member of the General Court Martial and is described in the Allegan newspaper as an "aid to Gen. Kilpatrick." According to an account in Dutcher's pension

---

Journal *it is recorded that "Captain Geo Smith of 3rd Cavalry, Co A has returned home." He later worked as a teamster for Daniel Gerber in Douglas.* ¶ *A third point in military service which generated a desire to desert was the long chilly weeks in winter quarters waiting for the war to resume in the spring. Then it seemed to many soldiers that they were being kept from family and pressing duties at home for no worthwhile reason.* ¶ *William T. Kimsey, a printer turned drummer with the 44th Indiana Infantry, deserted at the beginning of the winter on October 15, 1862, at Louisville, Kentucky. According to his military record, he returned to duty "at Indianapolis, sometime before the first of April 1863" under the President's proclamation which offered amnesty to deserters who returned to their units. The government furnished him with transportation from Indianapolis to Nashville where he rejoined his regiment. In July he was promoted*

to principal musician and later drum major, and served honorably until his final discharge on September 14, 1865. ¶ *It is hard to tell whether it was the long winter or the springtime promise of action that caused Ira Parrish of Co. F., 8th Michigan Cavalry to desert from the regiment's winter camp near Nicholasville, Kentucky on May 10, 1864. He had enlisted on December 16, 1862, in the same company as his older brother, William Henry Parrish.* ¶ *On March 18, 1863, Michigan approved an act to punish those deserters not claimed by federal authorities. If convicted in state courts the accused soldier could receive two years in prison. For resisting the draft, the maximum penalty was set at one year imprisonment and a $500 fine. But few deserters were pursued, there were too many of them and too many other pressing needs.*

file in the action at Brandy Station: "I was stunned by the bursting of a shell. The enemy charged our flank. Enemy pierced my right leg with sabre point. His horse striking my hips with his breast breaking same and running me down. Old wounds reopened." The wounded, including Dutcher, were evacuated by rail to the General Hospital at Georgetown, Washington, D.C.

William H. Rockwell was killed in Kilpatrick's charge. The October 26, 1863, Allegan newspaper noted:

> He was a brave and true man and a christian. He entered the service of his country from a sense of duty—leaving a wife and a large family of children in part dependent upon his labors, and whether in the field or languishing upon a sick bed in the hospital he was always cheerful—always the true soldier. We saw many traits of character in him to admire—none to regret.

THE BASSETT BOYS FROM ALLEGAN

Privates were not the only soldiers guilty of desertion. On June 23, 1863, Captain Elisha B. Bassett, of Co. B, 19th Michigan Infantry was dismissed for cowardice. When his company was engaged at Thompson's Station, March 5, 1863, he was discovered behind a large tree to the rear of the battle lines. When Colonel Henry C. Gilbert ordered him to his post, according to his later testimony, Bassett told him "that I must not depend upon him for anything, that the Lieut could command the Company & begged me to excuse him." Shortly afterwards Bassett took a cavalryman's horse and rode to the rear. The colonel concluded, "Capt. Bassett admits all the facts & only excuses himself in the pretense that he was sick. He was sick before the action commenced & it would have required no more physical ability for him to have remained and done his duty than it did to run away." ¶ So much of the regiment was captured at that battle that Bassett was left senior in command, a position which he did not handle well. He eventually simply deserted and was home in Allegan when the dishonorable discharge was rendered. Captain Bassett died in Michigan on November 25, 1865. The home folk seemed sympathetic to him. His obituary called him "one of our most benevolent, enterprising and public spirited citizens" and makes no mention of his war record. ¶ Captain Elisha B. Bassett should not be confused with his brother, Chauncey J. Bassett, an Allegan mechanic, who was one of the earliest officers to serve from Allegan County enlisting as a captain in the 6th Michigan Infantry in 1861. Chauncey had a distinguished military career and was killed in action on May 8, 1864, serving as a major with the 73rd U. S. Colored Troops.

132

1861 1862 1863 1864 1865 AFTER THE WAR

JAMES W. BILLINGS JOINS THE SIGNAL CORPS

James W. Billings, 16-year-old son of Walter and Sarah Billings of Peach Belt, Ganges Township, had enlisted in Co. B of the 13th Michigan Infantry in December of 1861, probably with his parents' permission. His father, Walter, would enlist in the 8th Michigan Cavalry a year later at the age of 44. James was promoted to corporal, and then sergeant and, on October 22, 1863, he was transferred to the Signal Corps. ¶ Although the first wartime use of the telegraph occurred in America during the Civil War, the government did not train their own men, but hired regular civilian operators. However, the signal corps was still responsible for other means of communication, especially the red and white signal flags used to direct tactics in the field. Young Billings may have gotten his new job because he was young and able to climb trees and rickety ladders easily and quickly. At other times men of the Signal Corps were carried aloft in large balloons to get a better view of the number and positions of enemy troops, then use their flags to wig-wag the information to men on the ground.

THE ACTION AT TUNICA BAYOU

While the 6th Michigan Infantry was stationed near the Mississippi River in Louisiana it began to run short of fodder for the horses. On November 8, 1863, the soldiers set out to obtain some, according to a later account:

> We had learned that up at Tunica, some 200 miles up the river from our camp, there was an old secesh planter that had several train loads of corn in cribs . . . . Six volunteers from each company were called for to go on the foraging expedition . . . . A staunch river steamer awaited us at the landing. Six mule teams were put on board with as many old heavy army wagons. We went on board under command of Col. Edward Bacon and soon steamed up the river, escorted by a river gunboat. In due time we reached the Tunica landing, disembarked our teams and carefully looking to our arms, proceeded along the road up the river to where the old planter lived. The boys said as they came in sight of the house that they saw a man hastily mount a horse and ride

1861 1862 1863 1864 1865 AFTER THE WAR

133

hurriedly away, but thought at the time that it was perhaps some Johnnie who had called there and seeing the Yanks approaching had decided to retire. Afterwards we could easily read the action of this horseman and his purpose.

Stacking their arms the soldiers set the plantation staff to work cooking them an elaborate meal while the corn was being loaded.

> We felt no uneasiness, as we had been told there was no Rebel force in reaching distance. . . . Matters went on quietly and satisfactorily until about four o'clock in the afternoon when the sound of the pickets firing alerted the rest that a large force of cavalry, estimated by one as 400 men, approached. Colonel Bacon decided the best chance was to run for it. Some made it to the river, others hid out in the dense underbrush until dark when the Union gunboat began a bombardment aimed at pushing the Rebels back so that those still able could make a run for the river vessels. [40]

At least four men were recovered in the darkness, three others turned up at camp about a week later, but Enoch Simpson, who had enlisted at 21, fresh from his father's Ganges farm; John Rollins, 18, a farm laborer from Casco Township, and Corporal Osborn Swaney of Ganges were taken prisoners. Rollins and Simpson died at Andersonville prison in Georgia; Simpson on April 18, 1864, and Rollins on December 9, 1864. Both were buried in the Andersonville Cemetery. Corporal Osborn Swaney died at the prison at Cahaba, Alabama, on April 17, 1864. All three had enlisted at Ganges on August 6, 1861.

DETERMINED FIGHTING IN TENNESSEE

On November 14 Confederate troops dispatched from Virginia to help out in the Tennessee campaign clashed with the Army of Ohio under General Ambrose Burnside at Louden in East Tennessee. On the 16th, the two armies met at Lenoir Station but were ordered to withdraw to Knoxville. The 17th Michigan Infantry was marching toward Knoxville, and the regiment had been detached from the main body of the brigade to serve as a rear guard when they were attacked by the enemy's advance guard about 9:30 a.m. at Campbell's Station, Kentucky. After "severe fighting" the 17th reached Knoxville where they helped defend the city. Sergeant Frank Fisher, a bugler with Co. I of the 17th Michigan Infantry, was killed in action. He had enlisted August 4, 1862, at Kalamazoo at the age of 22. ¶ Joseph Schuler of Saugatuck, a private with the 3rd Michigan Infantry, was wounded at Mine Run, a tiny tributary of the Rapidan River, southeast of Culpepper, Virginia on November 30. Federal troops under General Gouverneur K. Warren pushed south across the Rapidan River pursuing the Army of Northern Virginia, but misdirection and weather caused the attack to lose impetus. On November 30, the day planned for the great charge at Mine Run, the big guns had nearly finished their bombardment when frantic word was sent to the foot soldiers to "Suspend the attack until further orders." Schuler may have been wounded in the shelling.

THE U. S. COLORED TROOPS BEGIN SERVICE

On December 10, 1863, George H. Harris resigned as first lieutenant of Co. G, 6th Michigan Infantry to accept a commission in the Corps d'Afrique, later the 1st Louisiana Colored Troop. Chauncey J. Bassett of Allegan, who had served as captain of Co. G, had earlier resigned to enter the officer corps of the colored service. This regiment was one of the first Negro regiments. Recently discovered documents show that it was first mustered into Confederate service near the beginning of the war, before the South established the policy that barred freed blacks from military service. The men were mostly from the Creole community and had French-sounding names. Many were freed men of the New Orleans area, including some who were, compared to most men of color in the South at the time, both well educated and wealthy. On April 4, 1864, the regiment was mustered into federal service and redesignated the 73rd U. S. Colored Infantry. In the spring of 1864, Harris transferred to the 96th U. S. Colored Infantry, the federal designation for a regiment that had first mustered as the 2nd Corps de Af-

1861

1862

1863

1864

1865

AFTER THE WAR

135

rique Engineers. After six months of duty in Texas, the 96th USCT returned to Louisiana and was in charge of a pontoon train. They built a bridge over Vermillionville Bayou, on March 18 and another over the Cane River on March 30, 1864. Harris was discharged on January 29, 1866, at New Orleans. ¶ Another area soldier, Henry Hannibal Goodrich, son of Ganges physician Chauncey B. Goodrich, was discharged from the 10th Michigan Cavalry to accept a promotion as second lieutenant in the U. S. Heavy Artillery (Colored) and was promoted to captain just before the close of the war. Goodrich returned to Michigan in the spring of 1866. ¶ Although black hangers-on had been used to good advantage by both sides to do the dirty work of war, there was opposition in both the North and the South toward using the freed slaves in combat situations. The plan to use white officers in black regiments also drew criticism, and critics contended that only the dregs of the officer corps would volunteer for that kind of duty. Corporal Jacob Heringa of the 3rd Michigan Cavalry, however, wrote thoughtfully after the announcement was made:

> The raising of colored troops I think will be successful. The government wishes to have white men for officers. This getting men out of our army for negroes' officers may look despicable to the copperheads of the north, but never the less there are many good soldiers in the Union armies who will take ahold and destroy all opposition. [41]

FLLING HIS BROTHER'S PLACE IN THE REGIMENT

E. PENFOLD
FRONT 22

Henry Penfold of Ganges, 13th Michigan Infantry, died of disease in January of 1863. On December 16, 1863, his older brother, Edward Penfold, then 35, enlisted in the same regiment and company. He was sent, along with other replacements, to Chickamauga, Tennessee, where the 13th Infantry, organized with others as a brigade of engineers, was busy building warehouses and hospitals. While in the south, Edward suffered a severe stroke and was confined to the hospital. ¶ He was released from the hospital and mustered out of the army at Louisville, Kentucky, on July

25, 1865 and returned to Ganges and the large farm that he and his brother had begun in 1855. All of the farm buildings on the Penfold farm were destroyed in the great fire that struck the Fennville area on the same day as the Chicago fire in October of 1871, but they were rebuilt enough to continue to work the farm. He was a member of the GAR and "delighted in his associations with his old army comrades." Edward Penfold died in 1903.[42]

1861

1862

1863

1864

1865

AFTER THE WAR

AND THE BAND PLAYED "DIXIE"

Music was an important part of soldiering. Early in the war each regiment had its own enlisted band, and the popular song, "Dixie" had not yet been appropriated by the Confederates. A correspondent from the 13th Michigan Infantry, which was camped near Elizabethtown, Kentucky, reports a musical interlude in a February 19, 1862, letter that was printed in the March 3, 1862, issue of the Allegan Journal:

> We found on our arrival here one brigade consisting of 10 regiments. Our camp was between them. Monday morning 5 regiments moved past us on their way down the river, they were the 6th Ohio, 46th, 47th Indiana and 3rd Kentucky. They were travel stained and bronzed by exposure. . . . The 46th Indiana was a splendid body of men and had a very fine band; their music was of the first order, the best I have had the pleasure of hearing in years, at least so it seemed to me. They halted in front of our camp and played 'Dixie' for us, and in return for their compliment we gave them three rousing cheers.

The Saugatuck area furnished at least seven buglers, two drummers and two fife players in the war. In the 2nd Michigan Cavalry alone there were three local men on the bugle: Uri Nichols of Co. C; John Nies of Co. D and James Hutchinson of Co. H. Two more, Jacob R. Boas of Co. F and George Gardner of Co. I, served in the 5th Michigan Cavalry. In addition Frank Fisher served Co. I of the 17th Michigan Infantry, and Frederick A. Knickerbocker played for Battery G of the 1st Michigan Light Artillery. Sixteen-year-old Edward Breen enlisted in Co. B, 13th Michigan Infantry as a drummer, and William T. Kimsey rose to the rank of Principal Musician and Drum Major of the 44th Indiana Infantry. ¶ These men and others would return from the war and form brass bands in each community in western Allegan County, a tradition still being upheld by the Casco Band. ¶ In addition to music, the drummers and buglers were responsible for sounding the commands that helped direct the movements of the troops. At the height of the action the rest of the musicians were detailed as litter bearers to assist the wounded. Carrying on that tradition Saugatuck resident Johnson Fox was a high ranking bugler in World War II. ¶ Musical talent had its privileges. Private Lemuel W. Osborn, of the 13th Michigan Infantry wrote his wife on May 23, 1864, "There is not a private in the Regt. or a fellow in the Band, but what fairly begrudges me my faculty on the violin. Any would be glad to do the playing and play for cold victuals if they could only do the playing. They think I am highly honored that I can go in and play for aristocracy with the privilege of eating the good things that are left on the table." ¶ Charles L. Cummings of the 6th Michigan Infantry wrote about another kind of privilege for musicians. When the regiment was on the march one day, the drummer "confiscated" a couple of geese, took the head off the drum and tucked them inside. Not long after, the colonel rode up and asked him why he was not beating his drum. The drummer, replied, "Colonel, I want to speak to you." The officer drew closer and the drummer admitted, "I have a couple of geese in here." The colonel straighten up and gravely said, "Well, if you're sick and can't play you needn't." Then he rode on. "Needless to say, the Colonel had roast goose for dinner that night," Cummings concludes.

HM SILVER CORNET BAND PL. 45

1864

FOOD FOR BOTH HORSES AND HUMAN BEINGS WAS becoming scarce in the areas that the soldiers had visited. The needs of two armies in the field denuded most of the land. By 1864 it was evident that, even if northern soldiers "captured" southern territory, they did not have the manpower to guard their conquest. Instead, they burned the buildings and destroyed anything that would be of use to the rival army. When there was nothing left of value for the war effort, there was no need for guards.

HELPING OUT THE DUTCHMEN

Even the Northern troops were feeling the pinch. The 2nd Michigan Cavalry was stationed at Camp Strawberry Plains, near Atlanta, in January of 1864, when John Nies of Fillmore Township, who would finish the war with the enviable record of three years and 40 days of service without ever being absent from duty for injury or illness, found that others were less resourceful than he. One day he heard that the 25th Michigan Infantry was nearby. This regiment had an entire company made up of Dutch-speaking settlers from Holland, Michigan, so he went to see them.

And when I arrived they asked me if I had something to eat, and I handed my haversack to them as it contained some ham, etc., they were glad to get it, as they were poor on rations. When I got home after the war, Dr. Van Raalte sent for me to come and I went and such a spread I never sat down to and it was in my honor because I had given my haversack to the boys, his two sons being among them.[1] ¶ The father of the boys, the Reverend Albertus C. Van Raalte, had immigrated to southern Ottawa County with a small group of settlers in 1847, and the number grew rapidly. By the census of 1860, there were 2,777 people, mostly Dutch immigrants, living in Holland Township.

John Nies was discharged October 22, 1864, at Nashville, Tennessee. The following year he met and married Johanna Kruisenga whose parents had settled in Singapore. The bride was not anxious to be a farm wife and persuaded John to begin a business in Saugatuck, a small hardware store specializing in "General Hardware, Iron, Steel, Nails and Shelf Hardware." In 1887 he took into partnership his former apprentice, John Koning. In 1894 Nies sold out to Koning and moved to Holland where he began a second hardware business which lasted into the 20th Century on 8th Street. Nies died May 22, 1920, in Holland and was buried in Riverside Cemetery, Saugatuck.

CHRISTMAS ON THE CHICKAMAUGA

There was little fighting done in the wintertime, and boredom and the cold made discontented soldiers. Major W. G.

Eaton of the 13th Michigan Infantry (now joined with what was left of the 21st and 22nd Michigan Infantry and the 18th Ohio Infantry as a Brigade of Engineers) wrote on January 5, 1864, to a friend on leave at home:

> While you have been partaking of real enjoyments at home and among friends, we have been making some desperate attempts of a like nature in an army-like way . . . . The week before Christmas a family living up the Chickamauga about two miles invited the officers to attend a party . . . a very nice dance – gay, festive and respectable. The officers returned from the party with heads full of dance, and resolved to have a party in camp on New Year's night . . . . A good log house 32 x 18 [was] built, covered with canvas, with a good ante-room and 3 square tents for dressing rooms . . . .Two chandeliers were arranged to light the hall. Our old flag and banner and sundry swords were the chief ornaments and in justice to the committee on internal arrangements I must say that I believe but few halls at the north equaled it . . . . There were present 23 ladies, all dancers, and quite a number of the neighbors, and all seemed to enjoy themselves finely. A. Ward (the colored cook) served up the refreshments at 10, in his best manner, which surprised all the ladies present. ¶ Jeff C. Davis' division has moved out on our right about 2 miles up the creek but the 13th was here first – so the neighbors say. I understand that we have cavalry all along up the Chickamauga to Gordon's mills, but no infantry force beyond the river. We are getting out a fine lot of timber and logs and rafting them to Chattanooga.2

A GANGES ENGLISHMAN VIEWS THE WAR

James Hibberdine had come to Michigan from England before 1860 and bought a farm in Ganges Township, which, in 1864, was struggling. In addition to his own farm work, tending four acres of wheat, he was "working out" on nearby farms but not earning enough to buy food for his livestock and family. In a letter dated February 2, 1864, Hibberdine wrote his brother in England, giving an immigrant's view of American events:

> The people already begin to be excited about the election of another President. I should not wonder if Mr. Lincoln is re-elected. I look forward to rather

1861
1862
1863
1864
1865

AFTER THE WAR

141

a troublesome time & expect to see, if I live a few more years, quite a change in our government affairs. I little envy Maximilian [Ferdinand Maximilian Joseph, the brother of Austrian emperor Franz Joseph, was established as emperor of Mexico in 1864] his new throne, the American people will never long consent to an empire this side of the Atlantic. It is evident they mean to make themselves a first class fighting power both by sea & land & their present struggle must end before long. There is no doubt but when the leading spirits of the South are disposed of the people soon become loyal to the one flag.[3]

The family had some personal interest in the war and Hibberdine commented, "Martha [his wife] has a brother just returned from the army sick. I think it doubtful if he ever recovers but if he does he will probably be ruined for life, very few that return from the south sick ever wholly recover."

RE-ENLISTEES ENJOY THEIR FURLOUGH

Soldiers who re-enlisted were given furloughs home, usually 30 days. In addition to a chance to rest a little, these "vacations" were also seen as a time for the veteran soldiers to inspire those left at home to enlist. Quincy C. Lamoreux visited the editor of the *Allegan Journal* who wrote in the February 8 issue:

> A VETERAN FROM THE 8TH INFANTRY — We were visited on Saturday last by Mr. Q. C. Lamoreux, a re-enlisted veteran of this regiment. The 8th has passed through most of the hard fought battles of eastern Va. – was at the battle of James Island, S.C., and also at the siege of Vicksburg, and has now re-enlisted. Mr. Lamoreux has been wounded in three places, but is now in good health and spirits.

More than 30 veterans who had re-enlisted in Co. A, 3rd Michigan Cavalry, arrived in Allegan County for a 30-day furlough. The Allegan newspaper noted in the February 8, 1864 issue that the returned veterans "are looking well and are in the best of health and spirits." On arrival in Allegan the entire traveling group was invited to the Exchange Hotel for an oyster supper. Earlier returnees were treated to a

1861

1862

1863

1864

1865

AFTER THE WAR

142

"Pic Nic" supper at the new brick school house on the north side of the river. The evening ended with many toasts. Some of them were published in the February 8, 1864, *Allegan Journal*, including the last, by a local woman:

> The ships of our Navy
> And the Ladies of our land.
> May the first be well rigged,
> And the second well manned.

Charles Rubert of Co. A, 3rd Michigan Cavalry did not arrive home with the rest. He was left in a hospital in Memphis, Tennessee, where he died February 15, 1864, of wounds received in action. He had enlisted at Saugatuck on August 25, 1863, at the age of 18. Rubert was buried at the National Cemetery in Memphis.

THE DAHLGREN RAID ON RICHMOND

General Judson Kilpatrick had spent the winter working on a plan to raid Richmond and free Union prisoners, at the same time interfering with communications and industry. Grasping at anything to shorten the war the idea had the approval of President Lincoln. Kilpatrick was to lead 3,500 men to Richmond via Spotsylvania. A smaller force of 500 was to come in from the south and west under Colonel Ulric Dahlgren. ¶ Everything went wrong. William White of the 5th Michigan Calvary was taken prisoner on March 1, and John Hill was captured the following day. Dahlgren was killed and some papers on his body seemed to suggest that the raiders meant to capture or kill Confederate President Jefferson Davis. Angry Rebels mutilated Dahlgren's body and talked of hanging the captives in retaliation, but cooler heads eventually prevailed and the prisoners were incarcerated in Richmond lockups before being sent on to Andersonville.

TAKING A RISK FOR A PAIR OF SOCKS

It was difficult to know how much to trust the local residents, especially in the border states. On March 10, 1864, John Nies of Co. D, 2nd Michigan Cavalry, in camp near Calhoun, Tennessee, wrote to his mother and brothers:

1861

1862

1863

1864

1865

AFTER THE WAR

There are hereto, rebel citizens who have taken the oath of loyalty, but I don't care much for that kind. They did this in order to keep their possessions, not because they cared so much for the Old Government, or the present Administration. And yet among them all this kind of people we find a kind whose loyalty we can trust and indeed to such a degree that we believe hardly exists in the North . . . . I will tell you something about a Union family which lives near the mountains, near Chestua [Chestnut?] Creek, East Tennessee. John Vogel and I went out foraging, inquiring along the road where Jack lived (a noted rebel who had plenty of corn and fodder) when we halted at a house, the man of the house came out and we asked him where Jack lived and how far we were yet from his house, on which he replied, He lives about two miles from here in such and such a direction, but it is cold and rainy, won't you alight (dismount) and come and warm yourselves gentlemen? . . . The old lady asked us if we had been to dinner, on which we told her we had not. She prepared dinner for us and we ate. After dinner I went outdoors feeding our horses. On coming back I saw that one of the girls handed J. V. a pair of socks. I asked the girl at what price they were selling those socks? She told me she was not selling those socks but were making him a present of those, and if (she added) we had another pair we would give you a pair also. Here the old lady interrupted her daughter, said she, If you soldiers will stay here all night I will have the girls to work to knit you a pair too. This we did not like at first because we were nine or ten miles from camp, but at last we consented and stayed all night, and slept on a feather bed. [4]

WE GET LETTERS . . .

The army was being reorganized for what everyone hoped would be the final push in the spring. On March 24, 1864, the commanding officer of William T. Kimsey, chief musician with the 44th Indiana Infantry, received a detail from A. W. Wills for Kimsey, who was a printer in civilian life, to report for duty at the government printing house at Nashville. The officer's reply was to note that Kimsey was drum major of the regiment and "earnestly request that the detail be revoked as his services are very much needed with the regiment." In Kimsey's file the letter has a note written on it by Wills: "I was not aware that Kimsey was Drum Major of the Regt. at the time application was made for this detail. Under the circumstances I would not make the request and respectfully withdraw my petition." ¶ Although soldiers always complained about the mail service, it is amazing that it functioned at all considering the difficulties of transportation in the midst of the war. To avoid carrying heavy clothes on long marches in the summer when they were not needed many soldiers sent their warm clothing and blankets to their families for safe keeping, asking that they ship the items back in the fall. In a letter dated March 31, 1864, Lemuel W. Osborn of Co. B, 13th Michigan Infantry tells his family: "I with Pattison and Amidan shipped my overcoat and dress coat by express to Allegan. I wrote to Floyd to get them sometime when he is up and you will pay him your share of the expenses from Allegan." Osborn was also not pleased with some of the new recruits being gathered as replacements for the regiment. He wrote his wife on March 24, 1864: "The regiment is about 750 strong and I can tell you there is all sorts of customers here; I find a good many verry good quiet genteelmen; but there is some that is miserable ruff scruffs."[5]

SEARCHING THE WAR FOR YOUR REGIMENT

There was an awkward time as the third anniversary of a regiment's original muster date neared when those who re-enlisted were permitted a furlough, the men who had enlisted at a later date still had time to serve and, often, replacements for those who had not re-enlisted had not yet joined the regiment. This is where the 3rd Michigan Cavalry found itself on April 6, 1864, when a private wrote from Fort Pickering, near Memphis, Tennessee:

> A party of some ten new recruits for the 3rd Michigan Cavalry who were enlisted in December by Ike Wilson arrived here the other day. They had been sent to Nashville, Tenn., some time in January through mistake of the officers furnishing them with transportation. They are now here awaiting orders. . . . We hear that the rest of our Regiment is still at St. Louis, waiting for their horses. We look

1861

1862

1863

1864

1865

AFTER THE WAR

145

for them here every day or an order to be sent to our Regiment. Our boys are sick and tired of their confinement in Fort Pickering. . . . One reason for this is that the officers we have over us are entire strangers to us. They care very little about the men left in their charge.[6]

REBEL PRISONERS TAKE A STEAMBOAT NORTH

Skirmishes continued in Louisiana. John P. Parrish of the 6th Michigan Infantry wrote his wife on April 8, 1864:

General Banks has been pushing the rebs out of the northwest corner of this State. Shreveport is our possession since 8 or 10 days ago; it was where the rebs had pretended to keep the State government since we drove them out of New Orleans and Baton Rouge, two years since. Our troops have taken some hundreds of the rebels prisoners in this Spring campaign already and that without much fighting or loss on our side. . . . I saw a load of rebel prisoners on their way north this afternoon on one of our transport steamers. They were dressed in all sorts of fashions and of all colors from regular cotton white to brown, grey and butternut. I suppose they are to go to Chicago and be kept six months or a year before they can be exchanged for some of our soldiers that the Rebs have taken. Some of the rebs will take the oath of allegiance to the United States; and some of them are enlisting in the service of Uncle Abe Lincoln to fight against the south.[7]

SAD BUSINESS BACK HOME

Businesses that the soldiers left behind suffered in their absence. The military records of Lieutenant George W. Lonsbury of the 5th Michigan Cavalry include a letter he wrote to Captain E. B. Parsons, adjutant general of the cavalry on April 11, 1864:

I have the honor to request a leave of absence for fifteen days. Reasons, to visit my widowed mother in the State of Michigan who is very sick and wholly dependent on me for support. If I do not go now I shall probably never see her as she is now nearly eighty years of age. I have not had a leave of absence since the formation of the Regt but have been almost constantly on duty and have not seen my family in all this time, nearly two years . . . . My business is very much deranged and nothing but my personal attention will save it from ruin. Hoping you will grant this, my prayer."

The leave was granted.

A DUTIFUL FATHER BRINGS HIS SON HOME

Most soldiers who died during the war were buried where they fell, or in nearby cemeteries, but a few remains were shipped north to hometown graves. Sometimes when an officer fell in battle the men of his company or regiment would join together to pay the costs of shipping the remains home. On April 11, 1864, William H. Dunn, Sr. arrived in Allegan with the remains of his youngest son, Leonidas, who had been serving under his older brother, William Jr., in the 10th Michigan Cavalry. The young man died, probably of disease, at Camp Nelson, Kentucky, on March 1, 1864. ¶ Bringing bodies back to Allegan County was especially difficult because no railroad had yet been completed within the county. The April 18, 1864, *Allegan Journal* noted that the younger Dunn "gave up his life in the defence of those principles he held dearer than life." Burial was in Taylor Cemetery, Ganges.

BAILEY TAKEN PRISONER

The 3rd Michigan Infantry crossed the Rapidan River and camped near the old battlefield at Chancellorsville on May 4, 1864. Private George W. Bailey recorded in his diary:

> Thursday, May 5: Clear and warm. Marched at 5 o'clock A.M. and advanced about ten miles where we met the enemy. The 3rd Michigan ordered to the left and deploy as skirmishers when they immediately engaged the enemy losing 18 killed and about 50 wounded.

> Friday, May 6: As soon as it was light, the 3rd Michigan went in and fought and lost heavy. At 10:30 A.M. we were in a rifle pit and the enemy advanced. Our support all left us and the enemy flanked us on the left at 11:00 and Geo. W. Bailey, Dan Wilson of Co. F and several others of Co. K. were taken prisoners.[8]

1861 1862 1863 1864 1865 AFTER THE WAR

147

He would remain in southern prisons for seven months, but continued his diary.

FIGHTING IN THE MOUNTAINS OF GEORGIA

In a letter dated May 9, 1864, Joseph W. Ely of the 19th Michigan Infantry describes his regiment's assault on a mountain ridge near Dalton, Georgia. They dug in for a siege and Ely noted:

> I did not think a month ago we should have to build fortifications without spades, picks nor any proper tools but a long line of fortifications were thrown up in a short time with bayonets for picks and cups, tin plates and wooden spoons for shovels . . . .We had a long walk over the battlefield of Chickamauga. The bones of many a soldier lay scattered over the field, some of the graves are so shallow that their heads and feet can be seen entirely bare. 'Twas a horrible sight. . . . Skirmishing commences on the left again this morning about six o'clock. . . .We can see the smoke of the guns but can not see any of the troops on account of the woods and brush but we can hear very distinctly. Our division is lying here in the woods out of sight of the Rebs so that they will come this way and run into us without knowing that we are here. . . .You can not imagine the feeling of men lying here doing nothing when we know just a little way off our companions are lying wounded, dying and some fighting. [9]

By the end of the week the Confederates had fallen back to strongly fortified positions at Resaca, Georgia.

THE 8TH CAVALRY WITH LITTLE TO DO

The 8th Michigan Cavalry fought throughout January, but decided to go into winter quarters as February approached. On February 3 they turned their horses over to the proper department at Knoxville and started on foot for their camp between Mt. Sterling and Nicholasville, Kentucky. After a tedious march of 200 miles over the Cumberland mountains, they reached the winter quarters where they remained for four months, finally departing on June 3, 1864. ¶ But 18-year-old Ira Parrish was no longer enjoying the adventure of soldiering and deserted on May 10, 1864. Records show him absent without leave from Nicholasville, and he appears on a descriptive list of deserters issued May 12. He was serving in the same company and regiment as his older brother, William Henry Parrish, but letters home from William Henry, dated February 26 and June 18, 1864, do not mention Ira or his whereabouts.

MICHIGAN CALVARY BRIGADE AT YELLOW TAVERN

The Michigan Cavalry Brigade was on campaign with General Philip H. Sheridan about seven miles from Richmond at Yellow Tavern, Virginia, on May 11, 1864, when it encountered a large body of Confederate soldiers under General J. E. B. Stuart. The 5th and 6th Cavalry dismounted and the 1st and 7th fought mounted. Private Avery later wrote:

> Our company was on the left of the line and reached into a piece of woods, where we were pushing the rebs back from tree to tree. . . .The company was engaged in an open field in about the center of the line, where the brave Stafford and the heroic Lonsbury [who had been promoted to first lieutenant] were leading on the no less brave and heroic company, where the storm of leaden hail was dealing death and destruction in their path. Lewis Herner [Hirner] was killed, then Henry Werner wounded, and the balls came zip, zip, close to our ears, making a man duck his head without seeming to know it. . . . During the battle a ball struck Henry Werner in the mouth, passing out near the neck and breaking the jawbone. Lafayette Fox and myself [Avery] helped him to the rear and then went in again. To this day he cannot open his mouth enough to put the point of a ten penny nail between his teeth.[10]

Both Werner and Hirner were natives of Germany. Hirner had immigrated to the United States in 1844 and purchased a farm in Saugatuck Township in 1858. Werner had enlisted at Saugatuck on August 15, 1862. He was honorably discharged at Detroit on February 4, 1865. It was at Yellow Tavern that a sharpshooter from Co. E of the 5th Michigan Cavalry shot Confederate General J. E. B. Stuart causing a wound that led to his death. ¶ The campaign in Virginia

1861 1862 1863 **1864** 1865 AFTER THE WAR

149

continued. On May 31, 1864, Sergeant George H. Smith of the 5th Michigan Cavalry wrote his mother from Muller Corner, Virginia:

> We are having some hard fighting. We had a hard fight with the Rebs yesterday and drove them pellmell, killing and capturing lots of them and driving them to where we now are. We are all saddled and ready for them again. . . . The rebel infantry are now fighting on our right close by, and I presume they will try us again before night. Lieut. Lonsbury joined us last night. I think we shall soon have old Lee.[11]

George W. Lonsbury, an Allegan photographer who later moved to Fennville, had been on special detail at General Headquarters. ¶ On June 11, 1864, the busy 5th Michigan Cavalry met the Confederates at Trevilian's Station, eight miles from Gordonsville, Virginia. Sergeant George H. Smith, wrote his parents:

> We met the enemy on the 11th inst. in heavy force, but we charged them so hard that they gave way at first and we took a large amount of prisoners, horses, ambulances, caissons, &c. But they soon rallied and as no support came to us we were surrounded and our regiment got cut off and we lost heavily. We have only 12 left in the company. . . . I think none of them are killed.[12]

WITH SHERMAN MARCHING THROUGH GEORGIA

As General William T. Sherman continued his march toward Atlanta, skirmishing was heavy. The 19th Michigan Infantry lost its commander, Colonel Henry C. Gilbert of Coldwater, at Rescaca, Georgia, on May 15. Led by Major E. A. Griffin, the regiment encountered Confederate cavalry and massed soldiers in line of battle near Allatoona, Georgia. On May 26, 1864, Carlos Baker wrote from Dallas, Georgia, northeast of Atlanta:

> We met the enemy here Thursday the 26th inst at 4 o'clock P.M. and after a running fight of three miles we drove them into their defenses and held all the ground they had abandoned. We took a few prison-

1861 | 1861
1862 | 1862
1863 | 1863
1864 | 1864
1865 | 1865
AFTER THE WAR

ers and have gradually closed in upon them, in the
entire length of our line. We now hold Dallas, The
County Town of Paulding Co., Ga. and all reports
from the front are encouraging. [13]

Jacob Gunsaul, a farm laborer from Ganges Township, suffered a flesh wound across his right knee, but continued on
campaign.

"AN OLD AND FAITHFUL SOLDIER"

On June 20, 1864, during the Georgia campaign, Levi Tuttle
of the 4th Michigan Cavalry received a severe scalp wound
from a saber and also a thrust of the saber to the face that
affected his eye. The fighting was at Lattimer's Mills, near
Noonday Church, Georgia. Tuttle applied for a furlough of
30 days that he might go back to Michigan and recover from
the wound. In a letter to headquarters his commanding officer, Benjamin D. Pritchard of Allegan, noted that he had
approved the request based on the surgeon's certificate attached and added "Sgt. T. is an old and faithful soldier and
deserves any indulgence which can be bestowed upon him."
¶ Tuttle would return to service in November, 1864, and,
after several weeks of service with the headquarters staff, he
was with the regiment at the capture of Selma, Alabama,
in April.

ADVANCING ON RICHMOND

On June 3, 1864, the 8th Michigan Infantry attacked Confederate lines at Bethesda Church, near Cold Harbor, Virginia, hoping to drive to Richmond, 10 miles to the northeast. Here the regiment lost 52 men including Major W. Ely
Lewis and Color Corporal Owen Cook, who was killed in
action while carrying the flag. Cook had enlisted at the age
of 19 in Co. C of the 8th Infantry at Big Prairie, Newaygo
County, on September 23, 1861, and re-enlisted in December of 1863 in Tennessee. He was the son of Dr. J. B. Cook
who had begun a medical practice at Saugatuck in 1859. His
older brother, Amos, fought with the 2nd Michigan Cavalry
and received a discharge for disability, but died on the way

1861

1862

1863

1864

1865

AFTER THE WAR

151

home in 1862. ¶ Petersburg was considered the last obstacle on the way to Richmond. In July, 1864, during an unusual operation near Petersburg, Virginia, Charles Brandt of the 8th Michigan Infantry received a grapeshot wound to the head that affected his hearing. The 8th was part of the action at The Crater, July 30, where soldiers who had been miners in Pennsylvania blasted a hole in the rebel fortifications by setting off dynamite in tunnels under the structure. Their triumph was short-lived as Federal soldiers, attempting to enter the structure through the hole that was blown by the dynamite, got trapped in the resulting crater. ¶ On June 27, 1864, James B. Smith of Co. H., First Michigan Sharp-shooters, received a nasty wound to his thigh. The gunshot entered the upper leg from above and passed downward and inward. Five days later he died at Petersburg, Virginia, of complications from the wound. ¶ In mid-August, in an attempt to open a new front during the siege of Petersburg, the Union army, including the 8th Michigan Infantry, moved west of Petersburg and occupied over a mile of the vital railroad line to the south. They then turned north to approach Petersburg from the south. In the afternoon of August 19, A. P. Hill's Confederate corps collided with the Union infantry in the dense woods south of the town. Quincy Lamoreux of the 8th Michigan Infantry was taken prisoner at Weldon Railroad, Virginia.

CAVALRY UNITS FIGHT WELL IN SMALL BATTLES

Colonel Luther S. Trowbridge in his account of the 10th Michigan Cavalry tells of a brief skirmish in Tennessee under the leadership of William H. Dunn of Ganges in July of 1864:

> An affair occurred in Wilsonville [Tennessee] 25-30 miles from Sevierville. Lt. Dunn was ordered with 25 men to attempt to rescue Col. Fry of the East Tennessees, a valuable scout and guide captured by guerrillas. They soon found a party about the same size as his own robbing citizens. He followed them all day and part of the next until they reached the mountains and decided to return to camp. At Wil-

sonville, while still unbridled and unsaddled, feeding in the meadow, he was charged by the men they
were following plus about 60. They killed picket
Crammer of Ottawa County, but were met with
sharp fire from Spencer carbines and killed and
wounded six men and two horses. Pursuit was made,
but the rebels kept out of range of the rifles.[14]

In late July, the 8th Michigan Cavalry, under Lieutenant
Colonel Elisha Mix of Manlius Township, joined other
troops, under Major General George Stoneman, on a raid
into Georgia to divert pressure from General Sherman's
activities and, if possible, to free Union prisoners held in
Andersonville Prison. The Union campaigners were surrounded and Stoneman was prepared to surrender when
Mix asked for, and received, permission to lead his regiment, and anyone else who wished to follow, on a cavalry
charge through enemy lines. ¶ During the continued action
on August 2, 1864, Mix was shot off his horse and captured
with several of his men including Farrier Walter Billings
from Peach Belt and William Henry Parrish, who was serving in his second regiment, having earlier enlisted, along
with his father, in the 6th Michigan Infantry. An additional
contingent of the regiment was overtaken and captured on
August 3, but the rest, after riding almost continuously for
seven days and eight nights, rejoined the Union army.

"DAMN THE TORPEDOES"
James Reeve, an engineer at the Fennville sawmill, had enlisted early in the war in the 3rd Michigan Infantry. He was
discharged for disability, but by July of 1862 he had recovered his health enough to go to New York City where he enlisted in the U. S. Navy, putting his knowledge of engines
to work as a second class fireman. He was assigned to the
sloop Seminole in the fleet commanded by Admiral David
Farragut on the Gulf coast. A naval engagement in Mobile
Bay was set for dawn on August 5, 1864, to take advantage
of early morning high water which would help carry the
ships past the two forts at the head of the bay. Reeve later
described this day:

We were called to quarters and ordered to get ready for action. There were 15 ships in our fleet, including Admiral Farragut's flag ship. I was aboard the sloop Seminole. We proceeded down the channel to the bay with boats moving in pairs, being lashed together with cables and chains so that if one ship became disabled, the other could tow her out of danger. Fort Morgan frowned down upon us from the right and Fort Gaines on the left, looked equally formidable. Two of our ships struck mines laid in the channel and sank carrying 120 men down. The Tecumseh struck a mine and sank. We moved on down the bay under a heavy fire from the forts. Our vessels were badly splintered up before we got out of the range of the forts. We anchored and were just preparing for dinner when that old ram, the Tennessee came up and was going to clean up on the whole fleet. We poured shot into her from all sides and made her helpless. She surrendered after a two hour fight. My share of the prize was $80. [15]

It was during this battle, faced with a maze of underwater mines (called torpedoes at the time), that Farragut was said to have declared, "Damn the torpedoes, full speed ahead." ¶ The action gave the Union a staging area for planned operations against Mobile. ¶ There may have been a secondary reason for Reeve to return to war. He boarded at the home of sawmill owner E. A. Fenn. The Fenn's daughter, Irene, had been married to Henry Blakeslee who was killed in action with the 19th Michigan Infantry on March 6, 1863. Although Reeve had been discreet, his enthusiasm for young Irene and her infant daughter was obvious enough to make local tongues wag. It was an awkward time to pursue romance.

PHYSICIAN TO THE FREED SLAVES

E. B. WRIGHT
FRONT 23

Edwin B. Wright, an Illinois physician who would move to Saugatuck in 1871, worked with the Freedmen's Bureau, ministering to the needs of former slaves on Paw Paw Island in the Mississippi River near Vicksburg. Soon after he arrived there he was joined by his wife, Lydia, and foster daughter, eight-year-old Hattie Moffat. Lydia became ill and died of "acclimating fever" in October of 1864. Her obituary, found in an old scrapbook, says:

> She had but recently joined her husband and was enjoying to the full the delightful climate and opportunities for usefulness within her reach. Her husband being in charge of the Sanitary Interests of the Freed people of the post, she found abundant and welcome employment in relieving and preventing suffering. Her only child, a sweet little girl, made her domestic circle complete, and her happiness perfect. Now the widowed husband and the motherless little one share a grief with which no stranger can intermeddle. . . . She was buried on the 8th in the presence of a large concourse of dusky-faced but deeply sympathizing friends. [16]

Young Hattie, also caught the disease and was ill for many weeks, but recovered. In the spring of 1865, Paw Paw Island was flooded and operations moved to the mainland, then Dr. Wright was put in charge of the Refuge Home and Hospital in Vicksburg. In October, 1865, he married Phoebe, a school teacher, and they went to Lauderdale, Mississippi, to establish a hospital. In August, 1866, they took the train from Vicksburg to Columbus, Kentucky, traveled by boat to Cairo, Illinois, and took the train for Chicago, where they collected Hattie, who had been sent north by boat to the Illinois farm of her father's sister, Jessie, and Jessie's husband, Harvey L. House. In 1871 the family moved to Saugatuck where Hattie Moffat was married, in 1876, to Charles E. Bird, a Saugatuck druggist.

"AND THE BAND PLAYED YANKEE DOODLE . . ."

One of the major tactics that became especially important in 1864 was to destroy not only military property but anything that might aid and abet the Confederate efforts to wage war. One private in the 4th Michigan Cavalry chronicled a few days of the march through Georgia in a letter to the *Allegan Journal* dated August 18, 1864, and printed in the issue of September 26, 1864:

> We started from Sandtown on the extreme right of our army on the evening of the 18th reaching Fairburn Station on the Mobile & Atlanta R. R. about daylight the next morning. There the center of our column was attacked by a brigade of rebels, who fought quite desperately for a short time . . . . This

155

railroad had been torn up so we started east. After marching about six miles we again found the rebels. We dismounted and drove them across a deep narrow stream. They tried to destroy the bridge after them, but we hurried them away too soon. Gen. Kilpatrick helped repair the bridge and we were soon across . . . .We advanced to within sight of the depot when we had a slight skirmish with the rebels. . . .We then advanced and began tearing up the railroad (Macon and Atlanta). We burned the depot, one car load of leather, about one hundred bales of cotton, also three or four large store houses in the town of Jonesboro, besides destroying about three miles of railroad. We remained in town until about midnight burning and destroying rebel property. During this time we were cheered by good music from the 3rd Ky. Cav. band which played "Hail Columbia" and other patriotic airs. The glare of the fire reached for miles around and the air was highly perfumed with rebel whisky. The rebels attacked us while in the town, but a few volleys from our Spencers silenced them and the band played "Yankee Doodle" and the air rang with cheers. From there we marched south striking the same railroad the next day about noon at Lovejoy station.

1ST MICHIGAN COLORED INFANTRY

On August 29, 1864, a contingent of black and mulatto residents of Cheshire Township, Allegan County, south and east of Saugatuck, traveled to Kalamazoo to enlist in the 1st Michigan Colored Infantry. The 1870 census shows five men named Smith, all born in Kentucky, between the ages of 22 and 31 living in the area, all further described on the census as "mulatto." Samuel Smith, the youngest one on the census, and George W. Smith, the oldest, enlisted on that day in Co. F. Other members of the 1st Michigan Colored Infantry (taken into Federal service as the 102nd United States Colored Troops) from Cheshire Township who were counted on the 1890 veteran's census were James Perdue, 29; Alfred White, 28; Arthur Allen, 18 (a substitute for draftee James W. Allen); Andrew Boyd, 18; James Robinson, 21; William Howard, 18; William Ridgely, 33 and Joseph Crous. The two Smith brothers traveled south and joined the regiment on September 24, 1864, in Beaufort, South

Carolina. These were the first black soldiers from the area, although there were already several white officers serving with the Colored Troops.

NEW RECRUITS FROM ALLEGAN COUNTY

From September 2 to 28, 1864, the enlistment period was open for the newly-formed 28th Michigan Infantry. The commandant of the training camp was William B. Williams of Allegan who had been the original Captain of Co. I of the 5th Michigan Cavalry, later replaced with Douglas soldier George N. Dutcher. The 28th was mustered in during September and October of 1864 and local men included Hiram Ellis of Saugatuck, who transferred from the 5th Michigan Cavalry to accept a commission as first lieutenant and an assignment as adjutant to Colonel William W. Wheeler of St. Joseph; Smith B. Barker of Manlius Township; George A. Cook, a Ganges Township farm laborer; Judson Doud, a painter from Saugatuck Township; Ashley Nichols, 20-year-old son of a Ganges Township miller, and Peter Sargent, 38, a Ganges Township farmer.

H. ELLIS
BACK 24

THE ENGLISHMAN JOINS UP

On September 6, 1864, Ganges farmer James Hibberdine enlisted in the 17th Michigan Infantry. Although the outlook for his farm and family had looked bleak in February, matters were even worse by September. On May 2 his farm was sold at public auction for debt, and he wrote an impassioned letter to his brother in England asking for $60 to buy it back. "I expect to commence working out in about 10 days. I get good wages and think I shall be able to fetch everything round all right by next winter." [17] There is no notation or further letter to indicate that this sum, or any other sum, was sent or received. On August 30, 1864, the couple's only child, an eight-year-old son, Charles, died and was buried in the Loomis Cemetery. In despair Hibberdine enlisted in the Union Army hoping that the signing bonus and military pay would at least feed the rest of his family. ¶ To fill vacancies, a recruiter for the 17th Michigan Infantry

1861

1862

1863

1864

1865

AFTER THE WAR

158

had combed the area. He managed to sign up: Alvin H. Stillson. 25, who had arrived in 1838 in Ganges with his uncle, Harrison Hutchins, the first settler in Ganges Township, Stillson was a carpenter and sawyer and helped establish the first saw mill in Holland; James Hibberdine, 36, (mentioned above); Oliver P. Carman, 30, a Ganges farm laborer with a wife and two children; Marian D. Loomis, 24, the son of early settler Levi Loomis; Simeon Staring, 38, a Ganges farmer, with a wife and two children; Levi B. Davis, 34, a Ganges farmer with four children, and Julius U. Gardner, 42, a teamster with two children who lived in the Pier Cove area. ¶ Because most of the young men had already gone to war, recruits in 1864 tended to be older men, or younger boys who had not qualified for service earlier.

THE "WIDE-AWAKE REPUBLICANS" MEET IN SAUGATUCK

Back home patriotic fervor mixed with politics as local and national candidates campaigned for the fall election. On September 12, 1864, the Allegan newspaper carried the notice:

> MASS MEETING — The wide awake Republicans of the Lake Shore assembled in mass meeting in Saugatuck on the 12th to hear those champions of the Union cause, Upson and Fenny. The meeting was large and enthusiastic.

The same speakers moved on to Plainwell for a similar meeting the following day. The speakers were probably Charles Upson, Attorney General of Michigan, 1861-63 who was a candidate for the State Senate and other politicians running for state and local office.

MIX VISITS THE UNION LEAGUE

On September 27, 1864, Elisha Mix of the 8th Michigan Cavalry, a Manlius Township farmer who had been taken prisoner on Stoneman's Raid, August 2, 1864, was exchanged and returned to Union lines. Shortly after his return he was promoted to the rank of colonel. While he was home on furlough, Mix was interviewed by the Allegan editor who wrote in the September 27, 1864, issue:

> He was one of the officers placed under fire at Charleston, by the rebels. He says Charleston is a city of the most indescribable dearth, appearing as though it had been forsaken for 20 years . . . . Just prior to his being exchanged, the Colonel had the pleasure of being invited into a conclave of Union Leaguers and learned while there, by the reports, that these secret meetings are being organized in every direction.

The Union League was an organization formed in the North after the military defeats and Republican election losses of 1862. Southern men sympathetic to the Union cause and others, who felt the inevitability of defeat and saw it as a vehicle to political power, formed chapters in the South. Because Mix was taken to a meeting prior to being exchanged it is likely that the guards, or other officials of the prison, were connected with the organization. The Union League later became the main organization promoting the Republican cause among emancipated blacks. Mix is identified in an 1892 biographical volume as a Republican in politics.

THE WAR FOLLOWS DUTCHER OUT WEST

Former Captain George N. Dutcher of the 5th Michigan Cavalry, an engineer by trade, was hospitalized for injuries following the Battle of Brandy Station and was officially discharged for disability on November 2, 1863. He visited his mother and other family in Douglas, then went to Chicago where he had been working before enlistment. From Chicago he traveled to southern Illinois and joined his brother-in-law, Frederick H. May, who was building locomotives for the Northern Missouri Railway. ¶ According to a story recounted in his obituary in the Fennville newspaper, Dutcher took the first Northern Missouri Railway train into Jefferson City, Missouri, probably the first week of October, 1864. On that, or a later trip, he was taken prisoner by Confederate General Sterling "Pap" Price in Missouri. The assembled prisoners, including Dutcher, were led into Ironton where they were forced to strip to the waist and relinquish their boots. Then, with a noose around his neck to symbolize his fate as a "Northerner," he was paraded barefoot through the streets behind a column of Confederate soldiers. Dutcher later escaped and sought refuge with Union troops led by his old commander, General Pleasanton. ¶ This story is lent credence by an application in Dutcher's pension file dated October 3, 1864, which gives his home address as Kansas City, Jackson County, Missouri. In it he claimed to be "permanently lame & disabled" by "a gunshot wound through the right groin." Under description of his occupation he notes, perhaps not entirely truthfully, that he "has done nothing since discharge."

A LIEUTENANT TURNED PRIVATE

A. C. WALLIN
BACK 32

Alfred C. Wallin, one of Allegan County's first officers, had resigned his commission as second lieutenant of Co. G, 6th Michigan Infantry on July 1, 1862, after a service of just over a year. He returned to Michigan and resumed his study of law. Wallin was accepted into the Michigan bar in 1862 and the Illinois bar two years later. In October of 1864, with the war continuing, he re-enlisted, this time as a private in Co. A, 100th New York Infantry. He served as company clerk and was seldom in the thick of the action. He explained to his family in a letter written on April 20, 1865:

> You must understand that clerks are armed and must fight on the defensive; but by order of General Grant, they do not go out of the camp to fight for the reason that in case both the company commander and clerk are wounded, the accounts would be hopelessly confused. . . . I tried my mettle last fall, and know I can stand fire, and that is quite enough to satisfy me. [18]

REEVE PREPARES FOR A THIRD TERM OF SERVICE

James Reeve of Clyde Township was mustered into his third military service since the war began. He had enlisted on May 13, 1861, in the 3rd Michigan Infantry but was discharged for disability on August 7, 1862. He returned to

1861
1862
1863
1864
1865
AFTER THE WAR

160

Fennville to recover his health, then traveled to New York City where he enlisted in the U. S. Navy on July 20, 1863, as a second class fireman, serving with Farragut's fleet until early in 1864. He must have just returned home in time to be drafted from Clyde Township and assigned to Co. F of the 15th Michigan Infantry, where he served until July 26, 1865. ¶ When he finally returned to his job at the Fenn sawmill, it had been more than two years since the death of Irene (Fenn) Blakeslee's husband, Henry, with the 19th Michigan Infantry. She must have agreed to his marriage proposal in 1868. On the 1870 census the Reeve family consists of James, Irene, eight-year-old Hattie Blakeslee and one-year-old Nellie Reeve.

SMALL WARTIME INCIDENTS

Fernando Yemans, 8th Michigan Cavalry, was wounded and taken prisoner at Henryville, Tennessee, on November 23, 1864. Yemans had been in the army less than three months, having enlisted on August 24 at Saugatuck. He joined the regiment at Lexington, Kentucky, during its march south, and had been promoted to corporal on November 1. He was eventually paroled and discharged from the service at Detroit on June 6, 1865. ¶ Samuel Shaver of Saugatuck was a blacksmith and mule driver in the 5th Michigan Cavalry. For at least a portion of his duty he tended the headquarters wagon and was in charge of mail. The regiment was in camp near Winchester, Virginia, on November 24, 1864. Shaver had run his mules for miles into camp and, with other drivers, was out with teams after lumber and brick from old buildings for the officers to fix up their quarters, when enemy soldiers made a dash for them. The mule drivers escaped, the bugles sounded "Boots and Saddles" and a contingent of cavalry came to their rescue. ¶ On November 30 in Georgia the 102nd United States Colored Troops, including a contingent of black settlers from Cheshire Township, was part of the force that was responsible for the destruction of the Charleston and Savannah Railroad during Sherman's march through Georgia. On this day they

1861

1862

1863

1864

1865

AFTER THE WAR

161

engaged a force of Confederate soldiers at a place variously described as Honey Hill or Horney Hill:

> Here our forces sustained a charge and charged in return. In this affair the 102nd covered itself with glory; our regiment maintained the steadiest line of battle and fought with the greatest determination of any troops. The wounded refused to go to the rear, but kept on fighting. [19]

After a stronger Confederate charge, a general retreat was ordered. So many horses had been killed or wounded that two cannon directly in front of their sector had to be abandoned. The men of Co. D tried to rescue them, but were driven back with heavy losses including their captain. Then Lieutenant Orson W. Bennett "gallantly led a small force fully 100 yards in advance of the Union lines and brought in the guns, preventing their capture."

FOUNDER OF THE SAUGATUCK EPISCOPAL CHURCH SIGNS UP

As the war wore on, men who had not gone earlier, rationalizing that it "might not be necessary" were moved to do their perceived duty and sign-up. The Reverend J. Rice Taylor, 46, enlisted as a chaplain in the 123rd U. S. Colored Infantry at its organization on December 2, 1864, at Louisville, Kentucky. He was born in Niagara County, New York, and had attended seminary in New York City before moving to Allegan in 1858. There he led an Episcopal congregation that met at the courthouse. In 1863 he moved to Tecumseh, but that year he reported to the Bishop:

> I would respectfully report that on the 1st of September last I resigned the charge of St. Peter's, Tecumseh. My chief reason for leaving the parish was that I seemed to be gaining a subsistence without doing much good. After serving several weeks as a delegate under the Christian Commission from Michigan, I received and accepted an appointment as Chaplain to the 123rd Colored Infantry, stationed as post guard at Taylor Barracks, Louisville, Ky. Since then I have been engaged in the discharge of duties at this post, holding generally three services every Sunday and one week day service. We have

REV. TAYLOR
BACK 25

162

1861 1862 1863 1864 1865 AFTER THE WAR

now a chapel room, twenty-four feet wide by eighty-seven feet long, a small organ and full congrega-tions.[20]

The regiment's service was entirely within Kentucky. Taylor was mustered out with his unit on October 24, 1865, and moved to Saugatuck in 1869 eventually founding Episcopal churches in both Saugatuck and Holland. His son, Alfred, was the founder of the Fruit Growers Bank at Saugatuck.

PRISONERS STRAGGLE HOME

On December 7, 1864, George W. Bailey of the 3rd Michigan Infantry, who had been incarcerated in a number of different southern prisons since early May, finally managed to get in the line of those who would be paroled; the sick and convalescent were usually taken first. He wrote in his diary: "They commenced paroling this morning and are now examining the 8th hundred of the six thousand, I told the surgeon a good story and am now outside."[21] The men were marched to the railroad where they boarded a train for Charleston. At the wharf they boarded a Flag of Truce boat and were transferred to a Union Flag of Truce boat two miles below the ruins of Fort Sumter. Two days later they boarded the steamer Crescent City and set sail for Fortress Monroe, near Washington.

"NOT FIT FOR DUTY"

Walter Billings, a farrier with the 8th Michigan Cavalry who had been captured August 3, 1864, in Georgia, was paroled at Charleston, South Carolina, on December 11, 1864. He reported on December 15, 1864, and was sent to Camp Parole, Maryland, then back to Michigan to recuperate from his ordeal. A letter in his pension file dated January 24, 1865, from Ganges doctor, C. B. Goodrich, recommends an extension of furlough because "I have carefully examined the said farrier Walter Billings and find him suffering from chronic diarrhea and general debility and in my opinion he is unable to travel and will not be fit for duty in a less time than twenty days." In January and February Billings was at

W. BILLINGS BACK 26

Camp Chase, Ohio. He finally returned to his regiment, then encamped in Tennessee, on March 31, 1865. However his health did not improve and on June 15, 1865, Elisha Mix signed his discharge at Pulaski, Tennessee, and forwarded it to headquarters with a note that it was "respectfully forwarded approved. This soldier is too old and his health too poor since his release from Prison to be of any benefit to the Gov't." This despite the fact that both Mix and Billings were the same age, 45.

VISITING THE DENTIST ON FURLOUGH

George W. Lonsbury of the 5th Michigan Cavalry was promoted to captain of Co. M on November 10, 1864, and was mustered on December 19, 1864, at Winchester, Virginia. He went home on leave and during his furlough had all of his upper teeth removed in an effort to relieve "ague in the face and neuralgia" according to Dr. Abram R. Calkins, his Allegan physician. His mouth became "extremely ulcerated" and his leave was extended. In February he reported to Detroit where Surgeon E. F. Sawyer certified in a letter dated February 8, 1865, that he was "unfit for duty" in consequence of extraction of all of his teeth and severe neuralgia pains in the head. Lonsbury did not return to duty until March of 1865 and then was detailed to the 1st Cavalry Division Remount Camp in Pleasant Valley, Maryland, where unhorsed cavalry soldiers obtained new mounts. Despite his, possibly planned, extended furlough in 1864-65, when he was finally mustered out of service on June 19, 1865, he was brevetted a major "for gallant and meritorious service during the war." A brevet commission entitled an officer to take an honorary rank on discharge above his actual service rank.

BUTLER GETS OUT FROM BEHIND THE DESK

A letter from Brownsville, Arkanas, from the 3rd Michigan Cavalry correspondent to the Allegan newspaper, dated December 26, 1864, notes that Lieutenant James G. Butler, who had been serving on the headquarters staff of Colonel John K. Mizner, had been appointed captain of Co. F.

The regiment was dug in for the winter and had created such a fine camp that they sometimes called it "Michigan City." After working in the administrative end of the regiment, Captain Butler tried his hand at field command. Late in December he was in charge of Companies E, F, and G which, according to an account in the *Allegan Journal* for January 9, 1865: "went out and brought in 4 prisoners. They also killed one reb. They went out in the direction of Searcy." Searcy is north east of Little Rock. ¶ Butler's sojourn as a company commander was short lived. In February 1865 he was named acting assistant inspector general, and he spent most of 1865 serving as judge advocate on a military tribunal that heard court martial cases. He was promoted to the rank of major on November 9, 1865.

ONE MORE CHRISTMAS ON THE LINE

On December 23, 1864, Drummer Nelson W. Ogden, camped near Columbia, Tennessee with the 25th Michigan Infantry, reported that the civility that marked the early part of the war was eroding with the chances of the South for victory:

> When we were a coming from Johnsonville there was 3 Sergeants and 2 privates out of our regt. captured by Bushwhackers and killed and another from our company that got away after they took his money from him. They took from him $135. They are worse than the worst murderers that ever was heard of. They led them out and shot each one three times and then kicked them down the rocks. One fellow from the 130 Ind. got away after he was shot. The bullet just glazed the side of his skull and he told us all about it and described all of the boys that were killed. [22]

The Christmas of 1864 was celebrated by the 3rd Michigan Cavalry and other troops in Arkansas. Correspondent D. C. Henderson wrote in the January 9, 1865, issue of the *Allegan Journal*:

> Yesterday was Christmas and the boys fared pretty well on the whole. Rations of fresh meat were dealt out to the several companies, which with the game

and fowl which the men had laid in for previously, furnished us with a Christmas dinner which would have whetted the appetite of the veriest gourmand. Think of that you stay at home guards who think that soldiers have nothing to consume but 'hard tack and sow belly.'

The 5th Michigan Cavalry received a special kind of Christmas present. On December 28, 1864, they arrived at a camp they had used before near Winchester, Virginia and found waiting for them Sergeant William White, Private John Hill and Sergeant William Weeks who had been incarcerated in southern prisons since their capture on a raid in Richmond in March. Private Henry Avery wrote: "We were right glad to welcome them back again." [23] ¶ The interval since they had seen the three included a furlough home for the former prisoners. The December 19, 1864, *Allegan Journal* reported:

> Sergt. Wm. White of Saugatuck . . . just arrived in town from Andersonville, Ga. White was interned in loathsome Southern prisons for eight months! The sufferings and privations which these boys have undergone because of their devotion to the Union, baffle description.

White was luckier, or craftier, than most. He boasted that he had served nearly three years in the cavalry and never missed a meal. His hearty nature later backfired on him. After a 30 day furlough at home, White later told the pension board that he had not reported to the parole camp hospital as ordered because, "I had a dread of being in camp and thought best to go direct to my regiment & did so as promptly as I could. I did not go to Hospital after that but was treated while with my regiment." Later in life, the scurvy he had contracted in the Confederate prisons and "being compelled to use unwholesome food and bad water" caused health problems making it difficult for him to earn a living, but the pension board repeatedly denied his applications because he had not been treated in a hospital, so there was little documentation of his disabilities. In 1912 he was finally granted a pension of $30 a month. In April, 1865, White won "laurels for bravery" in the last push in Virginia. He was commissioned a second lieutenant on April 14, 1865. White was honorably discharged on July 20, 1865.

FOUR SURVIVORS ENLIST IN THE WAR EFFORT

Four of the area's Civil War soldiers already had a remarkable story of survival behind them when they started out for the war. ¶ On July 25, 1841, John H. and Mary Baragar Billings and six children, James, Peter Henry, Mary E., Hannah M. and the twins, John Darius and Jonathan Hosias, who were just over a year old, started from Saugatuck upriver in an open sailboat, bound for a visit with the Mann family near New Richmond. With them was Abigail (McDonald) McLaughlin, the wife of the boatbuilder James J. McLaughlin, and two or three of her children (accounts differ). ¶ A gust of wind struck the boat just as it hit a snag and the vessel capsized in the river. The elder Billings and the eldest sibling, Peter Henry Billings, rescued the twins, and all of the McLaughlin children, except the baby who was so tightly wrapped he simply floated ashore and was found caught in the reeds. Mrs. Billings, James, Mary and Hannah Billings and Mrs. McLaughlin were all drowned. ¶ One of the twins, Jonathan Hosias Billings, died in Hutchins Lake when he was about 12. He was returning from the home

R. MCLAUGHLIN
BACK 38

of a neighbor across the lake and chanced a shortcut across the ice when he fell through and was drowned. ¶ Peter Henry Billings enlisted in Co. I, 13th Michigan Infantry on October 22, 1861, at the age of 28 in Manlius Township. On the 1860 census both he and John Darius (below) were working as farm laborers on the family farm. By then his father had remarried and there were also eight half-siblings, aged two to 19, in the household. Peter Henry's Civil War career was short. He was discharged for disability, November 5, 1862. ¶ John Darius Billings, the surviving twin, enlisted, according to his obituary, "when the Civil War broke out" in Co. F, 9th Indiana Infantry and served until the end of the fighting. He returned to Saugatuck after the war and in 1868 received the franchise to operate the Saugatuck chain ferry. He later sold fan mills for E. A. Fenn, founder of Fennville, before moving to Iowa about 1870. ¶ James J. McLaughlin, the eldest son of that family, enlisted in Co. D, 10th Michigan Cavalry on October 3, 1864 for one year at Grand Rapids and rose to the rank of corporal. He had come to Michigan from New York State in 1837 when he was two years old. The family paused in Allegan where his father, James J. McLaughlin Sr., built a flouring mill for Alexander Ely, before moving on to Saugatuck where James Sr. built and refitted a number of Great Lakes boats. In 1849, the whole family moved to Northport with the Reverend George Nelson Smith and his Indian mission. After the war James Jr. lived in Elk Rapids where he died June 26, 1908 and is buried. ¶ Robert W. McLaughlin was born in Saugatuck Township, then called Newark, in 1837 and was four at the time of the boating accident. He ran away from home at an early age and shipped on the Great Lakes. When the Civil War began he enlisted in the 1st New York Marine Artillery and rose to the rank of captain. After the war, McLaughlin married and remained in New York State, although he frequently visited the family in Michigan. ¶ The mother of Robert and James McLaughlin, Abigail McDonald McLaughlin, was related to the McDonalds and the Scovills, who were among the founders of Douglas.

1865

FOR NEARLY FOUR YEARS EVERYONE, ESPECIALLY those in the north, had been expecting the end of the war "soon." Each time these hopes were thwarted and hostilities continued.

Fearing another disappointment,

recruitment continued.

On March 1, 1865 at Ganges, Daniel Eaton enlisted in the 13th Michigan Infantry, joining Willard E. Field who had enlisted at Saugatuck on February 23. On March 4, 1865, they were joined by Samuel Mosier. Some late enlistees missed the war altogether. John F. Tidd, enlisted in 24th Michigan Infantry at Saugatuck on March 14, and was mustered into service on March 25. He was mustered out at Detroit on June 28, apparently without leaving Michigan. ¶ On March 24, 1865, one of the area's youngest soldiers, John Utten, 17, of Fillmore Township, enlisted in Co. H of the 1st Michigan Cavalry. In 1860 he was working on the farm of his parents, John and Hermina Otten, who had come to Michigan with other immigrants from the Netherlands in 1847. After his war service, John Utten was married in 1867 at Singapore and in 1873 moved to Saugatuck where he was head sawyer at the Griffin and Henry sawmill. He later worked in the Douglas Basket Factory.

BIRD FAMILY NEARLY MISSES THE WAR

GEO. D. DEAN
AND
H. BIRD
BACK 27 & 28

George Dallas Dean, a Ganges farmer, who was married to Mary Bird, daughter of Henry and Desiah Bird of Saugatuck, enlisted with a friend, Ed Margeson, in the 10th Michigan Cavalry on February 13, 1865. They reported to the regiment at Knoxville, Tennessee, and shortly afterwards Dean became ill. Margeson later described Dean's ordeal for the pension board:

> . . . in April he was taken with what Dr called the Black Measles, and as we were just moving camp he was left sick in his tent. We only moved a mile or two. I went the next morning back with a teamster to the old camp after Headquarters goods. The ambulance had just come after George Dean to take him to the Hospital. He had remained there alone all night, I realized he was very bad off. I saw him again sometime in June. He was then just able to walk around.

Dean received a discharge for disability June 30, 1865.

Dean's brother-in-law, Henry Bird Jr., enlisted in May of 1864, in Co. H of the 141st Illinois Infantry. He contracted

1861
1862
1863
1864
1865
AFTER THE WAR
170

typhoid fever on the three-day train trip from Illinois to Kentucky where they were to be assigned to garrison duty. Because Bird was a Mason, he was placed in the care of the local Masonic hospital. He always credited the Masons with his eventual recovery. By the time he was well, his unit has already been discharged, so he returned to his studies at Wheaton College in Illinois. In 1868 the entire family moved to Saugatuck and Henry later started a drug store, run afterwards for many years by his brother, Charles. Henry later moved to Bozeman, Montana, where he died in 1932.[1]

ELLIS CITED FOR MERITORIOUS SERVICE

Hiram R. Ellis, along with the rest of the 28th Michigan Infantry, was on a train enroute to Annapolis, Maryland, when the regiment received orders to report instead to Alexandria, Virginia. Arriving there, they were assigned to the 23rd Corps and were put on ocean transport to Morehead City, North Carolina. One more rail journey and a march brought them to Wise Forks, North Carolina, where they met the enemy under Colonel William W. Wheeler of St. Joseph. On the morning of March 10, 1864, they were hit with a "fierce and determined charge," but the Union soldiers managed to hang on and then made their own charge at the double quick, driving the Confederates back from the position. About 2 p.m. on the same day, there was a "heavy and desperate onset on the left and center" that "most signally failed, the point having been strongly and promptly reinforced from the right." The Rebels retreated leaving their dead and wounded and a large number of prisoners and fell back across the Neuse River burning the bridge in their rear. ¶ For "gallant and meritorious service during the war" and especially the work at Wise Forks, Ellis was brevetted a captain. He had enlisted at Saugatuck in August of 1862 and mustered as a private in the 5th Michigan Cavalry. He was discharged to accept a promotion in August of 1864 and mustered as adjutant to Colonel Wheeler (formerly of the 13th Infantry) in the newly organized 28th Michigan Infantry. On the 1860 census, Ellis is described as a "clerk" and is living at a boarding house in Saugatuck Village with his mother, a dressmaker. He would return from the war and serve as the first clerk of the Village of Saugatuck and as postmaster before moving over to Douglas where his signature is prominent on the incorporation papers of the village in 1870. Ellis later moved to Grand Rapids and made a specialty of helping fellow veterans apply for pensions and other benefits from the government.

LUMBERMEN FROM MICHIGAN KNOW CORDUROY ROADS
Experienced lumbermen were often useful during the war. The *Allegan Journal* correspondent from the 3rd Michigan Cavalry wrote on March 13, 1865, from Brownsville, Arkansas:

> Captain [Isaac] Wilson of Co. K has for several weeks past had charge of a detail to make a wagon road leading to the Station (2 ½ miles) which we expect to use in a day or two to get out of this hole and to strike the railroad again. Captain W. is a competent man for such a purpose and knows the way to make a Michigan corduroy road. [2]

Already a "lumberman" on the 1860 census, Wilson had came home on furlough in June of 1864 and married Virginia Griffin, sister of Saugatuck lumberman W. B. Griffin. After the war, he returned to the Saugatuck area and became the foreman of the Stockbridge and Johnson mill and was in charge of the company's lumber camps in Pine Plains (later Valley) Township. ¶ On March 19, 1865, the left wing of General Sherman's army, commanded by General Henry Slocum, marched toward Bentonville, North Carolina, pushing back the Confederate cavalry as they advanced. A counterattack by Joseph Johnston's 20,000 men changed the battle to a defensive one until the arrival, the following day, of the rest of Sherman's army. James McCune and James S. Orr of Co. H., 13th Michigan Infantry, were wounded. The 13th Michigan Infantry lost 106 men including its commander, Colonel Willard G. Eaton of Otsego, who was killed in battle. These were the heaviest regimental losses on the Union side.

1861 1862 1863 1864 1865 AFTER THE WAR

172

WEEKS LOSES A FOOT

During Sheridan's battle of Five Forks, Virginia, on April 1, 1865, Lieutenant William Weeks of Co. I, 5ᵗʰ Michigan Cavalry, was severely injured in the left foot. The Allegan newspaper quotes intelligence gleaned from two regimental comrades who wrote home that "While in the front of battle, he was shot by a rebel sharpshooter, and has since suffered amputation of his left foot" and that he was "in City Point Hospital, doing as well as could be expected." The editor went on to muse in the April 17, 1865, issue:

WM. WEEKS
BACK 29

> In the many battles in which he has been engaged, Lieut. Weeks has had many narrow escapes, some almost miraculous, having had several horses shot under him. . . . Lieut Weeks has gained his present position as First Lieutenant in the company in which he enlisted as private, by his tried bravery, intelligence and soldierly deportment, gaining the friendship and good will of the men, the respect and esteem of the officers. The loss of a limb to one of his active temperament will be a sad blow . . .

Weeks spent nearly three months in the hospital before being honorably discharged on July 20, 1865. He returned to Allegan County and did not let the loss of his left foot slow him down much. He was elected Register of Deeds. In 1870, he and his brother founded an abstract company in Allegan. In 1874 he was married to Rose Mix, daughter of Brigadier General Elisha Mix, formerly of the 8ᵗʰ Michigan Cavalry, and, in 1876, William Weeks was elected Mayor of Allegan. He also had a large farm and engaged in breeding Durham cattle. Weeks was the nephew of Mary Elizabeth (Peckham) Morrison, who was the Saugatuck area's first schoolteacher and wife of early settler and tannery owner Stephen A. Morrison.

THE TATTERED COLORS OF THE SHARPSHOOTERS

The first regimental order of the new year, dated January 1, promoted Corporal Richard Campbell of Company I, First Michigan Sharpshooters, to color sergeant, replacing Henry C. Call, who had been wounded and discharged. There was little left of the regiment's flag to carry. During the

FLAG OF THE
1ST MICHIGAN
SHARPSHOOTERS
PL. 21

1861
1862
1863
1864
1865
AFTER THE WAR

Battle at Petersburg earlier, Color Sergeant George Caine thought that the regimental flag was in mortal danger of being captured so he tore the national colors into ſtripes and diſtributed it to the men. He then furled what was left of the regimental flag and the ſtate flag and buried it in the sand of the battlefield. The flags were retrieved after the battle. It was this tattered remnant that Campbell took charge of as the new year began. The firſt seven ſtripes and the blue canton were entirely missing. ¶ On April 2, 1865, during an assault on Petersburg by the Firſt Michigan Sharpshooters, Campbell tended the tattered national colors. Because of the ferocity and partial success of the engagement, five men were submitted for Medals of Honor including Campbell who "engaged in hand to hand conflict with the enemy," but no action was taken on the applications and the awards were not granted. Campbell was injured in the battle when a shell fragment ſtruck his left shoulder. He was not present the following day when the tattered colors of the Firſt Michigan Sharpshooters became the firſt Union flag to wave over the City of Petersburg under the care of Corporal James Walton of Co. I. Before dawn, their way lit by matches, members of the sharpshooters rushed to the roof of the courthouse before other U. S. troops could enter the city. Twenty minutes later the 2nd Michigan Infantry hoiſted its flag atop the cuſtoms house. Moſt regiments liſted the names of their battles on their flags. Since there was so little of the national flag left, the sharpshooters appended silk ſtreamers to the pole on which they recalled their battles before marching in the Grand Review.

LEE'S SURRENDER AT APPOMATOX

On April 9, 1865, the 5th Michigan Cavalry was in line of battle for a charge on the enemy near Appomatox, Virginia, when a Confederate soldier carrying a flag of truce appeared. The brigade was held ſtill in line, ready to swoop down on the enemy, but it proved to be the laſt line formed by them in the war. Lee surrendered. Still in line for the 5th Michigan Cavalry were Thomas Collier, George N. Gard-

NOTICE OF SURRENDER
PL. 22

FLAG OF TRUCE
PL. 23

1861
1862
1863
1864
1865
AFTER THE WAR

ner, Cornelius Gavin, John Hill, George W. Lonsbury, Samuel Shaver, Anthony Slack and William White. ¶ On the day of the surrender at Appomatox, Private Alvin Stillson of the 17th Michigan Infantry wrote his wife Minerva from Beasley's Farm near Petersburg, Virginia:

STILLSON BACK 30

> I seat myself this morning to write a few lines to let you know that I am STILL ALIVE and well for I'm tuff as a brick and I hope this may find My Dear Ones at home enjoying the same blessings. It has been a week since I have written a letter but it is not my fault for this is the first opportunity that I have had to write since the fight commenced at Petersburg. We have had a rather RUFF TIME of it but thank the Lord we came through all right. We cleaned the Rebs out Most Handsomely, but my dear, I can't say that I EVER want to see the sight again for it is a hard sight to travel for three or four miles over the bodies of dead men. But thank the Lord I don't think that I shall ever see another such battle for the fighting is about done . . . .You must keep up good courage and your old man will be with you before long. For My Part I can travel through FIRE or water to see the war ended.[3]

Company Clerk Alfred C. Wallin of the 100th New York Infantry, arrived just after the surrender. On April 11, 1863, he wrote in a letter home:

> We reached the front within one mile of the captured army of Lee about 7 P.M. We had marched 45 miles with hardly any rest. As soon as we reached our camp (the battle-field) we sank upon the ground, too tired to eat, and were asleep. It rained and I slept in a hole. In the morning I was lying in two inches of water – literally so. . . .Nothing has been officially said, we know nothing of terms; we look anxiously for papers to see what we have done. Grant came up with our column and often passed and repassed, looking absorbed – that's all.[4]

Wallin later described the final campaign in a letter dated April 20, 1865:

> I do not know that our corps has been particularly mentioned, but I am sure its marching was beaten by no other troops and equaled by few . . . . It has fought three days and nights and marched about two hun-

1861 1862 1863 1864 1865 AFTER THE WAR

175

dred miles in the past twenty-three days, [and has] actually run Lee down . . . . Lee gave up because his magazine and haversack were empty. But why were they empty? Because we made him shell out day by day and hour by hour . . . . He was bewildered by the ubiquitous cavalry. Cross-roads, cutoffs, ravines, all failed him. The merciless cavalry was always in his front, on his flank, among his trains and in his rear. I have conversed with many rebel officers. They are overwhelmed with the mortification of their defeat.[5]

JUBILATION IN MICHIGAN

On April 10, 1865, the news of Lee's surrender to Grant reached Allegan County. We have no accounts of how the news was received in Saugatuck, but it was probably similar to the activities in Allegan. The editor wrote happily in the April 17, 1865, issue:

GRAND JUBILEE! On receipt of the news Monday evening last, of the surrender of Lee and his rebel army, the event was celebrated in this village by the music of bands, the firing of guns, and on this occasion the privilege of ringing the old church bells was granted by the deacons. The official correspondence between Gens. Lee and Grant was read on the public square, and cheer after cheer went up from the excited crowd for the Union, the Army and the Flag and a "tiger" for General Grant. The greatest excitement prevailed and the rejoicing was kept up until daylight the next morning.

THE WAR CONTINUES IN THE WEST

Fighting continued in the west. The 10th Michigan Cavalry's assignment on Stoneman's raid was to destroy six large, beautiful bridges over the Roanoke river. The 11th Michigan Cavalry destroyed bridges over the New River. Then the 10th was sent to destroy some bridges between Greensboro and Salisbury over Abbott's Creek, along with some at High Point, North Carolina. The battalion succeeded in capturing two railway trains, loaded with supplies, and destroyed property that was estimated to be worth three million. On April 10, 1865, two units from the 10th continued on to Salisbury and met Ferguson's brigade of Rebel cavalry

1861 1862 1863 1864 1865 AFTER THE WAR

on the road. The Union soldiers were too tired to fight them, but they decided if they could draw them into a chase after the 10th they would not bother Stoneman's attack on Salisbury. Major Trowbridge later described the action:

> The 10th falling back by alternate squadrons, constantly presented an unbroken front to the enemy, wheeling out of column into line and steadily delivering their volleys from their Spencer carbines until they could see another squadron formed to receive the shock of the enemy. . . .The movements were all conducted with as much precision as if the place had been but a parade ground and the exercise but the sham fighting of the drill. . . .The fighting was constant and fierce, without a moment's interruption for nearly three hours, and extending over a space of about six miles when the enemy became discouraged at his failure to surround the handful of men and ceased his pursuit. . . . Maj. Dunn in this action bore a most conspicuous and gallant part, for which he received the commission of major by brevet from the Sec of War.[6]

William H. Dunn was the Ganges farm boy who had served as a private earlier in the war with the 5th Michigan Cavalry, saving Trowbridge (then a major) from capture at Gettysburg. When Trowbridge formed the 10th Michigan Cavalry, he offered Dunn a commission as lieutenant. Dunn had advanced to captain, and, as Trowbridge notes, was breveted a major for his heroics in the last days of the war.

DEATH OF PRESIDENT LINCOLN

On April 15, 1865, President Abraham Lincoln died in Washington D. C. shortly before 7:30 a.m., nine hours after being shot in the head while attending a play at Ford's Theater. ¶ Private Alfred Wallin, stationed nearby with the 100th New York Infantry, wrote his brothers at the Wallin tannery near Saugatuck on April 20:

> We are in possession of the details of the President's murder. It is not mere rhetoric to say that the sensation created in the army by the tidings is deeply solemn and profound . . . . No words can describe the burning desire of the soldiers to avenge the death of

1861

1862

1863

1864

1865

AFTER THE WAR

177

their commander-in-chief. 'Hunt the miscreants so long as they shall live,' is their cry . . . . But many Southerners are men of honor and purity, or the human face is meaningless. They have one sin: that sin is national. They are not consciously debased.[7]

The news dampened the joy of victory for the troops, many still in the trenches. On April 17, 1865, Private A. E. Calkins of Co. D, 8th Michigan Cavalry, wrote his mother from Pulaski, Tennessee:

> This has been the most solemn and effecting day I ever experienced since I have been in the Army. It has been observed as a day of mourning for the loss of our President. All labor has been prohibited in this Department. All places of business closed. All required to spend this day befitting the respect due the departed Statesman. . . . No morse [code] or disturbance has broken the quiet of the summer day except the booming of a cannon from Fort Rickly every half hour since sunrise, its thunder tones each time sending a shudder to my heart. . . . Yesterday we were rejoicing over the victories of our Armies and the prospect of speedy peace and today a deep gloom hangs over all but I think that is all, that it will not effect the end, unless to hasten it. Our Government don't depend upon the life of any one man. . . . Johnson will be the next to give up and perhaps Mobile, then what is left will leave the country, then a greater part of our Army will be mustered out to return home. . . . Not one American citizen will ever look back and say he is sorry for any sacrifices he made, and thousands are today regretting that they have not done more towards accomplishing this great end.[8]

"DON'T MAKE ANY NOISE, JOHNNY"

On April 18, 1865, Confederate forces were encamped near Henry Court House, North Carolina, when the 10th Michigan Cavalry attacked and drove them from the woods. According to an account later written by Colonel Trowbridge, "They mainly took refuge in a deep depression so common in the south and there huddled together, they formed an excellent target for Captain Dunn and his plucky boys. 27 killed."[9] ¶ Major Dunn added another feather to his military cap by thwarting the escape of a Georgia artillery regiment. The story was later told by the Confederate major during a visit to Detroit in the 1870s:

> In the spring of 1865, at the time of Lee's surrender, I was major of a Georgia regiment of artillery. I took a foolish notion that if I could steal away without being paroled and get across the Mississippi, I would like to help keep up the fight there. I thought I was not licked. I have changed by mind since then, but no matter. I had that notion then and so getting together the men of my bold battery, we set out to get across the big river. We got on well enough for a few days. We stole along the base of the mountains until we reached the Catawba river at a ford a few miles from Newton, in Western North Carolina. The citizens told us there had been some Yankee troops there a few days before, but whether they were still there they could not tell. The river at that point was very wide, and the ford led across an island in the middle of the river,. We approached very cautiously, keeping a sharp lookout for blue coats, but none were visible and we all got safely across to the island without seeing a sign of our enemies. From the island we scanned the southern bank of the river with the best eyes we could command but could see nothing to disturb us. At last I sent out two men with instructions to signal us if they found everything all right. Well, they went. We saw them go up out of the water, up the bank and disappear without giving us a sign. We waited and waited, but no signal came, and we concluded they had gone in search of a good square meal, for we were nearly starved. We thought it a mean trick anyway. After waiting a long time in suspense, and expressing hearty indignation at the greedy trick of those fellows, I thought I would go across, and I pledged my comrades that I would not leave them as the others had done. Upon reaching the bank of the river I noticed that the road had been cut down through the bank, making quite a deep cut, and directly across the road at the top of the hill some one, at some stage in the war, had dug a rifle pit. I was quietly speculating with myself as to whether I would have any trouble in getting my horse across the rifle-pit when a low voice, nearly over my head sounded in my ears. "Halt!" I looked up and saw lying on the top of the bank along the cut, a sergeant with a half dozen men, all covering me with their carbines. "All right, Johnny, come in out of the wet. You may just throw down what arms you have and then ride right up over the hill and you will be cared for. If you do as I say you will be

all right, but if you turn around or make any sign to those fellows over on the island, you will be in a bad fix. Don't make any noise, Johnny. We will treat you well, only do as I say." Of course there was nothing else for me to do, and I rode over the hill as my two men had done before me, without making a sign to my anxious comrades on the island. . . . I ſtaid there until afternoon and had the mortification of seeing my whole battery, about eighty in number taken in the same way . . . like turkeys walking into a pen . . . . In the afternoon Captain Dunn and his company were relieved and went to headquarters at Newton, of course taking us along.

SHARING
RATIONS
WITH
CONFEDERATES
PL. 24

At headquarters, the Confederate major asked Colonel Trowbridge if his men would be permitted to spend the night with nearby friends. Trowbridge assented and left no guard but asked them to report in the morning. The next day the members of the captured battery were furnished with animals for transportation and their side arms were reſtored. The major concluded, "You bade us good-bye with a hearty wish for our future happiness. The effeċt of such kindness on men as dispirited and broken in hopes and ex-peċtations as we were, can not be described."[10] Shortly af-terwards Dunn was named Inspeċtor of the 1ſt Brigade, 1ſt Cavalry Division, Department of the Cumberland.

NOT QUITE HOME

Private Quincy C. Lamoreaux of Manlius Township died in Plainwell on April 25, 1865, on his way home after be-ing released from a southern prison on March 1, 1865. The Plainwell correspondent to the *Allegan Journal* reported in the May 2, 1865, issue:

> He came here about a month ago, a paroled prisoner from the South and was on his way home, but was taken so seriously ill that he could proceed no farther on his journey. He had been in Southern prisons for 8 months, being changed from one to another, and had suffered all the horrors imaginable and was a mere skeleton when he arrived here.

He was the middle of three sons of Thomas and Abigail Lamoreaux who served in the Civil War. The oldeſt, Isaac,

1861 1862 1863 1864 1865 AFTER THE WAR

enlisted as a lieutenant with Co. L of the 4th Michigan Cavalry, but he had resigned his commission and returned to the family farm in March of 1863, after the death of his father. The youngest, Lyman, was a private in the 28th Michigan Infantry. Although they were the sons of farmers, the next generation was attracted to the lumbering business. On the 1860 census both Quincy and his older brother, Gilbert, are described as "sawyers" and another brother lists his occupation as "lumberman." Quincy was working as a sawyer in a mill in Pentwater when he enlisted in the 8th Michigan Infantry on August 24, 1861, at the age of 24.

Following Lee's surrender, Nelson W. Ogden, a drummer with the 28th Michigan Infantry, wrote from camp near Raleigh, North Carolina on April 26, 1865:

> I would like to stay at this place until our time is out, for this is a very nice city. It is very shady all over. We get plenty of rations all of the time. Johnston has not surrendered and won't for he don't like our terms. He offers to come under like Lee did but Grant & Johnson says that he must surrender unconditionally so I don't know how they will fix it unless we give them some cold iron and lead that will make them come to terms. Johnston has about 30,000 men and we have 150,000 to 175,000 on this side of them and Stoneman is on another side of them and the Army of the Potomac on another and Sheridan is about — somewhere.[11]

EXPLOSION ABOARD THE SULTANA

On April 27, 1865, more than 1,500 passengers, mostly released Union prisoners northward bound, were killed by the explosion and sinking of the steamer Sultana on the Mississippi River. Near the end of the war the Confederacy had agreed to move prisons to camps within territory controlled by the north. There they could be administered by the Confederates but would benefit from supplies of food and medicine furnished by the Federal government. Camp Fisk on the Big Black River, six miles from Vicksburg, was one of these. Prisoners were brought in by rail, mainly from the Confederate prison in Cahaba, Alabama. When word

SULTANA
PL. 25

1861

1862

1863

1864

1865

AFTER THE WAR

181

came that they had been freed they were moved to the river to be transported up the Mississippi to Cairo, Illinois, and then to Camp Chase in Columbus, Ohio.

Despite the presence of other boats that could have taken the excess, more than 2,000 passengers were crammed aboard the Steamship Sultana, a vessel that was rated for no more than 376 passengers. Traveling upStream againSt the spring floods with the vaSt weight of her human cargo overtaxed either a boiler that had been recently repaired, or one of the others. Eight miles north of Memphis, at 2 a.m., there was a tremendous explosion as one boiler burSt, followed by two others. The pilot house and cabins were shattered and support timbers cracked and crumbled. Men who survived the explosion jumped or were thrown into the water from the burning ship and fought each other in a panic.

A few escaped from the masses by swimming or hanging onto something that would float, even dead animals, until they were rescued. More than 1,000, moStly soldiers, were killed outright. About 520 were hospitalized after rescue and more than 200 of these died. No one knows the total of the men loSt that night, but the generally agreed on figure is in excess of 1,500. Among the dead was John A. Kinney of the 8th Michigan Cavalry, who had been taken prisoner at Dandridge, Tennessee, on January 19, 1864, and spent more than a year in Confederate prisons. He had enliSted on December 2, 1862, at Saugatuck at the age of 23.

THE CAPTURE OF JEFFERSON DAVIS

Jefferson Davis, the President of the Confederate States, his family, and some government officials were captured on May 10, 1865, near Irwinsville, Georgia by a segment of the 4th Michigan Cavalry under the command of Lieutenant Colonel Benjamin D. Pritchard of Allegan. Pritchard had left Macon on May 7 to take possession of ferries and scout the country for the purpose of capturing the Davis party. At 4 p.m. on May 9, he reached Abbyville and was told that a train of wagons had passed that way about midnight the previous night. He picked 128 men and seven officers to

B. PRITCHARD
BACK 31

continue the pursuit. The column arrived in Irwinville at about 1 a.m. on the 10th. As Pritchard later wrote:

> Here, passing my command as Confederate and in-
> quiring for "our train," representing that we were
> the rear guard left to fight back the Yankees, etc. I
> learned from the inhabitants that a train and party
> meeting the description of the one reported to me
> at Abbyville had encamped about dark, the night
> previous about 1 ½ miles out on the Abbyville road. I
> at once turned the head of my column in that direc-
> tion, impressing a negro for a guide.[12]

They arrived at the campsite in the darkness and sent 25 men on foot to surround the camp as they waited for the first light of dawn. Then the Union men crept forward and "were able to approach within four or five rods of the camp un-discovered, when a dash was ordered, and in an instant the whole camp with its inmates, was ours. A chain of mounted guards was immediately thrown around the camp and dis-mounted sentries were placed at the tents and wagons."

When the camp was charged by Pritchard's men, most of the inhabitants were still asleep. Shortly after guards were established, a Wisconsin regiment, which was also on the trail of the fleeing Rebel officials, approached from anoth-er direction and in the darkness mistook the 4th Cavalry men for Confederate guards. Leaving the guards in place Pritchard sped off to straighten things out. According to a narrative later written by Levi Tuttle of Saugatuck:

> During the time Col. Pritchard left this camp . . .
> to learn the cause of the firing upon his men, the
> request was made by Mrs. Davis to let her mother
> go to the branch for water. She came to the tent
> door after Mr. Davis, with tin pail in hand, had
> stepped out, when the guard discovered the boots
> that showed him to be a man; he was then halted.
> Then it was that Davis asked, "Is there a man among
> you?" when Mr. Munger answers, "Yes, I am one
> and if you move I will blow your brains out." About
> that time Col. Pritchard came up and Davis turned
> to him and asked if he was in command. He replied

1861

1862

1863

1864

1865

AFTER THE WAR

183

he was, when Davis remarked, "I suppose you think it is bravery to hunt down women and children, but I consider it vandalism and theft." Col. Pritchard then asked him, "Whom have I the honor to address?" when Davis replied, "You can call me what you are a mind to." Col. Pritchard then told him he would call him Jeff Davis, when he acknowledged that to be his name.[13]

When Davis had left the tent, pail in hand, he was wearing a waterproof sleeveless raglan which was similar to the one Davis himself wore, but which happened to be his wife's. As he left the tent that morning, she threw a black shawl about him. There was much editorial comment later in the nation's press about whether the waterproof and shawl were donned in a true attempt at deception or were just what the fleeing man could lay his hands on in the fervor of the moment. ¶ Pritchard gave his opinion in an 1889 interview:

JEFFERSON
DAVIS
CAPTURE
PL. 26

> It has never been denied that he [Davis] was dressed in his ordinary clothing at the time of his capture, but it is claimed that over his ordinary suit were worn articles of female attire, adopted by him as a disguise, with the purpose of eluding his pursuers by reason of the immunity from personal arrest and detention usually accorded to women under whatever circumstances they may be found; and there can be no more doubt that Mr. Davis was so disguised than there can be that he was captured at all, and the story of his disguise is no fabrication, as has been claimed years after his capture, but it was related to me within ten minutes after its occurrence by men whose veracity can not be questioned.[14]

Pritchard was later asked for a specific list of the men present at the capture of Davis and the list included Corporal William M. Oliver, a Saugatuck farmer, and Sergeant Benjamin K. Colf, who had enlisted at the age of 18, straight from his father's farm in western Manlius Township. Both were members of Co. L. Although his name is not on the list, Sergeant Levi Tuttle of the same company was known locally for being a part of the capturing party. He had only returned to the regiment on April 2, 1865, having recovered from the saber wound sustained at Noonday Church in June, 1864. His military records show that he was on de-

TRANSPORTING
DAVIS TO PRISON
PL. 27

1861
1862
1863
1864
1865
AFTER THE WAR

184

tached service with Colonel Pritchard. ¶ Records also show that Tuttle was part of a detail of 22 men which was charged with accompanying the Davis party to Fortress Monroe at the mouth of Chesapeake Bay. On May 12, they encamped near an old church and posted extra guards, according to Lieutenant Henry Albert Potter, "This being the last night before coming into town some thought Davis would try to escape. The guards were doubled and every precaution taken against surprise – but nothing of the kind."15 The next day they traveled from Macon to Augusta, Georgia, by train where they connected with a steamer in the Savannah River which took them to Savannah. From there they traveled by the steamer Wm. P. Clyde to Fortress Monroe and anchored for three days while accommodations were readied for the prisoners. Tuttle later described the transfer into the Fort:

> After the casemate for the safe guarding of the prisoner was ready Gen. Halleck [sic] came down from Washington and Gen. Miles who was in command at Fortress Monroe, came aboard the Clyde. There was a tug brought alongside whose upper deck was even with the lower deck of the Clyde. One half of the special guard was marched to the upper deck of this tug and stood at about face when Gens. Halleck and Miles, with the prisoners Davis and C. C. Clay, marched aboard followed by the balance of the special guard, and in this manner the transfer was made from our boat to the docks at Fortress Monroe. From there we formed around them and marched around to water battery when entrance to the Fort was made.16

Clay, a former U. S senator, had served as an envoy for the Confederate government and was suspected of being involved in the death of President Lincoln. Informed of the accusations, he turned himself in. He was later cleared. The guards from the 4th Michigan Cavalry were given quarters near the prisoners at the fortress and remained there for several days. ¶ In an account that Tuttle later wrote for the Saugatuck newspaper, he indicates that he was part of a detail which on March 23 received orders from the war department through General Miles to visit Mrs. Davis who was ſtill on the ſteamer Clyde, to obtain the lady's water-proof cloak which had been worn by Davis as a disguise at the time of his capture, and which was identified by the men who saw it on him at the time. On the following morning the balance of the disguise was procured. It was a shawl, which was identified and admitted to be the one worn by Davis. These articles were taken to Washington and turned over to the Secretary of War.

CELEBRATING THE VICTORY

Even before the final surrender in the weſt a two-day Grand Review of Union soldiers was held on Pennsylvania Avenue in Washington. In the reviewing ſtand were President Andrew Johnson and his cabinet and ſtaff along with such high-ranking members of the military who were not, at the moment, in the line of march. On May 23, 1865, marchers were veterans of the Virginia campaign, including Michigan's 1ſt, 2nd, 5th, 7th, 8th, 16th, 17th, 20th, 26th and 27th Michigan Infantry Regiments, the Michigan Cavalry Brigade and the 1ſt Michigan Sharpshooters. ¶ General Cuſter was riding a bay thoroughbred named Don Juan, and he was finely dressed for the occasion in a dark blue blouse, red necktie, jet black boots, and gold spurs said to have been worn by Santa Anna at the siege of the Alamo, white gauntlets and a black turn-up hat. The feiſty Don Juan was ſtartled by flowers tossed by adoring ladies at the general and bolted as they neared the reviewing ſtand. When Cuſter tried to raise his sword in salute as he passed at a gallop he succeeded in knocking his hat off. Finally he dropped the sword and used both hands to bring his mount under control. A friend, Lieutenant Fred Dent Grant, General Grant's eldeſt son, retrieved the sword and the hat, and Cuſter doubled back and repassed the president and the other dignitaries assembled in a more sedate manner.

GRAND REVIEW PL. 28 On the following day, May 24, 1865, the Grand Review was held for the armies of the Weſt, or at leaſt those regiments which were no longer engaged and could get to Washington. These included the 10th, 13th, 14th, 15th, 19th, and 21ſt

186

1861 1862 1863 1864 1865 AFTER THE WAR

Michigan Infantry Regiments and Batteries B and C of the Michigan Light Artillery.

THE AREA'S CONFEDERATE PRIVATE

On the day after the Grand Review in Washington, the last semblance of Confederate armed force disappeared with the surrender of New Orleans to General Edward R. Canby on May 26, 1865. One soldier being surrendered was Andrew Plummer, the son of Benjamin and Elvira Plummer, who had come to Allegan County in 1834 and built a sawmill at the outlet of Goshorn Lake. Andrew was the first white child born in Saugatuck Township to survive to adulthood. He had left Michigan in 1856 for Minnesota and then wandered south, settling in Texas about 1860. ¶ According to the 1890 veteran's census, Plummer was "Pressed into Confederate service and kept in shop in Texas until close of war." In May of 1862, "A. Plummer, Allegan Co., Michigan" turns up on the rolls of the 7th Texas Infantry. The regiment had an active war from Tennessee to Georgia, and the main body of men was surrendered at Durham Station, North Carolina, April 26, 1865. That Plummer became a prisoner of war at the time of the New Orleans surrender, when all remaining Confederate soldiers were formally surrendered to the Federal troops, supports the claim that he was "kept in Texas" and did not actively participate with the regiment in the field. The family had not heard from him for several years and thought that he had died. It was a big surprise when he returned to Ganges Township after the war. Plummer eventually owned a 100 acre farm including both fruit trees and general farming. He died in 1917. Most of the Western Allegan County Plummers of today are descended from him.

PLUMMER
RECORD
AND
PLUMMER
FARM
PLS. 29 & 30

A SOLDIER'S VIEWS OF RECONSTRUCTION

Alfred Wallin, the lawyer turned soldier, pondered the task of reconstruction before the nation and in a letter dated May 4, 1865, wrote his father:

A. WALLIN
BACK 32

> In common with the intelligent men both North and South, I presume you are thinking of how (to

use the words of the late lamented President) to bring the Rebel States back to their practical relations with the government. I see Gen. Butler has elaborated a scheme and evolved it in a recent speech . . . it is much too severe in my judgment. The North needs no securities against future revolts other than those which the abolition of slavery and banishment of the chief conspirators secures. If the people, so long accustomed to self-government, are balked and embarrassed at every stage of their reorganization, their existence will be intolerable, even if they are allowed to keep their lands . . . . ¶ The people, white and black, after being relieved of the incubus of slavery and the domination of certain unscrupulous leaders need only to be let alone, and discreetly assisted to grow wiser. They must be made wiser. They will not take kindly to schooling at first, and if harshly dealt with they may never learn, but either continue among us as an element of discontent and strife, or emigrate, or in some way disappear before their more powerful foes. ¶ History has a number of parallels to our present national crisis. After a war the question always arises what shall be done with the spoils, and to what extent shall the conquered people be punished. I believe that whenever in history the victors have dealt out sweeping measures of vengeance under the guise of retributive justice, such measures have recoiled with dreadful visitations upon those who have forgotten in justice to remember mercy. [17]

188

Wallin served out his term of service and returned to the practice of law, first in Minnesota and, in 1883, in Fargo, North Dakota. In 1889 he was elected as a Judge of the Supreme Court of North Dakota, a position he held until progressive deafness caused his retirement from the bench in 1902. Wallin died in California in 1923.

NOT ALL SOLDIERS WERE SENT STRAIGHT HOME from the Civil War after the conclusion of the fighting. Some units were detailed to guard Southern cities and railroads to make sure that Southern guerrillas did not continue the battle. Others, especially the cavalry units, were sent out West to do battle with the Indians. The 5th Michigan Cavalry was mustered out at Fort Leavenworth, Kansas, near the end of June, 1865, but men of the 3rd Michigan Cavalry were held in service until February of 1866, when they were finally mustered out at San Antonio, Texas, and required to make their own way back to Michigan.

SOME NEVER DID GET "HOME"

Some soldiers chose to remain in the communities where they had been stationed. James G. Butler, son of Saugatuck's founder, sent in a request on February 12, 1866, that he "be mustered out of service and receive final discharge and payment at San Antonio, Texas," stating that he was not requesting this privilege "for the purpose only of receiving from the government additional pay in the nature of traveling allowances" but because he "desires in good faith to remain in the south." Apparently other soldiers had made similar requests so that the traveling allowance would be paid to them in cash. After a visit to Michigan, where he was married to Margaret Leggat of Grand Haven, on October 15, 1868, the couple settled in St. Louis, Missouri, where Butler became a director of the American Tobacco Company and the Mercantile National Bank. Only one visit to Saugatuck is recorded in the weekly newspaper. In 1892, the couple returned for the dedication of the tall pylon that marks the grave of James' father, William G. Butler, and his three wives, in Riverside Cemetery, Saugatuck. James G. Butler died August 22, 1916, and is buried in St. Louis. ¶ Butler's counterpart, George N. Dutcher, son of William F. Dutcher, founder of Douglas, had been discharged from service for disability in 1863. After further work as an engineer on the Northern Missouri Railroad, he returned to Michigan and Chicago, according to an 1892 biography, "shattered in health and still suffering from his wounds."[1] His doctor told him that a sea voyage would do him good, so, after a visit to relatives in Pennsylvania and New York, he embarked May 23, 1869, on the whaling ship Florida. A journal kept by Dutcher relates adventurous tales of shipwreck near Africa, mutiny near Australia, an interlude in San Francisco and a return trip across the isthmus of Panama, finally arriving in Buffalo, New York, on September 29, 1870.[2] Dutcher worked in Chicago until 1894 when he returned to Douglas and lived in a small white house on Union Street. He died in April of 1909 and is buried in the Douglas Cemetery.

AN EDUCATION ON THE MARCH

DR. PARRISH
BACK 33

Although the 1860 census had described John P. Parrish of the 6th Michigan Infantry as a physician, he probably had received very little training. The Civil War would be his university. He had enlisted as a wagoneer but his medical work began with the nursing of his son, who suffered pneumonia on the march south. Parrish was then put in charge of all of the sick members of the company, eventually being named wardmaster of the hospital. After his unit arrived in Louisiana he took on the duties of cooking for the hospital where he ate with the surgeons and learned from their conversation. He did his job so well, and was enjoyed as a conversationalist, that when the dining group decided to charge each member extra for non-issue food obtained, the others agreed to pay Parrish's fee. The head surgeon, Dr. Milton Chase of Otsego, wrote in 1874:

> Dr. John Parrish, a private of Company G, from this county, and now a resident of this county, had more ingenuity in cooking for the sick than both of the women had. He could get up twenty different and palatable dishes out of hard tack and bacon, and he would make something out of them for the most delicate stomach. He was an old man, and as near the perfect Christian as any man I ever knew. There was no man in the regiment of more value to the sick during the three years he was with it than he was. He was always cheerful, always hopeful, always willing to do what he was told to do and was never at his wits' end . . . . A woman could not cook by an out-of-doors fire with green cottonwood, but Doctor Parrish could.[3]

In August of 1863 Parrish was relieved of his pots and pans and given the position of pharmacist in the regimental dispensary where he handed out medicine, making most of his own pills. He also acquired a medical book "that has a good many things in it."[4] Parrish was mustered out August

1861

1862

1863

1864

1865

AFTER THE WAR

191

23, 1864, and returned to Allegan County where he served as school inspector and Pine Plains Township clerk in 1865 before moving to Pier Cove where he hung out his shingle as a physician. Before 1880 he moved to Van Buren County, locating in Irvington, the north portion of the settlement later called Lacota, where he opened an office at the corner of Baseline Road and Broadway (later called Main Street). Parrish died March 9, 1906, and was buried in the Lacota Cemetery. ¶ As the soldiers returned home from the battlefield, it did not take long for yesterday's privations and horror to fade into the background and their military service to become today's fond memories. Printers created elegant certificates on which soldiers could record the highlights of their service. The *Allegan Journal* of December 26, 1879, announced that Lieutenant William White had received "an elegant certificate of life membership of the Andersonville Survivors Association" and goes on to note, "Mr White was a prisoner in that southern prison for one year and escaped in a better condition than the majority of the sufferers who endured its torments." Shortly after the war he gave up farming near Peach Belt and moved to a house he called Kalamont which still stands on Randolph Street in Douglas. Over the piano in the parlor he hung a large engraving of Andersonville Prison as a remembrance.

A REBEL FLAG IN THE PUBLIC SQUARE

Old enmity between the sections of the country did not end overnight. An incident occurred in Saugatuck on the 4th of July, 1870, which was indicative of the times. The July 9, 1870, *Saugatuck Commercial* reported:

> Probably but few of those who were in town on the 4th knew that some cowardly puppy hoisted a rebel flag upon the staff in the Public Square. We cannot see how any human being can so lose all sense of honor, as to offer so mean an insult to the friends of the dead, an insult more bitter because the cause for which they fought is lost forever. The people of the South, some of them at least, believe they were right, and now acknowledge their defeat. It is unmanly to

keep their wounds open by referring to them in an unkind spirit. ¶ The flag has two broad stripes of red, with one of white between; in the upper corner is a broad field of blue with seven stars. Upon the red strips are printed the words – Vicksburg, Gettsyburg, Cedar Springs, Atlanta, Shenandoah Valley, Libby Prison, Andersonville, Wirtz and J. Wilkes Booth. Upon the white stripe, looking as if sketched with a scoop shovel and engraved with a plow, is a picture of Jeff Davis, as he appeared when circumstances and the Michigan boys made it advisable for him to go away in his wife's clothes. In mockery this shabby imitation of a flag was hoisted half mast, a sign usually, of sorrow and sympathy, but in this case a proof of devilish rejoicing over those who lost friends, brothers, fathers, lovers, good name and honor, in a vain attempt to destroy our country.

Two weeks later when Walter Philbrooks, a clerk in the O. R. Johnson store who had lived many years in the south, shot, and apparently killed, a man who he said had threatened him, the speculation quickly shifted to the idea that instead of trying to embarrass the southerners, the flag had been hoisted on the staff by someone, namely Philbrooks, trying to revive the Southern cause. ¶ After the shooting, which took place outside the Johnson store in downtown Saugatuck, on Water Street, the editor, who was himself an eyewitness, wrote:

> . . . a low hoarse murmur ran through the crowd, gathering force as it grew, until from every hand came cries for justice. 'Bring out the coward! Shoot the secession scoundrel who comes here to insult us with his rebel flags. Lynch the traitor, the murderer, the Southern hound . . . '

However, cooler heads prevailed and Philbrooks was taken first to the Saugatuck post office where "the crowd surged about the doors and glass windows and threatened each instant to tear the building to pieces" and then to the jail in Allegan. ¶ The case was dampened when the injured man did not die but rallied. The Allegan newspaper was also careful to point out that Philbrooks had seen no military service, had not "shot many a blue coat" as the Saugatuck

1861   1862   1863   1864   1865   AFTER THE WAR

193

editor claimed, and had, in fact, been only a clerk in the Confederate Treasury Department at Richmond. The clincher came when a Saugatuck restaurant worker took the blame for raising the rebel flag on the 4th of July. Philbrooks was found innocent at the trial, but the incident shows how easy it was to expect the worst from those who had formerly been "the enemy," even six years after the surrender.

ON THE MOVE AFTER THE WAR

On May 20, 1862, President Lincoln had signed the Homestead Act, which stated that any citizen at least 21 and head of a family could obtain up to 160 acres of unoccupied government land by living on land and cultivating it continuously for 5 years or get clear title at any time after six months by paying the minimum government price. Southern states had opposed this idea since 1854. The bill became effective January 1, 1863, and Michigan, which had large tracts of unoccupied land, benefited more than most states. More than 2,500,000 acres were homesteaded.

Many of the Civil War veterans, having seen a part of the country beyond their home county, returned from the war with a wanderlust for new places and experiences. There was a marked influx in the Saugatuck-Ganges area of veterans from New York, Pennsylvania, Massachusetts, Ohio and Indiana looking for new homes in Michigan. A letter from a Saugatuck correspondent to the *Allegan Journal* was dated February 14, 1866:

> The prospects for this place for the next few years are quite flattering. Indeed there is no point in Western Michigan where are better or more favorable opportunities for investing money with a prospect of a larger return of profits than here. The fact that the Harbor Improvement question is settled and the work to be commenced without delay has stimulated a spirit of enterprise which is manifesting itself by adding permanent improvements to the place and with the increased immigration already pouring in upon us we find that more room is needed, and I understand that our worthy townsman, Stephen

A. Morrison is intending to vacate a portion of his valuable farm, platting it into Village lots. Mr. E. Judson is intending to vacate a part of his farm for the same purpose, thereby giving to the new comer a chance to locate where it may beſt suit him.[5]

SAUGATUCK MAP
1873
PL. 6.2

The correspondent concluded that Saugatuck only lacked "a good foundry for caſting agricultural implements," "a machine shop," "a ſtock of Hardware" (a need that would soon be filled by returning veteran John Nies), and "a merchant tailor to clothe our people for which a fair remuneration would be cheerfully given."

1861

1862

1863

1864

1865

SISTER VILLAGES: DOUGLAS AND DUDLEYVILLE

The communities south of the river were less than a decade old when the war began. The same, or another correspondent in a letter dated February 12, 1866, described them and had some advice to offer:

> To our ſiſter villages across the little lake I would call your attention. Douglasville [sic] and Dudleyville with three ſtores and mills and tannery are operating upon a large scale. T. B. Dutcher's company is doing a big business, so are Messrs. Carpenter & Conger, Messrs. Gerber & Schenck drive a large Tannery. It also affords some of the beſt mechanics in the State. It has a well regulated Hotel owned by Jonathan Wade, who is well calculated to run a firſt-class Hotel and please the public generally. These two villages in the opinion of your correspondent should be consolidated and have a Poſt-office. I for one would hold up both hands for it. Saugatuckians are in for it generally.[6]

AFTER THE WAR

195

The Douglas poſt office was opened March 27, 1866, (although it was on the Dudleyville side of Center Street), and the two settlements were incorporated as the Village of Douglas on Oſtober 14, 1870.

HEADING WEST

At the same time that Eaſtern veterans were moving in, some native Saugatuck-Ganges men were traveling farther weſt. Hiram R. Ellis of the 28th Michigan Infantry, and former druggiſt George H. Harris left for the business opportunities of Chicago; Alfred Wallin went to Minnesota, then North Dakota, and finally California; Caleb A. Ensign, who had been the first president of the Village of Douglas, left for Chicago in 1877 and moved on to California in 1888; Samuel Buchanan Anacortes, of the 17th Michigan Infantry left for Washington State, and James G. Butler, of the 4th Michigan Cavalry settled in St. Louis. ¶ The country seemed a much smaller place after the war. The children of veteran Walter Billings of the 8th Michigan Cavalry were part of the westward movement, settling in Iowa, Kansas, Nebraska, Dakota and Indian Territory. After the death of his wife, Billings made several trips out west, visiting each offspring in turn. Henry Hudson Hutchins wrote that Billings, with his horse named Billy and a dog he called Watchie My Son, made the trip, sometimes two or three times in one year, "camping out nights the same as in soldier life." Billings used the same horse but was obliged to provide a new buggy for each trip.[7]

W. BILLINGS
BACK 26

REUNIONS KEEP THE MEMORIES ALIVE

REUNION
RIBBONS
PL. 33

Reunions were a popular pastime for years after the end of the war. The August 13, 1886, *Lakeshore Commercial* reports on a reunion held at Saugatuck of :

CO. I , FIFTH MICHIGAN CALVARY.

The above Company was recruited in August, 1862, by W. B. Williams , who now resides at Allegan, and who was chosen captain. Being unable to endure the rigors of the service, Capt Williams resigned the position and was succeeded by Geo N. Dutcher , now of Chicago. Subsequently Dutcher was wounded and furloughed and the captaincy of the company fell upon the shoulders of Chas H. Safford. At the recent reunion held in our village, seventeen of the surviving members of this company were present, and singularly enough all three of the above mentioned officers. None of these members had seen Captain Safford since the close of the war, 22 years ago, and more than one bronzed face was wet with tears of joy at meeting him on this occasion. Capt Safford lives at present at Black River, Alcona Co., this state, and came to Saugatuck on purpose to meet his old comrades. He is a pleasant and fine appearing man, as may also be said of his two predecessors.

Attending the reunion were: Captain William B. Williams, Captain George N. Dutcher, Captain Charles H. Safford, Lieutenant William White, Anthony Slack of Douglas, Frank Miller, Samuel Shaver of Saugatuck, Henry Werner, Hannibal Hart, Lafayette Fox, George E. Munn, George W. Lonsbury of Allegan, William McWilliams, Henry Zoermann, William H. Dunn of Ganges, Sam Clark, and Raphael Ross. ¶ Some of the same old soldiers gathered in 1919 at the residence of Mr. and Mrs. W. G Tisdale on the west shore of Lake Kalamazoo, with Mrs. Tisdale's father, Lieutenant. William White, as co-host. According to the Saugatuck newspaper, "At each plate was a silk souvenir necktie in remembrance of the Custer Brigade of which Mr. White and William H. Dunn were members. The banquet featured the army rations of 1861-65 consisting largely of coffee, beans, crackers and doughnuts gotten up and served in such an attractive style by Mrs. Tisdale as to leave the guests under the impression they were partaking of a six course dinner." [8]

MONUMENTS

Both sides of Allegan County undertook efforts to create monuments honoring the men of the county for their service during the war. In Allegan the effort was organized on November 17, 1889, "by the patriotic women of the community." Their stated aim was "to erect a suitable soldiers' monument." Funds increased only slowly, and it was 14 years before enough funds were in hand to let the contract for the monument. The cornerstone was laid on Decoration Day, 1903, and the stone shaft soon after erected. The Allegan County Board of Supervisors appropriated $600 for a "suitable figure" and the completed monument was dedicated Decoration Day, 1904. ¶ On the west side of the county the Woman's Soldiers Monument Society of Ganges was formed and began to raise money for the erection of a monument in Taylor Cemetery. One project created

ALLEGAN
MONUMENT
PL. 6.5

a signature quilt that was raffled off and won by Lillian Grimes Eddy of Douglas, formerly of Ganges. Many of the signatures on the quilt were Civil War veterans and include their regiment and company. The base of the monument was dedicated on Decoration Day, 1902, with General B. D. Pritchard of Allegan offering the address. The contract for the statue on the top was awarded to E. A. Bovee of the Grand Rapids Monument Company and it was in place for the dedication of the completed monument on May 30, 1906. The Ganges monument also includes, on the sides of the base, lists of men from the area who served in the Civil War as well as members of the Ganges G.A.R. post.

GANGES
MONUMENT
PL. 35

MARKING THE GRAVES

As part of their benefits, each veteran was entitled to a government-furnished tombstone which included the soldier's name, rank and unit. The first of these headstones arrived in October of 1888. ¶ Andrew Bee of Co. L, 4th Michigan Cavalry, died at his home in Martin Township on September 15, 1894. Bee was one of the group of Michigan soldiers who participated in the capture of Confederate President Jefferson Davis and is said to have been the first to recognize the president of the Confederacy in his disguise. He was buried in the Martin Cemetery, and a gravestone erected over his grave reads, "First man to lay hands on Jeff Davis at his capture." ¶ After the war there was a scramble to find the graves of loved ones who were killed on the battlefield or died of disease. Although bodies were frequently interred on the field where they fell, there was an effort to rebury them in an orderly fashion as soon as possible. National cemeteries sprang up in the vicinity of major encampments or battlefields; however, the record keeping under wartime conditions was not always reliable. ¶ Elmon Lafayette Raplee, the son of Private Madison Raplee of the 4th Michigan Cavalry, who was only two when his father died of measles at Nashville, Tennessee, tried to locate his father's grave, but was not successful. The task was taken up by his daughters, Alice May (Raplee) Wight-

RAPLEE
GRAVE
PL. 36

198

man and Gertrude (Raplee) Van Hartesveldt of Fennville, who were similarly unsuccessful. Finally a granddaughter, May (Wightman) Winne, applied pressure through Congressman Guy VanderJagt's office, and the record keepers discovered that the handwritten name "Raplee" had been misread as "Bipler." A new stone with the name correctly spelled was ordered for his grave in the National Cemetery in Nashville. "It was about 70 years too late for my grandfather to know," the granddaughter pointed out.

THE GRAND ARMY OF THE REPUBLIC

Even before the end of the war, the veterans had formed an organization called the Grand Army of the Republic (G. A. R.) and posts were set up around the country. There were 14 posts in Allegan County alone. The posts in each state were numbered according to the date of formation. Local posts included W. G. Eaton #34 in Otsego, Jacob G. Fry #46 in Ganges, and C. J. Bassett #56 in Allegan, which were among the earliest. The George N. Dutcher #148 in Douglas was chartered June 6, 1863, but changed its name frequently. It was called the John Kirby post until 1884, when the reports were filed under the name Peter Van Arsdale, before returning to the name John Kirby which was still being used when the post made its last report in 1895. The post in Fennville was named for A. H. Fenn #371. ¶ For some reason, Saugatuck was very late in organizing its Civil War veterans, a task it did not begin until 1903. The men most active in organization of the post were Richard Baker, who had served with the 22nd New York Cavalry, and Joseph E. Cohenour, formerly of the 34th Illinois Infantry, both recently-arrived in Allegan County. General Benjamin Pritchard of Allegan was the mustering-in officer. The post became the James M. Pond #460, although G.A.R. records show that Saugatuck was earlier served by the Nahum Gilbert Post #422. James M. Pond had risen to the rank of acting captain with the 18th Massachusetts Infantry. He moved to Saugatuck after the war and held several public offices including that of chief engineer of the

Saugatuck Fire Department at its organization in 1873. ¶ The G. A. R. was a potent political force for many years, especially concerning veterans' rights. The final encampment of the national organization was held in 1949 at Indianapolis. Only six surviving Civil War veterans were able to attend.

MEMORIAL DAY IN GANGES

GANGES
PARADE
AND
BAND
PLS. 37 & 38

With so many Civil War veterans in Ganges Township, Memorial Day (first called Decoration Day because it was the day the graves were decorated with flowers) was always celebrated with enthusiasm. Treva (Miller) McKeown, whose grandfather, Adam Miller, was both a Civil War veteran and a member of the Ganges band, wrote:

1861
1862
1863
1864
1865

AFTER THE WAR

200

> About the years 1906 to 1912 Civil War veterans were guests of honor at the Memorial Day services at the Ganges Methodist Church. After the benediction and tributes to those tired old men. and a program of local talent, including the reading of the "Gettysburg Address," all who cared to "marched" to the Taylor Cemetery. On one such occasion that I remember vividly Major W. H. Dunn, a veteran cavalry officer, decided to ride a horse in the procession. As the assemblage was being organized, Major Dunn rode up on a fine looking well-groomed horse. Everything went well until the horse became excited and thrashed about and became unruly. For a few minutes much concern was felt for the elderly rider, and all those standing nearby, but with the good horsemanship of Major Dunn, and the aid of several men, the horse was quieted down. The procession finally started with the accompaniment of our local Fife and Drum Corps, consisting of George Gaze on the fife, Marion Pressler on the bass drum and my father, Bertrand Miller, on the snare drum. After reaching the cemetery the children placed the lilac and snowball bouquets on the graves of veterans. [9]

THE VANISHING ARMY

James Hibberdine of the 17th Michigan Infantry was right about the effects of war on the health of those who enlisted. He returned from the war with chronic kidney problems and never fully recovered. He moved to Saugatuck, to the one-story house on the northeast corner of Allegan and Maple Streets, where he died in 1888 at the age of 60. He wrote a last letter to his family in England in 1876 which said in part:

> What a checkered life ours is to look back, many seasons of joy, many of disappointment and bereavement . . . . I still look for better brighter days but it will take some time to get started again, we are so badly torn to pieces . . . all I can do is the best I can.[10]

Anthony Slack, who served as a teamster in the 5th Michigan Cavalry, went to Monroe, Michigan, on June 4, 1910, for the unveiling of an equestrian statue erected in honor of General George Armstrong Custer. Slack was one of about 400 survivors of the old Michigan Cavalry Brigade which was given a place of honor in the parade and ceremonies. At Monroe, he suffered a paralytic stroke. After recuperating for a time on the east side of the state, he returned to the home of his daughter, Blanche (Slack) Ellis, on Ellis Street, Douglas, where he died July 10, 1915. ¶ William T. Kimsey, who had served as drum major for the 44th Indiana Infantry, attended "the great musical contest" at Soldier Field in Chicago, on August 23, 1930. Before 150,000 people he spoke over the radio stating, according to the August 29, 1930, *Commercial Record*, "that Douglas, Saugatuck and western Michigan were resort and scenic sections of the central west. He also gave some statements in regard to the battles of the Civil War that were received with much enthusiasm by that great audience. It was heard from coast to coast over the radio." He was chosen to play the long roll on the very drum that he had carried in the war, calling the troops into action at Fort Donelson, Shiloh, Stone River, Chickamauga and Nashville. ¶ He celebrated the 70th anniversary of the First Congregational Church of Saugatuck in July of 1930 with a demonstration of the long roll. Saugatuck historian May Francis Heath wrote, "The audience was deeply thrilled by this unusual demonstration; and

CUSTER
STATUE
PL. 39

CIVIL WAR
PARADE
PL. 40

1861 1862 1863 1864 1865 AFTER THE WAR

201

some of us didn't know that from so small a drum there could be brought forth such a tremendous volume of inspiring sound." [11] Kimsey moved from Saugatuck to Douglas in 1930. In October of 1932, at the age of 93, he attended the 53rd reunion of the old regiment at Fort Wayne, Indiana. Once again with the old drum he was paired with regimental fifer William H. Hannen, and there is a newspaper picture of the duo playing "war-time music." [12] Kimsey died two days later, on October 9, 1932, at his nephew's home in Fort Wayne. Piper Hannen accompanied the body back to Douglas for burial. ¶ At the Congregational church anniversary celebration in 1930 four old men, three of them Civil War veterans, staged what would be a "last parade." At the fore playing "spirited martial music" and "other patriotic tunes . . . with all the fervor of the battlefield"[13] was drummer William T. Kimsey, 92, and fifer William "Whistling Bill" Hasselgren. Major William H. Dunn of Ganges, 86, of the 10th Michigan Cavalry and Joshua Brown, 86, veteran of the 14th Illinois Cavalry served as color bearers. ¶ Joshua Brown, Saugatuck's last Civil War veteran, died on September 5, 1939, at the age of 95. He was born in Sheboygan, Wisconsin, and was so frail as a young man that doctors told him that he needed to find work in outdoors if he expected to live. In 1861 he enlisted in Co. M of the 14th Illinois Cavalry and served until the close of the war. Afterwards, he became a house painter and, from 1879 to 1880 served at the life-saving station in Ludington. He moved to Saugatuck in 1880 and resumed his work as a house painter and decorator. Brown built a home on the southeast corner of Griffith and Mason Streets in downtown Saugatuck that is still standing. ¶ The last Civil War veteran in Allegan County died in 1946. He was Ralph Towner, a Trowbridge Township farmer and letter carrier, who had enlisted in Co. F of the 186th New York Volunteers as a substitute in July, 1864. Towner moved to Michigan in 1871 and to Allegan County in 1872. At the time of his death the newspaper noted there were just four Civil War veterans living in Michigan, and only about 193 in the nation.

KIMSEY
CLIPPINGS
PLS. 41-43

44TH INDIANA
INFRANTRY
PL. 44

J. BROWN
BACK 35

1861 1862 1863 1864 1865

AFTER THE WAR

202

A LAST LOOK BACK BECOMES A LOOK FORWARD

In 1921, for the 56th reunion of the 1st Engineers and Mechanics regiment, Lieutenant Caleb A. Ensign, who had moved to California, summed up the soldiers' experiences in a letter:

LT. ENSIGN
BACK 36

Our ever present subconscious identity seems to continuously mirror back the days "when we were young" as but "yesterday;" the "scenes of youth" as but "tales just told!" But when reminiscently I try to picture again the form and face of the "old time friend," and to review the incidents of comradely services or even essay to speak the names of associates in achievements; or when I would recall notations of the events of the past years of my fellows of the War, and the various trends of their lives and work, which I have sometimes heard – what a "far look" is that which is impressed upon me thru the haze of Time Past! n¶ After all I take it, it is not the Past, that can make us most glad, tho we have therein somewhat whereof to glory, as that we have had, under God, a part "in preserving us a Nation," as did our forefathers in making it! Shall we not more rejoice that we are living in this ADVANCING AGE? And as we continue to FACE FORWARD we may ever find occasion to sing, "Mine eyes have seen the glory of the coming of the Lord!" and we shall sing in the gladness of hope for our children and the generations to come. [14]

VETERANS
BACK 37-46

1861 | 1862 | 1863 | 1864 | 1865 | AFTER THE WAR

203

1861   [1]   *Civil War Diary and Biography of George W. Bailey*, (G. R. Post: Colleyville, Texas) 1990. p. 99.

[2]   *Portrait and Biographical Record of Kalamazoo, Allegan & Van Buren Counties,* (Chapman Bros.: Kalamazoo) 1892.p. 249.

[3]   Bailey, p. 103.

[4]   *Official Record of the Union and Confederate Navies in the War of Rebellion,* Series I, Vol. 5 (Government Printing Office: Washington, D. C.) 1897, p. 729.

[4]   *Autobiography of Scott Wilmoth Eddy,* typescript, p. 2. Eddy Family Archives.

[5]   *Nies family in early Holland,* typescript, Ch. 1, p. 2, John Nies Collection, Holland Museum Archives and Research Library, Holland, Michigan.

[6]   William H. Parrish to Ira Parrish, October 27, 1861, Thayer-Parrish Family Archives.

[7]   James M. Ducomb to Maria Ducomb, November 20, 1861, Sheridan Family Archives.

[8]   John P. Parrish to Margaret Parrish, December 7, 1861, Thayer-Parrish Family Archives.

[9]   John P. Parrish to Margaret Parrish, March 4, 1864, Emma-Jean Hoag Collection.

1862   [1]   May Family Scrapbook, May-McManus Family Archives.

[2]   John P. Parrish to Margaret Parrish, June, 1863, Emma-Jean Hoag Collection.

[3]   William H. Parrish to Margaret Parrish, January 26, 1862, Thayer-Parrish Family Archives.

[4]   Nies, *Civil War Account of John Nies,* p. 2, John Nies Collection, Holland Museum Archives.

[5]   James M. Ducomb to Maria Ducomb, April 17, 1862, Sheridan Family Archives.

[6]   Nies, *Civil War Account,* p. 2, Holland Museum Archives.

[7]   Eddy, p. 4-5.

[8]   Eddy, p. 7.

[9]   *Allegan Journal,* May 26, 1862.

[10]   *Allegan Journal,* June 9, 1862.

[11]   John P. Parrish to Margaret Parrish, May 9, 1862, Emma-Jean Hoag Collection.

[12]   *Allegan Journal,* December 8, 1862.

[13]   *Official Records,* Series I, Vol 13, p. 75

[14]   *Allegan Journal,* April 21, 1862.

[15]   Nies, *Civil War Account,* p. 5, Holland Museum Archives.

[16]   *Allegan Journal,* September 1, 1862.

[17]   Henry Blakeslee to Irene Blakeslee, August 25, 1862, Crane Family Archives.

18 *Allegan Journal,* September 8, 1862.

19 *Allegan Journal,* October 6, 1862.

20 William H. Rockwell to Polly A. Rockwell, October 1, 1862. William H. Rockwell Collection, Western Michigan University Archives and Regional History Collections, Kalamazoo, Michigan.

21 Avery, James Henry, *Under Custer's Command: The Civil War Journal of James Henry Avery,* (Brassey's: Washington, D. C.) 2000, p.15.

22 John P. Parrish to Margaret Parrish, September 17, 1862, Emma-Jean Hoag Collection.

23 Henry Blakeslee to Irene Blakeslee, October 27, 1862, Crane Family Archives.

24 Henry Blakeslee to Irene Blakeslee, October 29, 1862, Crane Family Archives.

25 Obituary in the Billings family scrapbook, Kit Lane Collection.

26 *Allegan Journal,* December 29, 1862.

27 Crotty, Daniel G., *Four Years Campaigning in the Army of the Potomac* (Dygert Bros. & Co.: Grand Rapids) 1874. Reprinted in 1995 by Belle Grove Publishing Co., Kearny, New Jersey, p. 73.

28 William H. Rockwell to Polly A. Rockwell, March 7, 1863, WMU.

29 William Henry Parrish to Margaret Parrish, June 18, 1864, Thayer-Parrish Family Archives.

30 Ira Parrish to Margaret Parrish, August 3, 1863, Emma-Jean Hoag Collection.

31 Avery, p. 19.

32 *Allegan Journal,* January 19, 1863.

33 Henry Blakeslee to Irene Blakeslee, [November] 25, 1862, Crane Family Archives.

34 *Allegan Journal,* January 19, 1863.

35 Eddy, p. 11.

1863

1 Kidd, J. H., *Personal Recollections of a Cavalryman* (Sentinel Printing Company: Ionia) 1908. p. 75-76.

2 *Allegan Journal,* January 27, 1862.

3 William H. Rockwell to Polly A. Rockwell, January 4, 1863, WMU.

4 Henry Blakeslee to Irene Blakeslee, January 21, 1863, Crane Family Archives.

5 *1864 Annual Report of the Michigan Soldier's Relief Association.* Library of Michigan, Lansing.

6 Civil War Letters of Members of the Hardin Family, Allen County Public Library, Fort Wayne, Indiana.

7 Diary of Jacob Heringa, entry for January 28, 1863, Allegan County Historical Society, Allegan, Michigan.

8 Kidd, p. 90-1.

9 *Personal Reminiscences of Samuel Harris,* (The Ryerson Press: Chicago) 1897, Rare Book Room, Library of Michigan.

10 Henry Blakeslee to Irene Blakeslee, February 22, 1863, Crane Family Archives.

1863, cont'd.

11 *Allegan Journal*, April 20, 1863.

12 Henry Blakeslee to Irene Blakeslee, January 24, 1863, Crane Family Archives.

13 Judson L. Austin to wife, September 12, 1863, Judson L. Austin Collection, Michigan Historical Collections, Bentley Historical Library, University of Michigan, Ann Arbor.

14 John Nies to "mother and brothers," April 2, 1863, John Nies Collection, Holland Museum Archives and Research Library, Holland, Michigan.

15 Avery, p. 19-20.

16 Harris, p. 13.

17 William H. Rockwell to Polly A. Rockwell, April 17, 1863, WMU.

18 Bailey, p. 34-35.

19 Bailey, p. 48.

20 John P. Parrish to Margaret Parrish, March 4, 1864, Emma-Jean Hoag Collection.

21 Eddy, p. 13.

22 Johnson, Ben C. *A Soldier's Life: The Civil War Experiences of Ben C. Johnson* (Western Michigan University Press: Kalamazoo) 1962, p. 96.

23 *Allegan Journal*, June 29, 1863.

24 Avery, p. 31.

25 Account by Hiram Ellis in July 27, 1863, *Allegan Journal*.

26 *Ibid.*

27 Avery, p.37.

28 William H. Rockwell to Polly A. Rockwell, July 9, 1863, WMU..

29 Avery, p. 40-41.

30 William H. Rockwell to Polly A. Rockwell, August 18, 1863, WMU.

31 Obituary in May-McManus family scrapbook.

32 McCline, John Slavery in the Clover Bottoms (University of Tennessee Press: Knoxville) 1998, p. 84.

33 Heringa diary, entry for August 24, 1863.

34 John P Hanchett to "My dear aunt", October 18, 1863. Letter owned by Jim Gowen and Ray Riker.

35 *Michigan in the War*, p. 339

36 *Allegan Journal*, October 12, 1863.

37 *Allegan Journal*, October 12, 1863.

38 *Allegan Journal*, October 5, 1863.

39 Avery, p. 50.

40 Johnson, p.105-107.

41 Heringa diary, entry for May 13, 1863.

42 Thomas, Henry F. *A Twentieth Century History of Allegan County, Michigan* (The Lewis Publishing Company: Chicago) 1907, p. 204.

1   Nies, *Civil War Account*, p. 7, John Nies Collection, Holland Museum Archives.

2   *Allegan Journal*, January 18, 1864.

3   James Hibberdine to brother, February 2, 1864, Hibberdine Family Archives, Devonshire, England.

4   Nies, to "mother and brothers," March 10, 1864, John Nies Collection, Holland Museum Archives.

5   Lemuel W. Osborn to Eunice Osborn, March 31, 1864, Lemuel W. Osborn Papers, Michigan State Archives, Lansing.

6   *Allegan Journal*, April 18, 1864.

7   John P. Parrish to Margaret Parrish, April 8, 1864, Emma-Jean Hoag Collection.

8   Bailey, p. 66.

9   Joseph Ely to "Friends at Home," May 9, 1864, Allegan County Historical Society.

10 Avery, p. 72.

11 *Allegan Journal*, June 13, 1864.

12 *Allegan Journal*, July 11, 1864.

13 *Allegan Journal*, June 13,1864.

14 Trowbridge, L. S. *A Brief History of the Tenth Michigan Cavalry* (Friesema Bros. Print. Co.: Detroit) 1905.

15 Recounted in James Reeve obituary in obituary files of Herrick Public Library, Holland, Michigan.

16 Bird-House family records, Katharine House Allen Collection.

17 James Hibberdine to brother, May 2, 1864, Hibberdine Family Archives, Devonshire, England.

18 *In memory of Alfred Curtis Wallin, Justice of the Supreme Court of North Dakota, 1890-1903*, n.p., n.d., p. 100.

19 *Record of service of Michigan Volunteers in the Civil War, 1861-1865, First Michigan Colored Infantry*, p. 4.

20 Smith, Franklin Campbell, *The Diocese of Western Michigan: A History*, (Diocesan Historical Commission: Grand Rapids) 1948, p.116.

21 Bailey, p.95.

22 Nelson W. Ogden to "Sister & Mother." December 23, 1864. Nelson W. Ogden Collection, Holland Museum Archives and Research Library, Holland, Michigan.

23 Avery, p. 127.

1864

1   Bird Family Archives, Ken Howe, Shoreline, Washington.

2   *Allegan Journal*, April 3, 1865.

3   Alvin H. Stilson to Minerva Stilson, April 9, 1865.

4   Wallin, p. 98-99.

5   Wallin, p.99-100.

6   Robertson, Jno. *Michigan in the War* (W. S. George & Co., State Printers & Binders) 1882, p. 724..

1865

1865, cont'd.   7   Wallin, p. 101.

        8   Unidentified and undated newspaper clipping in Allegan Public Library, vertical file.

        9 Trowbridge, L. S., *A Brief History of the Tenth Michigan Cavalry,* Library of Michigan.

        10 *Michigan in the War,* p. 727.

        11 Nelson W. Ogden to "Sister," April 26, 1865, Nelson W. Ogden Papers, Holland Museum.

        12 Account by Pritchard reprinted in the *Allegan Gazette,* November 30, 1907, on the occasion of his death.

        13 Account by Tuttle reprinted in Lane, Kit, *The Day the Elephant Died and Other Tales of Saugatuck,* (Pavilion Press: Douglas, Michigan) 1990, p. 14-21.

        14 *Allegan Gazette,* November 30, 1907.

        15 Entry for May 12, 1865, Henry Albert Potter diary, Henry Albert Potter papers, Michigan State Archives, Lansing.

        16 Tuttle, *op. cit.*

        17 Wallin, p. 18-19.

AFTER THE WAR   1   *Portrait and Biographical Record of Kalamazoo, Allegan and Van Buren Counties,* p. 202.

        2   The handwritten journal of Dutcher's journey around the world is now in the archives of the Saugatuck-Douglas Historical Society.

        3   "Blue Coat Sketches" by Milton Chase in *Allegan Journal,* February. 21, 1874, in scrapbook in Milton Chase Papers, Bentley Historical Library, University of Michigan, Ann Arbor.

        4   John P. Parrish to Margaret Parrish, March 4, 1864, Emma-Jean Hoag Collection.

        5   *Allegan Journal,* January 29, 1866.

        6   *Ibid.*

        7   Hutchins, Henry Hudson, *Western Allegan County Pioneer Days* (Pavilion Press: Douglas, Michigan) 1995, p. 44.

        8   *Commercial Record,* October 16, 1919.

        9   McKeown, Treva Miller, *Western Allegan County History* (Curtis Media) 1988, p. 361.

        10 James Hibberdine to brother's family, 1876, Hibberdine Family Archives, Devonshire, England.

        11 *The Seventieth Anniversary of The First Congregational Church of Saugatuck, Michigan, 1860-1930,* [1930] p. 18.

        12 *Fort Wayne Journal-Gazette,* October 7, 1932, and *Fort Wayne News-Sentinel,* October 10, 1932.

        13 *The Seventieth Anniversary of The First Congregational Church of Saugatuck, Michigan, 1860-1930,* [1930] p. 3.

        14 Sligh, Charles R. *History of the Services of the First Regiment Michigan Engineers & Mechanics,* (Grand Rapids) 1921, p. 92.

BIBLIOGRAPHY

Anderson, David D., ed. *Lieutenant Wm. E. Sleight and the 102nd Reg. U. S. Colored Infantry in the Civil War* (The Midwestern Press: MSU, East Lansing, Michigan) 2003.

Anderson, William M. *They Died to Make Men Free: A History of the 19th Michigan Infantry in the Civil War* (Morningside: Dayton, Ohio) 1994.

Bacon, Co. Edward. *Among the Cotton Thieves* (The Free Press Steam Book and Job Printing House: Detroit) 1867. Reprint 1962, Committee for the Preservation of the Port Hudson Battlefield.

Bailey, George W. *The Civil War Diary and Biography of George W. Bailey* (G. R. Post: Colleyville, Texas) 1990.

Bertera, Martin and Ken Oberholzer *The 4th Michigan Volunteer Infantry at Gettysburg: The Battle for the Wheatfield* (Morningside House, Inc. (Dayton, Ohio) 1997.,

Catton, Bruce *America Goes to War: The Civil War and its meaning to Americans Today* (Wesleyan University Press: Middletown, Connecticut) 1958.

—*Reflections on the Civil War* (Doubleday & Co., Inc.: New York) 1981.

Col. R. H. G. Minty and the 4th Michigan Cavalry [1864?]

Crotty, Daniel G. *Four Years Campaigning in the Army of the Potomac* (Dygert Bros & Co.: Grand Rapids) 1874. Reprinted Belle Grove Publishing, Kearney, N. J., 1995.

Cummings, Charles L. *A poetical description of the Sixth army corps campaign during the year 1863 by George E. Reed, Together with a sketch of my life and service in the Army . . .* (S. E. Shade: Harrisburg, Pennsylvania) [1887?]

Decoration Day 1902 (Archives of the Ganges United Methodist Church)

Doyle, Julie A., John David Smith and Richard M. McMurry. *This Wilderness of War: The Civil War Letters of George W. Squier, Hoosier Volunteer* (University of Tennessee Press: Knoxville) 1998.

Genco, James G. *To the Sound of Musketry and Tap of the Drum: A History of Michigan's Battery D Through the Letters of Artificer Harold J. Bartlett, 1861-1864* (Ray Russell Books: Rochester, Michigan) 1983.

Harris, Samuel *The Michigan Brigade of Cavalry at the Battle of Gettysburg, July 3, 1863 Speech delivered at the annual reunion of Co. A., 5th Michigan Cavalry, at Cass City, Michigan, June 14, 1893.* (Reprint: Custer Ephemera Society) 1973.

Harris, Samuel *Personal Reminiscences of Samuel Harris* (The Rogerson Press: Chicago) 1897.

Herek, Raymond J. *These Men Have Seen Hard Service: The First Michigan Sharpshooters in the Civil War* (Wayne State University Press: Detroit) 1998.

Hesseltine, William B. *Civil War Prisons: A Study in War Psychology* (Frederick Ungar Publishing Co.: New York) 1930.

History of the Michigan Organizations at Chickamauga, Chattanooga and Missionary Ridge, Second Edition (Robert Smith Printing Co.: Lansing, Michigan) 1899.

Husby, Karla Jean and Eric J. *Wittenberg Under Custer's Command: The Civil War Journal of James Henry Avery* (Brassey's: Washington DC) 2000.

In Memory of Alfred Curtis Wallin, Justice of the Supreme Court of North Dakota, 1890-1903. [1923]

Johnson, Ben C. *A Soldier's Life: The Civil War Experiences of Ben C. Johnson* (Western Michigan University Press: Kalamazoo) 1962.

Kidd, J. H. *Personal Recollections of a Cavalryman with Custer's Michigan Cavalry Brigade in the Civil War* (The Sentinel Press: Ionia) 1908.

Longacre, Edward G. *Custer and His Wolverines: The Michigan Cavalry Brigade, 1861-1865* (Da Capo Press) c. 1997.

May, George S. *Michigan and the Civil War Years, 1860-1866, A Wartime Chronicle* (Michigan Civil War Centennial Observance Commission: Lansing) 1964.

McCline, John *Slavery in the Clover Bottoms, John McCline's Narrative of Life During Slavery and the Civil War* (University of Tennessee Press: Knoxville) 1998.

Overmyer, Leonard G. *Forest Haven Soldiers: The Civil War Veterans of Glen Lake & Surrounding Leelanau* (Overmyer Historicals: Grand Rapids) 1999.

Ponder, Jerry *General Sterling Price's 1864 Invasion of Missouri* (Ponder Books: Mason, Texas) 1999.

Record of Service of Michigan Volunteers in the Civil War, 1861-1865.

Rerick, John H. *The Fourty-4th Indiana Volunteer Infantry* (Published by author: LaGrange, Indiana) 1880.

Robertson, Jno. *Michigan in the War* (W. S. George & Co., State Printers & Binders) 1882,

Rummel, George III *Calvary on the Roads to Gettysburg: Kilpatrick at Hanover and Hunterstown* (White Man Books: Shippensburg, Pennsylvania) 2000.

Sligh, Charles R. *History of the Services of the First Regiment Michigan Engineers & Mechanics* (Grand Rapids) 1921.

Trowbridge, L. S. *A Brief History of the Tenth Michigan Cavalry* (Friesema Bros. Print. Co.: Detroit) 1905.

Trowbridge, L. S. *Michigan Troops in the Battle of Gettyburg,* Microfiche (University Publications of America: Bethesda, Maryland) 1993.

Trowbridge, L. S. *The Stoneman Raid of 1865* (Ostler Print. Co.: Detroit) 1888.

Vaughan, Coleman C. *Alphabetical General Index to Public Library Sets of 85,271 Names of Michigan Soldiers and Sailors Individual Records* (Wykoop Hallenbeck Crawford Co.: Lansing) 1915. 1984 reprint.

Wallin, Van A. *The Michigan Wallins* (Toren Craftsmen: Grand Rapids) 1933.

MANUSCRIPTS

Babbitt, Darwin H., Diary, State Archives of Michigan
Blakeslee, Henry, Letters, loaned by the Crane family.
Ducumb, James, Letters, loaned by the Sheridan family
Eddy, Scott, Autobiography, loaned by the Eddy family
Hanchett, J. P., Letter, loaned by Jim Gowran and Ray Riker
Heringa, Jacob, Diary, Allegan County Historical Society
Nies, John, Civil War Account and Letters, Holland Museum Archives and Research Library
Ogden, Nelson W., Papers, Holland Museum Archives and Research Library
Osborn, Lemuel W., Papers, State Archives of Michigan
Parrish Family, Letters and History, loaned by Dorothy and Terry Mc-Neil
Potter, Henry Albert, Papers, State Archives of Michigan

NEWSPAPERS

Allegan Journal, Allegan Public Library
Saugatuck Commercial

PHOTO CREDITS

FRONT 1 History of Allegan and Barry Counties, 1880
2 Charles J. Lorenz Collection
3 Allegan County Historical Society
4 Kit Lane
5 Frances Wallin Shaw
6 Archives of All Saints' Episcopal Church, Saugatuck
7 The Civil War Dairy and Biography of George W. Bailey, G. R. Post, Colleyville, Texas
8 Eddy Family archives
9 Saugatuck-Douglas Historical Society Archives
10 Dutcher Family album from David Babbitt
11 Dr. Milton Chase Collection, Bentley Historical Library, University of Michigan, Ann Arbor.
12 Bob and Lue Crane
13 Dutcher Family album
14 Allegan County Historical Society
15 SDHS archives
16 John Nies Papers, Holland Museum Archives and Research Library.
17 Portrait and Biographical Record of Kalamazoo, Allegan and Van Buren Counties, 1892
18 SDHS archives
19 10th Cavalry Regimental History, Library of Michigan, Lansing
20 White Family archives
21 Allegan County Historical Society
22 History of Allegan and Barry Counties, 1880
23 Mary Lea (Bird) Jones, Brooklyn, New York.

PLATES 1 Bill Kemperman
2 1864 wall map
3 Norm and Connie Deam
4 1864 wall map
5 1864 wall map
6 Allegan Journal file, Allegan Public Library
7 Kit Lane
10 National Archives and Records Administration (NARA)
12 DHS archives

13 Allegan Journal file.
18-20 Jim Gowran and Ray Riker
21 Michigan Capitol Committee, Peter Glendinning, photographer.
22 Allegan Journal file.
29 NARA
30 Portrait and Biographical Record of Kalamazoo, Allegan and Van Buren Counties, 1892
31 Kit Lane from Inez Billings
32 1873 Allegan County Atlas
33 Bill Kemperman
35 Larry and Priscilla Massie
36 Wightman-Winne Family archives
37 Larry and Priscilla Massie
38 SDHS archives
39 Dedication program for Custer monument, 1910
40 Kit Lane
41-42 Allen County (Indiana) Public Library newspaper collection
43 NARA
44 Allen County Historical Society, Fort Wayne, Indiana
45 SDHS archives

BACK 24 Kit Lane
25 Archives of All Saints' Episcopal Church, Saugatuck and Sharyn R. Brackett
26 Allegan County Historical Society
27 Gerald Clark, Florida.
28 Ken Howe, Shoreline, Washington
29 Bill Bleeker, Saugatuck
30 SDHS archives
31 Allegan County Historical Society
32 Frances Wallin Shaw
33 Dorothy and Terry McNeil, St. Joseph, Michigan.
34 SDHS archives
35 SDHS archives
36 1st Michigan Engineers and Mechanics regimental history
37 Willard Prentice
38 Mrs. Oliver M., Snyder
39 Treva Miller McKeown
40 May Wightman Winne
41 Frances Wallin Shaw
42 Joan Shriver VanLue
43 History of Allegan and Barry Counties, 1880.
44 Dutcher Family album
45 SDHS archives
46 Eddy Family archives

INDEX

214

215

216

217

219

THIS BOOK WAS DESIGNED BY KEN CARLS FOR THE SAUGATUCK-DOUGLAS HISTORICAL SOCIETY WITH PHOTOGRAPHS PREPARED BY JACK SHERIDAN. THE TEXT IS SET IN CASLON TYPES. ONE THOUSAND COPIES WERE PRINTED AT CROUSE PRINTING IN CHAMPAIGN, ILLINOIS WITH ASSISTANCE FROM SHIRLEY CROUSE AND KEVIN NETHERTON. | *A special numbered edition of this book has been hand bound in cloth over board by Christopher Hohn and Tedra Ashley at Lincoln Bookbindery in Urbana, Illinois.*

This is No. _____ .

Ken Carls is Professor and Associate D of the School of Art + Design at the Un of Illinois at Urbana-Champaign.

24	25	26	36	37	38
27	28	29	39	40	41
30	31	32	42	43	44
33	34	35	45	46	

24 Hiram Ellis
28th Michigan Infantry

25 Chaplain J. Rice Taylor
123rd U. S. Colored Infantry

26 Walter Billings
Enlisted in the 8th Michigan Cavalry at the age of 44.

27 George Dallas Dean
10th Michigan Cavalry

28 Henry Bird
141st Illinois Infantry

29 William Weeks
5th Michigan Cavalry

30 Alvin Stillson
Formerly of the 17th Michigan Infantry, about 1909

31 Benjamin D. Pritchard
*4th Michigan Cavalry
Near the end of the war*

32 Alfred C. Wallin
*6th Michigan Infantry and 100th New York Infantry
Later served on the Supreme Court of North Dakota*

33 Dr. John P. Parrish,
Formerly of the 6th Michigan Infantry, returned from the war and hung out his shingle as a physician in Pier Cove

34 Anthony Slack

35 Joshua Brown
On his 90th birthday. Died five years later at the age of 95, the last Saugatuck area Civil War veteran

36 C. A. Ensign
1st Engineers and Mechanics

37 Warren Prentice
4th Michigan Cavalry

38 Robert McLaughlin
1st New York Marine Artillery

39 Adam Miller
13th Michigan Infantry

40 Adsit Raplee
9th Michigan Infantry

41 Edwin Wallin
8th Michigan Cavalry

42 Henry Shriver
74th New York Infantry

43 E. J. Stow
13th Michigan Infantry

44 G. N. Dutcher
5th Michigan Cavalry

45 R. B. Newnham
U. S. Navy

46 C. C. Billings and Scott Eddy
On their joint 80th birthday

C. A. Ensign

E. J. STOW.